LITERARY CRITICISM AND CULTURAL THEORY

T0314626

Edited by
William E. Cain
Professor of English, Wellesley College

A ROUTLEDGE SERIES

LITERARY CRITICISM AND CULTURAL THEORY

WILLIAM E. CAIN, *General Editor*

GENDERED PATHOLOGIES
THE FEMALE BODY AND BIOMEDICAL DISCOURSE IN THE NINETEENTH-CENTURY ENGLISH NOVEL

Sondra M. Archimedes

LONDON AND NEW YORK

Published in 2005 by
Routledge
Taylor & Francis Group
711 Third Avenue
New York, NY 10017

Published in Great Britain by
Routledge
Taylor & Francis Group
2 Park Square
Milton Park, Abingdon
Oxon OX14 4RN

First published in paperback 2012

International Standard Book Number-13: 978-0-415-64795-3 (Paperback)
International Standard Book Number-13: 978-0-415-97526-1 (Hardcover)
Library of Congress Card Number 2005017435

Library of Congress Cataloging-In-Publication Data

Archimedes, Sondra M.
  Gendered pathologies : the female body and biomedical discourse in the
  nineteenth-century English novel / by Sondra M. Archimedes.
      p. cm. -- (Literary criticism and cultural theory)
  Originally presented as the author's thesis (Ph.D.)--University of
  California, Santa Cruz, 2003.
  Includes bibliographical references (p.   ) and index.
  ISBN 0-415-97526-3 (alk. paper)
  1. English fiction--19th century--History and criticism. 2. Body,
  Human, in literature. 3. Literature and medicine--Great
  Britain--History--19th century. 4. Women and literature--Great
  Britain--History--19th century. 5. Sex role in literature. 6. Medicine
  in literature. 7. Women in literature. I. Title. II. Series.

PR868.B63.A73 2005
823'.8093561--dc22   2005017435

Routledge
Taylor & Francis Group
New York London

Contents

Acknowledgments

I would like to express my gratitude to the friends, colleagues, and institutions that helped make this book possible. This project began as a doctoral dissertation at the University of California, Santa Cruz, where I received fellowships from the Institute for Humanities Research, the Division of Graduate Studies, and the Literature Department which allowed me much needed time to engage in research and writing. While in the graduate program there, I had the pleasure of working with John Jordan, my advisor, whose kind encouragement and practical advice helped guide me through the early stages of the dissertation and throughout the revising of the manuscript; to him I owe my deepest thanks. Also important have been the contributions of the other members of my committee: Murray Baumgarten, for his unfailing support and Carla Freccero, for her incisive criticism.

Numerous friends and colleagues have contributed to this project, both by providing crucial help when needed and in making my life bearable during the writing process. Of these, I would like to thank Mary Waters for sharing ideas on every possible aspect of academic (and nonacademic) life. I was also privileged to enjoy many delightful meals and lively discussions with friends such as Penny Barkin, Caralinda Lee, Leslie Pahl, Helena Younossi, and Soraya Younossi that have sustained me throughout the years. To Sherri Helvie I owe a special debt of gratitude, both for her thoughtful attention to the minutia of my life and for many inspiring conversations. Most of all, however, this book could not have been written without the wry sense of humor, expert film knowledge, and infinite kindness of my best friend and life partner, Steve Shorb.

Introduction

"Derangements of the Uterus" and Other Mysteries

In the 1863 edition of a popular medical text on women's diseases, Gunning Bedford, a New York physician, applauded modern science for finally uncovering the mysteries of the female body:

> [W]ith the speculum and toucher alone, we would have learned only the existence of lesion of structure . . . whilst the various nervous disturbances in different portions of the economy, dependent on organic and functional derangements of the uterus and its annexae, would have remained sealed mysteries, but for the light which modern physiology has thrown upon them. . . .
>
> The ample means, therefore, which we now possess of investigating uterine disorders, and the comparative facility with which the true nature of these diseases is arrived at, give to this class of special maladies an identity, which formerly did not belong to them; and hence what in the remote periods of our science were regarded as idiopathic affections of the head, chest, abdomen, etc., are now recognized to be symptomatic disturbances, or merely effects of disease in the uterine organs. This is really progress; not that progress which travels beyond judgment, and leads often to fatal issues, but a progress the result of truthful and philosophical investigation.[1]

For Bedford and others in the medical profession, the female reproductive system, with its "derangements" and "sealed mysteries," was the ultimate enigma, a secret buried so deep that it surely contained the answers to the most pressing medical questions of the time. Obscure feminine maladies, as Bedford observes ("idiopathic affections of the head, chest, abdomen, etc."), were now revealed to be "merely effects of disease in the uterine organs." The intra-uterine revelations that medical science afforded promised an answer to potentially all of women's diseases; headaches, fatigue, and transitory discomforts now could be confidently assigned to the uterus and its environs. The final unearthing of this very remote recess was nothing short of astounding, for this was the unveiling of *truth:* "light" now shone on the "true nature" of the female body. Part adventure, part mystery, part philosophical treatise, the gynecological text was a quest narrative of the first degree.

Medical interest in female reproduction came at a time when social configurations and gender roles were undergoing rapid transformations. In Britain, the second half of the nineteenth century saw frequent economic fluctuations and increasing class mobility, while middle-class women sought higher education and work outside the home. For many, these alarming changes brought with them a desire to categorize and classify social and physical phenomena in an attempt to impose order on an unruly world. Women came under special scrutiny from scientists and doctors wanting to explain human behavior and social occurrences in terms of biology. Medically, the female body was constructed as radically "other" to the male body, weakened by an unstable reproductive system and subject to mental and physical malfunctions. According to medical researchers, reproductive disorders might be the cause not only of troubling physical problems, but also of wayward social conduct. Transgressive feminine behavior (such as rude speech, masturbation, or prostitution) which at one time would have been defined simply as immoral or illegal, increasingly was defined in medical terms. Middle-class women content in traditional gender roles constituted the social and biological norm, while others stood in an inferior relationship to their bourgeois counterparts. These others—the socially delinquent or the economically disenfranchised— came under especially close investigation. To the medical eye, the transgressive woman, in particular, was a sick woman. She might be classified as neurasthenic, hysterical, or "morally" insane; yet more to the point, she was seen as "unnatural" and even "deviant."[2] The label of "unnatural" connected the biological aberration to the social, suggesting that the one was the logical precursor to the other and opening up a Pandora's Box of medical pathologies. While not all problems could be attributed to the uterus, in the middle decades of the century it was the first and last resort of the ladies' physician.[3]

The nineteenth-century medical community's fascination with gynecological "truths" coincided with the public reception of another kind of reproductive revelation: the narrative of evolutionary biology. Darwin's theory of natural selection was, first and foremost, a theory about reproduction and species development. *The Origin of Species,* published in 1859, brought to popular attention a new way of envisioning social organization, not as a disparate assortment of various classes and economic groups, but as related parts of a single biological network. The *Origin,* with its emphasis on the manner in which entire species change and develop through the reproduction of particular traits, suggested that human beings, like the rest of the natural world, comprised a group of related organisms—a species or "race" in themselves—susceptible to the same reproductive vicissitudes as any other species.[4] Although Darwin did not present a full theory of human evolutionary development until the publication of *The Descent of Man* in 1871, the parallels between human development and that of the plant and animal world were clearly apparent in the earlier work. In this context, reproductivity was not merely a feminine trait, but a paradigm for biological and social relatedness in the human family.

The concept of biological relatedness in evolutionary discourse was a resonant one which lent itself to broad analogies in both the natural and the social sciences. Disciplines such as biology, anthropology, and sociology envisioned the individual human body as embedded within a larger biological network, joined to other organisms at a cellular level. Under the logic of the new scientific thinking, the social body was also a human body, subject to the same "laws of nature" as any other living organism. A primary example of this logic is evident in Herbert Spencer's theory of the social organism, delineated in embryonic form in his 1851 *Social Statics* and developed more fully in 1860 under the title "The Social Organism."[5] Spencer's concept of the social organism made explicit the connection between the individual organism and the larger social sphere. According to Spencer, there was a direct parallel between "the body politic and a living individual body" ("Social Organism" 269); like the living organism, the social body grew, developed and adapted itself to changing conditions. Spencer's formulation of the social body—what I will call the "biological metaphor"—codified the thought of many eighteenth- and nineteenth-century social theorists. Although comparisons between the social body and the human body were nothing new,[6] it was not until the nineteenth century that the correspondence was seen in the context of the emerging field of social science. Spencer, in particular, pursued the analogy over many years, delineating in minute detail the biological foundation of his thought. Social theorists such as Adam Smith and Thomas Malthus, writing in the eighteenth and early nineteenth centuries, prepared the way by advancing theories of self-regulating social and economic functions that lent themselves to the envisioning of an organic social body. Adam Smith's concept of *laissez-faire* economics, for example, demonstrated that the market was part of an interconnected system that adjusted itself automatically if left to its own devices.[7] Later nineteenth-century writers

(Spencer, for instance) conceived of Smith's system as organic or "natural." In a more specific reference to the natural world, Thomas Malthus, in his writings on population, cautioned that the "laws of nature" must be observed for society to function properly. In his view, economic differences between rich and poor reflected these "laws" and were thus, at some fundamental level, equitable.[8] In both cases, social theories found justification in the "natural" order of the world.

My analysis focuses on the convergence of the two trajectories briefly outlined above: the pathologization of the female body and the construction of the social body in Victorian Britain. In particular, I examine nineteenth-century literary representations of "deviant" female sexuality in relation to biomedical discourses on women and society. As I argue, in novels by Charles Dickens, H. Rider Haggard, and Thomas Hardy, the deviant woman's body is closely connected to the social domain through biological analogy; the social body is an extension of the female body, literally and figuratively linked to its referent through tropes of reproductive peril. Each of these texts relates the story of a troubled society, threatened in some way by a collective social deterioration imbued with biological connotations. Like the transgressive women at the center of these texts, the communities show signs of compromised reproductive capacity and a generalized decline in vitality. My point is that both "bodies"—the social body and the female—were constructed by the same biological "laws" and shaped by the same biological narratives. Such narratives were both enabling and troubling, consolidating the populace as a unified entity on the one hand, while also suggesting the possibility of species decline on the other. Yet, as I am asserting, these novels effectively shift attention away from the problems of the social sphere and displace it onto the bodies of deviant women, thus "solving" problems that the text cannot solve in its own terms.[9] In other words, by pathologizing the female body, the afflictions of the larger social body are sidestepped, seemingly remedied by exposing the "truth" about deviant female sexuality.

While there are numerous studies which focus on female sexuality or gender ideology in the nineteenth century, scant attention has been given to correspondences between the female body and the Victorian social body.[10] In an article on Dickens's *Great Expectations*, Susan Walsh compares the postmenopausal female body to the ailing economic body, arguing that both were subject to "constrictions," in the medical language of the day. As a starting point for her analysis, Walsh refers to Catherine Gallagher's essay on the social body as conceptualized by Thomas Malthus and Henry Mayhew.[11] One of Gallagher's insights is that while eighteenth-century writers saw a "link between healthy individual and social bodies," Malthus's *Essay on the*

Principles of Population actually contradicts accepted beliefs when it warns that healthy, vigorous reproduction in the individual will create an unhealthy social body by straining its capacities to provide for all ("The Body" 83). My investigation shares some assumptions with Gallagher's and Walsh's studies, yet departs from theirs in significant ways. Gallagher's analysis does not concern itself with the female body, for example, nor does it focus on biology or sexual deviance. Similarly, while Walsh's essay explores the metaphorical connection between the ailing female body and the ailing economic/social body, she does not analyze the social body as a biological entity in itself. Where Walsh is looking at analogies between post-menopausal women and economic instability, I am specifically looking at the way in which female sexual deviance and tropes of problematized reproductivity relate to biomedical views of the social domain. Walsh's argument is not about sexual deviance or the biological relatedness of the social sphere, but about the cultural lampooning of the elderly female body.

Interestingly, Walsh's analysis is one of the few feminist investigations that takes up Herbert Spencer's thought on the social body. In the context of women's studies, much attention has been directed towards Spencer's theory of women's biological inferiority, yet his work on the social organism usually receives only a passing glance.[12] Cynthia Russett, for example, in her critique of Victorian sexual science, summarizes Spencer's concept succinctly, stating that "the study of society was seen as a kind of extension of biology to be pursued according to the methods and concepts of the natural sciences" (*Sexual Science* 86); Russett does not elaborate much further, however, but turns instead to Spencer's theories of sexual difference.[13] In contrast, rather than focusing exclusively upon the portion of Spencer's work that addresses sexual difference, I examine the connection between the individual biological organism and larger social sphere within the framework of Spencer's concept of the social body and nineteenth-century gendered science. By so doing, I wish to illuminate the changes that occurred under the gender-inflected model. One of my assertions in this study is that while the Spencerian model is often used to support the status quo, the feminized version of this model introduces cultural anxiety into the mix. When the social body finds its referent in the female body, in other words, concern with the health and longevity of the social domain increases.

My analysis has been influenced by several related fields of inquiry, especially feminist scholarship on Victorian gender ideology and critical studies of disease, sexuality, and the body.[14] The field of Victorian gender ideology is extensive, but certain studies have had a particular bearing on my work. Several publications that do not deal with literature in any sustained manner but which have been especially useful to me in sorting through various scientific approaches to sexual difference in the nineteenth century include Russett's *Sexual Science: The Victorian Construction of Womanhood* and Jill Conway's "Stereotypes of Femininity in a Theory of Sexual Evolution." Other important works are Elaine Showalter's *The Female Malady: Women, Madness and English Culture, 1830–1980* and Sally Shuttleworth's "Female Circulation: Medical Discourse and Popular Advertising in the Mid-Victorian Era"; both studies explore the medical regulation of women, the first in relation to insanity and the second in relation to menstruation. Additionally, Carroll Smith-Rosenberg's "Discourses of Sexuality and Subjectivity: The New Woman, 1870–1936" and *Disorderly Conduct: Visions of Gender in Victorian America* address the attitudes of sexologists toward female social and intellectual autonomy in the late nineteenth and early twentieth centuries, specifically in relation to the New Woman.[15] There have also been several studies examining medical and social discourses of prostitution and their relation to social attitudes towards gender. The best known among these is Judith Walkowitz's *Prostitution and Victorian Society: Women, Class, and the State,* which charts the rise and fall of the Contagious Disease Acts. Mary Poovey uses a more literary approach to this subject matter in "Speaking of the Body: Mid-Victorian Constructions of Female Desire," which looks at the effect of prostitution discourses on women's subjectivity as evidenced in Charlotte Brontë's *Jane Eyre.*[16]

In addition to critical investigations that focus specifically on the female body there are those that cast a wider net and examine alterity across several fields. Two studies in particular that have had a substantial impact on the formation of my ideas are Sander Gilman's *Difference and Pathology: Stereotypes of Sexuality, Race and Madness* and Peter Stallybrass and Allon White's *The Politics and Poetics of Transgression,* both of which posit the deviant or transgressive body as "other" to the dominant culture. Gilman's work is enlightening in that it examines a relationship between the prostitute's body and disease, thus making tangible the connection between social transgression and pathology while also clarifying the ways in which the medical domain constructs deviance. Stallybrass and White's work has been especially illuminating for me, and in some ways my approach is an extension of theirs. In particular, my analysis, like theirs, looks at the ways in which widely-held beliefs about the physical body help to organize ideas about the social order. Yet where Stallybrass and White focus specifically on the cultural categories of "high and low," I focus on normality and pathology, with the emphasis on the latter category and with the added inflection of gender. The imposition of gender on this model changes the relationship between high and low, self and other, or dominant culture and marginalized body when examined in the context of biology. Because the female body was associated with reproduction, parallels between that body and the larger social body as a product of evolution were inevitable. Thus, while Victorian science marginalized many kinds of bodies—female, criminal, working class, homosexual, non-white, and others, as Gilman, Stallybrass, and White explore— only the female body was capable of representing the entire species in its reproductive capacity. Women's bodies, because they were associated with nature, biology, and reproduction, were the perfect analog to the increasingly biologized social body. Consequently, the female body occupied a paradoxical position: it was always already "other," yet also the "same" in reference to the social domain.

Other studies of sexuality and the body that have had a bearing on my work include Jeffrey Weeks's *Sex, Politics and Society: The Regulation of Sexuality Since 1800* and *Sexuality and Its Discontents: Meanings, Myths & Modern Sexualities.* Both volumes contain much information on the cultural preoccupation with sexuality in the nineteenth century, especially as a means of social regulation. Most important, however, have been Michel Foucault's *The Birth of the Clinic* and the first volume of *The History of Sexuality. The Birth of the Clinic,* for instance, traces a major epistemological shift in European medicine which transformed the role of the doctor, the regard for the patient, and the understanding of disease. Before the late eighteenth century, Foucault explains, doctors viewed disease as something mobile and abstract, having as much to do with a patient's own observations and complaints as with a specific defect in the body. In contrast, late eighteenth- and nineteenth-century medical approaches focused complete attention on particular organs and areas of the body which were considered to be the sites of pathology. Patients' complaints or symptoms were thus devalued, and the doctor became a glorified sleuth acting upon an object rather than a subject. In a sense, the body was divorced from the patient as it came under the purview of the medical gaze. The shift, then, was from healing the invalid to finding the disease. Such an epistemological shift was packed with ideological significance: the doctor became a privileged authority, the patient was disenfranchised, and disease assumed a heightened value, justifying the specialized authority of the "expert" and maintaining the balance of power. Foucault's formulation is central to my purposes in that it demonstrates the logic fundamental to a medical culture in which pathology takes precedence over other aspects of physical functioning. In this framework, the body becomes an important, malleable signifier, not only for relationships of power, but also for widespread cultural anxieties.[17]

Along with *The Birth of the Clinic,* Foucault's *History of Sexuality* has been invaluable to me in developing my ideas about deviance and the social sphere. One of the main assertions Foucault makes here is that in the nineteenth century, European "experts" of various kinds—doctors, scientists, educators, parents—became preoccupied with locating and defining unnatural or deviant sexualities. The focus was not so much on the legality or illegality of any particular act, but on whether the act was deemed "natural." Foucault's study demonstrates the way in which the pursuit of deviance sustained its own growth as a field, supporting the authority of self-described "experts" and creating an outlaw society—those labeled as "perverts"—that took pleasure in evading the experts. Both Foucault's and Weeks's analyses, then, have been useful to me in tracking the cultural construction of deviance. My study seeks to extend these analyses by looking at the larger culture itself (the social body) as a deviant or unhealthy culture, united through a common biological destiny.

My view of the social body as a biological entity has been inspired, in part, by Mary Poovey's *Making a Social Body: British Cultural Formation, 1830–1864.* This book argues that the concept of the "social body" was very much a nineteenth-century formation, emerging from a variety of literary and cultural texts which emphasized the notion of a single mass culture in spite of recognized differences of class, gender and race (*Social Body* 2). Poovey analyzes the social body as a unitary vision of British national identity and charts the way in which the phrase "the *great body of the people*" (*Social Body* 7) (used, for instance, in Adam Smith's *Wealth of Nations*) shifted in meaning, from denoting in the eighteenth century only the laboring poor to designating in the early nineteenth century either the laboring poor as a separate group or "British (or English) society as an organic whole" (*Social Body* 8). While Poovey does not formulate the concept of the social body as a specifically biological entity, some of the language she uses, such as "organic whole," captures the sense that I wish to tease out (*Social Body* 8). This connotation of the social whole as a biological entity, or as imaginatively constituted through attention to biomedical discourses, is implicitly suggested in Chapter Six of Poovey's study, which examines Edwin Chadwick's 1842 report on sanitation conditions in London. In his report, Chadwick investigated the sanitary habits of the working classes, linking poor sanitation and disease to "immoral" behavior.[18] In Poovey's view, despite the very obvious polarization between the bourgeois and working classes that such a report generated, it nonetheless offered unifying ideas about the British populace as a social aggregate; "ideas about domesticity, the social domain, the nation, and public health," she comments, helped create the sense of a citizenry united in its goals for a healthy nation (*Social Body* 131).[19]

Chapter One of my study, "Science, Gender, and the Nineteenth Century," focuses on nineteenth-century scientific discourses in relation to the female body, the social body, and the construction of deviance. This chapter is divided into four main parts. The first section, "The Social Body and the Biological Metaphor," examines the analogy between the individual human body and the larger social domain as developed in nineteenth-century thought. I pay particular attention to Herbert Spencer's theory of the social organism here because it provides an essential biological and metaphorical link between the individual organism and the larger social sphere. Additionally, I examine how evolutionary discourses brought ideas about reproduction and the species of the human "race" to public attention, thus emphasizing the biological connectedness of the social sphere. In the second section, "The Normal and the Pathological," I trace the development of the idea of pathology as something separate and distinct from the normal. It is this division between normal and pathological that enables the concept of deviance to become an important focus of nineteenth-century science and medicine. Foucault's theories of the medical gaze and changing attitudes toward disease are central to my ideas in this section, as are his observations on perversion as a nineteenth-century obsession. The scientific construction of the female body is the focus of the third section, "The Female Body and Biomedical Discourse." Here I discuss the relation of Victorian domestic ideology to theories of sexual difference. I am especially concerned in this section with medical views on female reproduction and the reformulation in the cultural sphere of female social transgression as medical pathology. The last section, "The Reproductive Imperative," outlines the broader claims of my argument, connecting the female body to the social body through the concept of reproduction. The main point I am making here is that vigorous, "healthy," heteronormative reproduction became a guarantee of female normality in the nineteenth century imagination, just as for the larger social body it guaranteed the continuance of the species.

In my second chapter, "Towards a Discourse of Perversion: Female Deviance, Sibling Incest, and the Bourgeois Family in Dickens's *Hard Times*," I turn to literary representations of the deviant female body in Charles Dickens's *Hard Times,* a novel about the deleterious effects of industrial culture on the middle-class family. My focus in this chapter is on the incestuous relationship between the central female protagonist, Louisa, and her brother, Tom, and its connection to the ills of industrial society. I am asserting here that although incest, as legally defined, was commonplace in the nineteenth-century novel and even condoned when it brought families closer together—through the marriage of first cousins, for instance—the incestuous sibling relationship in *Hard Times* is censured because it illustrates the complete breakdown of family alliances and the destruction of normal affective ties. That breakdown is best illustrated here through the trope of nonreproductivity as represented in Louisa's deviant body. At stake is not only the collapse of the bourgeois family, but also the future of industrial society, metaphorically portrayed as an interrelated organic entity. My goal in this chapter is to demonstrate that although biology is not an overt theme in this text, correspondences among the family, the larger social domain, and the natural world illustrate the extent to which biological assumptions permeated popular thought in the 1850s.

My next chapter, "Women, 'Savages,' and the Body of Africa: Rider Haggard's *She* as Biological Narrative," looks at correspondences among gender ideology, nineteenth-century science, and European discourses of colonial domination and racial stereotyping. *She* is a male adventure novel about two Englishmen who travel to Africa and encounter Ayesha, a seductive woman of the *femme fatale* mold. Haggard's African landscape, a "dark continent" of underground tunnels and secret passages, bears a suspicious resemblance to the female body. It is, moreover, a diseased landscape, with subterranean caves full of decaying corpses, an image which renders the female body as living tomb. Emanating from the caves are numerous canals, rivers, and swamps, all containing poisonous vapors and fever-inducing gases, also suggestive of a diseased body. The Amahagger, the African tribe over which Ayesha rules, is an extension of the diseased landscape. Although two of the Africans are portrayed along "noble savage" lines, the rest engage in degenerate practices, cannibalizing their prisoners and intermixing with other races. In the context of late-Victorian discourses of degeneration and racial science, these practices signal a biological decline, supported in the novel by a lack of healthy reproduction. Yet, as I am arguing, Ayesha's transgressive (and nonreproductive) sexuality takes center stage, rendering the social decline of the Amahagger virtually invisible. It is Ayesha, rather than the Amahagger, who takes on the text's various allusions to racial and sexual degeneration. I am concerned, in particular, with female nonreproductivity as a paradigm for social and biological deterioration.

The fourth chapter, "'Shapes like our own selves hideously multiplied': Sue Bridehead, Reproduction, and the Disease of 'Modern Civilization,'" turns to Thomas Hardy's *Jude the Obscure* and scientific discourses about nervousness and gender. This novel focuses on the character of Jude, whose frustration over failing in his intellectual ambitions is exacerbated by an erratic romantic relationship with his cousin, Sue Bridehead. Throughout the narrative, Jude's profound depression is mirrored by Sue's nervous demeanor. By the story's end, their older children have died, Sue's infant is stillborn, she suffers a mental collapse, and Jude dies from ambiguous physical and emotional causes. While Sue's nervousness (and to a much lesser extent, Jude's) has been commented upon by many critics, my study looks at the entire social sphere of *Jude* as affected with neurasthenia, a nineteenth-century catch-all diagnosis for nerve-related problems. I argue that Sue's emotional turmoil detracts attention from more widespread nervous disorders in the social domain. Nervous sensibility in *Jude* is shown to be both the mark of the sensitive and intelligent, but also an impediment to emotional stability and fulfilling sexual relationships. Misfortunes involving sex, reproduction, and biological inheritance suggest that an unhealthy populace is eroding from within, and only a few sturdy pockets of rural (but socially, morally, and intellectually backward) society will be able to carry on the species. It is a bleak view of the future, enacted by Sue in her hesitations about sexual relations and her difficulties with childbirth and the raising of healthy children. It is not Jude who is "obscure," then, but the "modern society" which he inhabits, a society whose reproductive future is uncertain. Sue's fragile body is the analog to that uncertain future.

Lastly, my Afterword considers the issue of female deviance in light of twenty-first-century politics and culture. As I argue, in today's environment, assumptions about innate gender characteristics continue to inform ideas about female social transgression. A brief look at prominent news stories of the past year suggests that tropes of feminine pathology speak to the cultural sphere today in much the same way as they did in the nineteenth century.

Gender ideology in the nineteenth century provided a reference point for biomedical discourse of the period and evolutionary thought. According to scientific reasoning, the biologically-construed social body was vulnerable to the same problems as the female reproductive system. If reproductivity in the female body signaled frailty and proneness to breakdown, then it signaled much the same for the human species. In both, vigorous reproduction was a sign of health, yet the reverse was also true: faulty reproduction signaled social decline.[20] Fiction of the later nineteenth century explored some of these themes and expressed anxieties about the longevity of the existing social domain in varying ways. As I argue, these anxieties were displaced onto the bodies of sexually transgressive women and associated with female reproduction and the raising of children. By so doing, literary works disconnected the concept of problematic reproduction from its larger cultural context and projected it onto the pathologized woman's body, thereby solving an insoluble dilemma, at least at the level of narrative. Moreover, this projection onto the female body had the effect of exposing a hidden "truth." Just as

Bedford believed that by discovering the "sealed mysteries" of the uterus medical science had found the cause of all the disparate ailments women suffered, so too did the nineteenth-century novel produce a diagnosis of female sexual pathology as the answer to perplexing social problems. Foucault's comments on "the truth of sex" spring to mind here:

> The essential point is that sex was not only a matter of sensation and pleasure, of law and taboo, but also of truth and falsehood, that the truth of sex became something fundamental, useful, or dangerous, precious or formidable: in short, that sex was constituted as a problem of truth. (*Sexuality* 56)

Paradoxically, as Foucault explains, the nineteenth century simultaneously produced sex as an object of knowledge and hid it from view. The more that the "experts" looked to sex as the hidden source of knowledge, the more elusive sex became, and thus was the hunt perpetuated. While Foucault is talking about a range of sexual subjects, his words have a particular relevance to the female body, for although in the nineteenth century that body was constantly yielding up its secrets, it also veiled the very thing it promised to disclose; women were still the mysterious sex, whose actions remained infinitely unknowable. In a similar manner, the novels examined here enact the paradox of "the truth of sex." The Victorian narrative of female sexual deviance, in other words, promises much but never tells all.

Chapter One
Science, Gender, and the Nineteenth Century

THE SOCIAL BODY AND THE BIOLOGICAL METAPHOR

The communities portrayed in each of the novels I am analyzing here are, in varying ways, diseased societies, threatened by the spectre of their own demise. In the case of *Hard Times,* industrial society and a mechanistic social ethic produce dysfunctional family relationships. *She,* on the other hand, ventures outside of bourgeois England and portrays a small African society marked as diseased according to the terms of Victorian anthropology. Similarly, in *Jude the Obscure* the widespread desire for social and intellectual advancement, added to the pressure of changing gender paradigms, render "modern civilization" a breeding ground for nervous disorders. In each case, the depiction of society as diseased is enabled by an underlying biological metaphor envisioning the social sphere as a living organism or social body. Each story in its own way sees the community in which narrative events take place as a biological entity: a living organism comprised of many smaller organisms, capable either of development or decline. It is this concept that allows us to see *Jude's* "modern civilization," for instance, as pathological—not only disease-producing, but also an unhealthy organism in itself. The biological metaphor allows the narrators of all three of these texts to cast the social body as subject to the same kinds of infirmities as the human body. The same metaphor that links organism and social domain joins the pathologized female body to the social body, but results in very different constructions of the social sphere. Whereas the connection between human body and social domain was often deployed as a means to uphold the existing social order, the connection between female body and social domain was used to reveal problems in that domain.[1] The female body, associated with reproductive and physical or mental frailty, was the counterpart to the diseased or at-risk society, the society on the brink of reproductive decline. In the texts I am examining, the deviant female body which engages in nonprocreative sex or experiences problems associated with reproduction signifies the uncertain reproductive future of the diseased community in much the same way that the individual organism in nineteenth-century thought represented the larger species in a biological system.

These associations—between society and biology, individual and species—were fundamental to much scientific thinking in the second half of the nineteenth century. Herbert Spencer, in particular, underscored these correlations by making the link between society and organism a cornerstone of his thought, refining his theories over a number of years. George Stocking observes that as early as 1851, Spencer, in *Social Statics,* introduced the outlines of his concept of the "social organism," making this one of three major principles of his social theory. As Stocking explains:

> One can find in *Social Statics* the germs of each of what have been called Spencer's "three sociologies": the contractual individual, the social organic, and the cultural. The first is evident in his conception of society as an aggregation of individual social atoms, whose individual natures determine by summation the character of the social whole; the second, primarily as an occasional metaphor—the "social organism"—tacitly opposed to the "mechanism" of state administration; the third, implicit (as it was to remain) in the relation of social forms and national character. (132)

Spencer developed his thoughts on the metaphorical relationship between the social whole and the living organism more fully in an 1860 essay entitled "The Social Organism." In it he posited outright "an analogy between the body politic and a living individual body," emphasizing the thought that "society is a growth and not a manufacture" (269). For Spencer the concept of "manufacture" entailed an artificial imposition of a plan that was rigid and unchanging, whereas an "organism" grew, developed, and adapted itself to changing conditions, becoming larger and more complex while individual units became more interconnected. Spencer's concept of the social organism, with its explicit biological referent, was a fairly novel way of thinking about society at the time; although the basic metaphor between individual body and social body had a long history, the scientific framework was something new. In this, Spencer was representative of larger cultural trends, illustrating the increasing tendency for scientists and laypeople alike to look to biology rather than religion or philosophy to explain and evaluate human relationships, human institutions, and human desires.

The nineteenth-century debate over evolution, perhaps more than any other scientific debate, elevated the tenets of biology to public prominence. As Russett observes, "[b]iology in the second half of the nineteenth century was steeped in an atmosphere of evolution. Though the concept had not awaited the *Origin of Species,* Charles Darwin's collection of facts and powerful reasoning made evolution central to biological inquiry" (4). Nineteenth-century biological evolutionism offered two basic lines of thought as to how characteristics were inherited and passed on to the next generation.[2] The theory of natural selection, first suggested by A.R. Wallace but developed in detail by Darwin in the *Origin,* asserted that animals which were best suited to a particular environment survived, passing their innate characteristics onto their offspring; in this way, over many generations, characteristics which favored survival became prominent, while characteristics unsuitable to a particular environment tended to diminish. Darwin's concept of natural selection diverged from the widely accepted idea, promoted by Jean Baptiste Lamarck, that characteristics acquired during an individual's lifetime could be passed on to his or her offspring. According to Lamarck's logic, the rustling of wind on an animal's coat, for instance, could stimulate more fur to grow, thus causing animals in cold climates to have thicker fur than those in warm areas. In the *Origin,* Darwin considers "the direct action of the severe climate" to alter inherited characteristics a possibility, but believes the greater probability to be that "[t]he structure of an organism . . . is primarily determined by its response to other organisms and to the environment rather than by the direct effect of external conditions" (389). Yet despite his comments here, as Russett notes, "Darwin was far from denying a role to the Lamarckian inheritance of acquired characteristics, and indeed he expanded that role as time went by" (65). Darwin's continued consideration of Lamarck's ideas illustrates one reason why both theories remained influential throughout the century. Both within and outside of the scientific community, the notion of acquired characteristics continued to be associated with evolution for several decades, even in the face of new information. As Janet Oppenheim comments, "Down to the end of the century, natural selection and the inheritance of acquired characteristics coexisted as plausible alternative explanations of evolutionary change, both attracting staunch adherents and acerbic critics. . . . Lamarckism was never eclipsed by Darwinism during the Victorian era because there was no tidy distinction between the two" (Oppenheim 290). In fact, it was not until the 1880s, when August Weismann discredited Lamarck's ideas with his findings on the germ-plasm, that the scientific basis for natural selection was clearly established; yet in the minds of the general public, the two theories continued not only to coexist with one another, but also to be thought of as a single theory.[3]

Theories of evolution, whether based on natural selection or acquired characteristics, emphasized the importance of heredity and reproduction, while at the same time drawing attention to the concept of the "species." The individual was not merely an independent unit, but part of a larger biological entity to which it was intimately bound. The close connection between individual organism and species was exemplified in an important scientific maxim of the nineteenth century, succinctly expressed as "ontogeny recapitulates phylogeny" (Russett 50). This phrase explains the theory of recapitulation, which Russett defines as "the concept . . . that every individual organism repeats in its own life history the life history of its race, passing through the lower forms of its ancestors on its way to maturity" (50). Thus, the individual human being, in passing from an embryonic stage to physical maturity, goes through the same developmental phases as the human species did over millions of years. Russett's point is that recapitulation theory was used extensively in the sciences, including the social sciences, where it was employed to impose a biological model onto one of social hierarchy, with women, children and "savages" ranking far below the adult white male on the "phyletic ladder" (Russett 51). Yet it is also interesting to note the more rudimentary idea that recapitulation theory formalized the relationship between individual and species, making what was essentially a metaphor into an absolute equivalency. Although recapitulation was not established as a theory until the 1860s, an 1852 article by Spencer in support of evolution describes biological relationships in a similar way.[4] "Surely," Spencer writes, "if a single cell may, when subjected to certain influences, become a man in the space of twenty years; there is nothing absurd in the hypothesis that under certain other influences, a cell may, in the course of millions of years, give origin to the human race" ("Development Hypothesis" 6). In this view, society is not merely *like* an organism in terms of social development and growth, as it is in "The Social Organism," but more specifically *is* an organism, stripped to its cellular essence. The social body is almost literally an extension of the human body.

Spencer's comments and the ensuing interest in recapitulation theory suggest the extent to which the concept of biological unity between individual organism and "the race" or larger species permeated both the natural and the social sciences.[5] Moreover, such reasoning reconfigured social concepts that elevated the status of the individual in relation to society, so important to eighteenth-century political thought. The biological model automatically invoked the concept of species in any examination of an individual, so that the idea of health or disease in a human being could apply similarly to a large social network. Here, as elsewhere in evolutionary discussions, the notion of the species subsumed social organization under that of the biological, laying the groundwork for a powerful metaphor that resonated far beyond the scientific community.

Parallels between the social sphere and biological organization were especially apparent in a kind of thinking loosely known as "social Darwinism," an idea which gained ascendance in the second half of the century. The popular catchphrase "survival of the fittest"—the legacy of Spencer and not Darwin—captured the essence of social Darwinism in assuming a direct relationship between the social sphere and the natural world of plant and animal biology. "Survival of the fittest" followed the general logic of natural selection, but implied that the most physically "fit" organism was also the most capable in other categories, such as intellectual and moral. Thus, in the social sphere, social Darwinism was used to justify the status quo and oppose government intervention to remedy social or economic imbalances; there will always be some individuals who are poorer and weaker than others (so the logic goes), but the "law of nature" which necessitates this imbalance guarantees the survival of the larger social body—and rightly so. Spencer's *Principles of Sociology* outlines much of the rationale behind social Darwinism. Spencer reasons, for instance:

> To be slow of speed is to be caught by an enemy; to be wanting in swiftness is to fail in catching prey: death being in either case the result. . . . On glancing up from low types of animals having but rudimentary eyes and small powers of motion, to high types of animals having wide vision, considerable intelligence, and great activity, it becomes undeniable that where loss of life is entailed on the first by these defects, life is preserved in the last by these superiorities. The implication, then, is that successive improvements of the organs of sense and motion, and of the internal coordinating apparatus which uses them, have indirectly resulted from the antagonisms and competitions of organisms with one another.
>
> A parallel truth is disclosed on watching how there evolves the regulating system of a political aggregate, and how there are developed those appliances for offence and defence put in action by it. (*Principles of Sociology* 520)

Thus, conflict, disparity, and imbalance contribute to the strengthening and improvement of the social body in the same way as they do to the human body. In this reasoning, certain animals are more highly evolved than others, and the struggle between disparate organisms and groups benefits the species by improving the physical and mental attributes of the survivors. Some individual members may suffer, but that is necessary for the good of the whole. The implication is that inequalities of wealth or social status among individuals or groups are somehow "natural."

Spencer enlarges on the idea of the natural social body—or "body politic," in Spencer's words—when he turns to the issue of internal regulation. The body politic is a self-regulating mechanism, like the human body, with no need of outside interference. Consequently, Spencer asserts, "[t]he general result, then, is that in societies, as in living bodies, the increasing mutual dependence of parts, implying an increasingly-efficient regulating system, therefore implies not only developed regulating centres, but also means by which the influences of such centres may be propagated" (*Principles of Sociology* 538). To support his praise of the "efficient" self-regulating system, Spencer provides the example of the British banking system, wherein "this kind of regulation is effected by the system of banks and associated financial bodies which lend out capital" (*Principles of Sociology* 546); he argues, in short, that where one sphere experiences a great flow of capital, another sphere experiences a diminishment, which keeps the larger organism healthy. Not surprisingly, in a later section, Spencer laments the intrusion of government, complaining that "in London the Metropolitan Board having proposed that the rate-payers should spend so much to build houses for the poor in the Holborn district, the Secretary of State says they must spend more!" (583). Spencer's conclusion is that free trade and a general loosening of state interventions will improve the quality of life for the social aggregate. In this formulation, Spencer recasts Adam Smith's *laissez-faire* capitalism more specifically as an organic model. Spencer's ruminations about the "efficiency" of self-regulating free markets, for example, added a biological rationale for opposing governmental regulation and advocating the free flow of capital.

Analogies between the human body and the "natural" social body similarly rationalized the policies of Thomas Malthus, who believed, as Jeffrey Weeks puts it, "that population arrived naturally at its own correct level" (*Sex, Politics* 123). In *Essay on the Principle of Population*, for instance, Malthus states:

> [I]f any man chose to marry, without a prospect of being able to support a family, he should have the most perfect liberty so to do. Though to marry, in this case, is in my opinion clearly an immoral act, yet it is not one which society can justly take upon itself to prevent or punish;

> because the punishment provided for it by the laws of nature falls
> directly and most severely upon the individual who commits the act,
> and, through him, only more remotely and feebly on the society. When
> nature will govern and punish for us, it is a very miserable ambition to
> wish to snatch the rod from her hands, and draw upon ourselves the
> odium of executioner. To the punishment, therefore, of nature he
> should be left, the punishment of severe want. (262)

Malthus advocates a policy that is basically non-interventionist, although he
also cautions individuals to regulate their own reproductive functions lest
"nature" use her harsher methods of population control. Moreover, he
believes that society should not intercede because the punishment falls
exactly where it should—on the delinquent individual and not on the community. In this way, Malthus sees a direct correlation between the "proper"
functioning of the individual and a healthy society, suggesting that the individual who is healthy in a moral sense contributes to a healthy social sphere
with manageable population numbers.[6] Like the "low types of animals" who
are eclipsed by the "animals having wide vision [and] considerable intelligence" of Spencer's description, the person who bears children without sufficient means (and a crystal ball to see into the future) will be justifiably
punished by "nature."[7]

THE NORMAL AND THE PATHOLOGICAL

In the field of nineteenth century medicine, "normality" was the functional
equivalent to "natural." Like social theorists who believed in the validity of
"nature's laws," doctors and scientists believed that an understanding of the
"normal" processes of the human body would yield the answer to a larger com-
prehension of all the problems of human suffering. Normality, however, was
the counterpart to pathology; and herein was the key to a major shift in medical thinking. In the early years of the nineteenth century, Parisian doctors
moved away from the idea of disease as a process involving a certain amount of
abstraction and mobility towards something more concrete and localized. Foucault terms the earlier mode of diagnosis "classificatory medicine," which
imagined disease as having a free movement in space rather than being located
at a particular site in the body. Classificatory medicine visualized "a free spatial-
ization for the disease, with no privileged region, no constraint imposed by
hospital conditions . . ." (*Clinic* 18). Nineteenth-century medicine, in contrast,
confined disease to a specific anatomical space: "the illness is articulated exactly
on the body, and its logical distribution is carried out at once in terms of
anatomical masses" (Foucault, *Clinic* 4). It is not, as Foucault explains, that

eighteenth-century medicine ignored anatomy, but rather that it treated "localization in the organism as a *subsidiary* problem, [defining] a fundamental system of relations involving envelopments, subordinations, divisions, [and] resemblances" (5; emphasis added). The eighteenth-century method was more all-encompassing than the nineteenth-century approach, taking into account the patient, his or her body, symptoms, and individual history in a comprehensive and interrelated manner. The nineteenth-century method, on the other hand, perceived disease as an object or thing which could be made visible in the same way that organs in the body could be made visible through dissection. Such an approach had decisive implications for medical thought, which began to focus on locating and defining pathology rather than treating the whole patient.[8]

One consequence of the new approach to disease was that the patient was figuratively obliterated from medical investigation. In Foucault's terminology, the patient became the object of the medical gaze, disenfranchised from authority over his or her own body. As Foucault asserts, "[the nineteenth century] is the period that marks the suzerainty of the gaze, since in the same perceptual field, following the same continuities or the same breaks, experience reads at a glance the visible lesions of the organism and the coherence of pathological forms . . ." (*Clinic* 3). The gaze is the outcome of a medical approach that values visibility above all else, yet it is a visibility that only the trained expert can perceive. By asserting its absolute authority and objectivity, the gaze dismisses the patient as an unreliable source. Roy Porter, in his history of Western medicine, *The Greatest Benefit to Mankind*, describes this change in attitude as a "shift from reliance upon the symptoms of sufferers reported (not depreciated as subjective) to signs (praised as objective signifiers of lesions)" (313). As patients and symptoms became less important, doctors and the pursuit of visible signs became more so. Porter further remarks:

> The nuances of this or that patient were brushed aside, for such symptoms were now viewed as mere foam on the surface of what Jean Louis Alibert (1768–1837) called the "uncharted ocean of disease." What killed were underlying lesions—tumours, inflammation, gangrene—so attention had to focus on diseases understood as conditions with laws of their own, afflicting all alike; medicine's job was to establish the patterns of pathology. The new doctor was a detective, using the investigative tool of clinical-pathological correlation to be tirelessly on disease's trail. (306–07)

Thus, as medicine's focus slowly shifted, the patient suffered a drop in status. Rather than being a distinctive individual with a unique history, he or she became an assortment of parts—organs, membranes, tissues. The doctor-detective, in turn, rose in status, endowed with the twin attributes of expertise and objectivity.

As these changes took place between doctor and patient, the study of pathological anatomy assumed central importance in the medical field. Disease became the be-all and end-all of medical endeavor, changing it in fundamental ways. As a diagnostic model, disease was very different from everything that had come before, drawing attention and giving shape to ideas that had previously been formless. Porter points out, for instance, that "the idea that disease was quite a different state from health" was entirely novel and hotly contested (*Greatest Benefit* 313). Moreover, as doctors came to accept the notion that disease and health were radically different, the concept of health itself underwent a transformation. In the new schema, health had to be as sharply defined as disease and as clearly visible. Health was, however, an inadequate antithesis to the newly-conceptualized state of disease. Under the sway of the disease model, the notion of "health" was supplanted by a term more compliant with the suppositions of pathological anatomy. Health connoted something all too vague—a state of well-being experienced by an individual, a condition that was more subjective than objective. Biomedical discourse cast health in a new guise, not merely as an indeterminate state contingent upon the assertions of this or that individual, but as a quantifiable standard known as "normality." The normal and the pathological were two interdependent states, each constructed by the other. Georges Canguilhem has stated that:

> "[N]ormal" and "pathological" are concepts that arose in the nineteenth century out of developments in instrumentation, statistics, anatomy, and physiology. The "pathological" does not exist as an isolated and objective phenomenon, but in contradistinction to what is arbitrarily designated the "physiological." Similarly, the "normal" applies to an arbitrarily delimited range of possibilities around the statistical "norm" (average).[9]

"Normal," then, does not connote the kind of vitality that "health" suggests, but instead appeals to statistics and averages—all those quantifiable factors that can be measured in a laboratory without regard to an individual's subjective perceptions. Yet at the same time, paradoxically, there is a curious non-scientific implication in "normality"; it does not claim to mean a disease-free condition—presumably the antithesis of pathology—but something arrived at by general consensus. This change of terminology is not insignificant, for in itself the "normal" was merely a statistical average, but when pitted against the "pathological," it assumed a kind of moral authority. Foucault's comments on "normality" capture something of this implication:

> Generally speaking, it might be said that up to the end of the eighteenth
> century medicine related much more to health than to normality; it did
> not begin by analysing a "regular" functioning of the organism and go
> on to seek where it had deviated, what it was disturbed by, and how it
> could be brought back into normal working order; it referred, rather, to
> qualities of vigour, suppleness, and fluidity, which were lost in illness
> and which it was the task of medicine to restore. . . . Nineteenth-cen-
> tury medicine, on the other hand, was regulated more in accordance
> with normality than with health. . . . (*Clinic* 35)

The pathological was a deviation, then, and the standard from which it deviated was the "normal"; normality, in turn, was the thing that did not deviate. Under this formulation, normality was not so much a thing in itself as it was a tautology, existing to add weight to the claims of pathology.

The reconceptualization of disease in the nineteenth century as an abnormality or deviation from a norm illustrated a decisive change in social theory and in attitudes towards social groups. Concepts of normality and pathology easily adapted themselves to conventional beliefs about particular classes and ethnic groups, hardening divisions by ascribing a biological basis to social differences. Such nineteenth-century attitudes diverged markedly from those of the eighteenth. Russett comments, for instance:

> One measure of the European turn away from the Enlightenment faith
> in natural rights was the increasing emphasis laid by the social sciences
> on individual and group differences. It had been characteristic of social
> theory in the late eighteenth century to stress the commonalities shared
> by all human beings. . . . Eighteenth-century theorists did not deny the
> existence of differences among races and national groups; they did not
> even deny that some groups were better, or more advanced, than others.
> But in the main they did reject the notion that such differences were
> inborn or hereditary, and hence permanent. . . .
>   This congeries of ideas gradually gave way in the nineteenth cen-
> tury to a stress on differentiation and hierarchy. (6)

Nineteenth-century doctors and scientists reproduced their own cultural biases, emphasizing differences between the middle classes and their social "others," and placing the white, male body at the top of the biological hierarchy. Recapitulation theory offered one way of linking the social to the biological by establishing a scientific rationale for the thought that some people—such as women, children, and "savages"—were less "developed" than others—specifically, the white, middle-class male (Russett 51). The disease model offered another way to reproduce cultural biases within a scientific framework by accentuating the idea of difference and appealing to the self-interests of the dominant classes. Just as categories of normal and pathological opposed and defined each other, so too did categories of social difference: middle class and working class, men and women, white and black.

Yet biomedical ideas about social and ethnic differences reached far beyond the scientific sphere. As early as the 1840s in Britain, groups and individuals who did not uphold the same standards as the Victorian middle class stood the chance of being branded "diseased" even among the lay population. Chadwick's 1842 report on sanitation, for instance, gained an "enormous readership" because, as Poovey explains, "Chadwick, ever the entrepreneur . . . sent proof copies to luminaries such as Carlyle, John Stuart Mill, and Dickens, not to mention all the newspapers and quarterlies likely to run a review" (*Social Body* 117). Chadwick's report capitalized on bourgeois disapproval of working class behavior by linking moral laxity and even criminal tendencies to the sanitary conditions of the poor. According to Chadwick, overcrowded rooms and sloppy housekeeping, for instance, "mark the depraved and blunted state of [the inhabitants'] feelings, and the moral and social disorder which exists" (qtd. in *Social Body* 123). Untidiness in house and dress was one step away from disease, crime, and prostitution. Thus, bourgeois values were imposed upon the poor and working classes through a proposed system of regulation involving cleanliness, living arrangements, and even food and clothing. As Stallybrass and White observe, Chadwick's insistence upon "'regularity of diet' [and] 'clean or respectable clothes'" (qtd. in Stallybrass 126) had as much to do with the bourgeoisie's ideas about their own middle-class bodies as with "the body of the Other" (126).[10] While the Victorian middle class imagined itself as clean and orderly in both a moral and a physical sense, in its social "others" it saw a deviation from all that was pure and healthy. "In the slum, the bourgeois spectator surveyed and classified *his own antithesis*," as Stallybrass and White remark (128). Moreover, I would note that Chadwick's report conveniently situated disease in opposition to the "normal" middle-class body, appealing to a public receptive to an emergent biomedical discourse.

The bourgeois preoccupation with "the body of the Other" fueled interest in scientific divisions of normal and pathological. The "other" was diseased, abnormal, and deviant, whether by virtue of racial, sexual, class, or national difference. Such ideas about difference supported the slow shift from moral into biomedical discourse, with the latter reproducing the former's biases.

Thus, instances of crime, prostitution, and other social issues, which had traditionally been discussed in relation to religious or philosophical beliefs, began to be seen within a scientific framework. In the new terminology, criminals, prostitutes, and alcoholics alike were not merely morally corrupt or socially abhorrent, but medically deviant, a label which combined both social disgrace and physical disease in one expression. Cesare Lombroso, for example, the nineteenth-century Italian criminal anthropologist, sorted criminals into distinct physical types in an attempt to demonstrate that criminal behavior had a biological basis. Lombroso made use, in part, of the theory of recapitulation, identifying criminal types as biological primitives, similar to "normal" individuals but less developed through evolutionary "backwardness." Daniel Pick notes, for instance, that "[c]riminality for Lombroso was not 'unnatural' sin, nor an act of free will, but the sign of a primitive form of nature within an advanced society" (122–26).[11] More specifically for my analysis, the idea of the "primitive" type existing within an "advanced" society suggested linkages between racial and social prejudices, for the idea of blackness was inherent in the idea of the criminal as primitive.[12]

The same correspondences between biological deviance and racial or social otherness can be seen in nineteenth-century concepts of the prostitute. In an essay examining nineteenth-century comparisons of white female prostitutes to black women, Gilman examines the way in which medical descriptions of black female genitalia and buttocks were linked to corresponding descriptions of prostitutes. These descriptions were carefully documented with photographs and drawings, ostensibly to prove that so-called physical anomalies "were inherent, biological variations rather than adaptations" (*Difference* 89). Moreover, as Gilman explains, "the deformation of the labia in the [African woman] is accounted a congenital error, and thus incorporated into the disease model" (*Difference* 89). Both the black women and the white prostitutes were seen to be pathological types, their pathologies apparent through biological deformities inscribed upon the body. Like Lombroso's criminals, the prostitute deviated from the norm constituted by the white bourgeois body.

The turn to biology, a preoccupation with disease, and an assumption that the white, middle-class body and its associated social practices comprised a scientific norm all laid the groundwork for a transition from a moral discourse to a biomedical one. Scientific discourse reproduced bourgeois moral codes, concealing religious and social beliefs behind a facade of objectivity. Nowhere was this shift more apparent than in the field of sexuality, where anxieties about crime, poverty, class and racial otherness could be expressed through discussions about public health and safety. Jeffrey Weeks observes, for example:

> Sexuality becomes a symbolic battleground both because it was the focus of many of [the changes in relations between the sexes], and because it was a surrogate medium through which other intractable battles could be fought. Anxieties produced in the bourgeois mind through large gatherings of workers, men *and* women, in factories, could be emotionally discharged through a campaign to moralise the female operatives, and exclude them from the factories. Worries over housing and overcrowding might be lanced through campaigns about the threat of incest. Fear of imperial decay could be allayed by moralising campaigns against prostitution, the supposed festering carrier of venereal infection, and hence of the weakening of the health of soldiers. (*Sexuality* 74)

It was on this "symbolic battleground" that the war was fought to uphold bourgeois ideology. By the second half of the nineteenth century, sexuality was central to many public dialogues on a variety of social problems. Weeks remarks that "a preoccupation with the source, manifestation and effects of the bodily pleasures" (64) was not new to the nineteenth century, but "[w]hat *was,* however, new . . . was the sustained effort to put all this on to a new, 'scientific' footing . . ." (*Sexuality* 65). Whether it be through an interest in the living arrangements of the poor or the genital configurations of prostitutes and black women, sexuality constituted the Ur-pathology, containing the visible trace of all social otherness.

Although the form of discourse about sexuality changed over the course of the century, moral concerns did not disappear completely from medical observations. Medical discourse often sought to obscure its social and moral assumptions, while at other times such considerations were foregrounded. An example of lingering moral anxieties can be seen in changing discussions of child sexuality and masturbation. Gilman notes that in the late eighteenth and early nineteenth centuries, masturbation was considered "the major deviancy" among medical authorities and that concern about masturbation often centered around anxieties about the sexuality of children (*Difference* 91). In particular, Gilman states:

> The initial interest in masturbation as a sexual pathology appeared in the early eighteenth century, and its impetus was clearly theological. The first widely circulated tractate on the subject, *Onania, or the Heinous Sin of Self-Pollution* (1726?), reads not as much like a series of medical case studies as like the testimony of sinners presented in the

newest church on Grub Street, the Tabernacle of Public Opinion. . . .
[C]learly the earliest popular or pseudomedical interest in sexuality was
a manifestation of corruption in the child. . . . Masturbation was an
indicator of the potential for perversion inherent in humanity because
of the fall from grace. (*Difference* 191; question mark in original)[13]

Gilman further notes that both Heinrich Kaan, author of "[t]he first comprehensive nosology of human sexual pathology," published in 1844, and
Bénédict Augustin Morel, a French psychiatrist whose 1857 and 1860 publications influenced research into degeneration, shared a belief that universal
sexual deviancy was the result of humanity's fall from grace (*Difference* 192).
Both men felt that sexual deviancy was present in society, at least potentially,
either through the child or the primitive, who mirrored the sexuality of early
humanity. As Gilman explains, "[t]he child is the primitive form of human;
the primitive manifests humanity's early sexuality" (*Difference* 192). Such
chronological primitivism was apparent in Morel's view, which held that the
degenerate was like the primitive who "bore the scars of a fall from grace"
(*Difference* 192). Again, the stamp of recapitulation theory is evident here,
yet this time it imposes the concept of sexual deviancy onto a model of
degenerate development.

   With the appearance of sexology in the latter decades of the nineteenth
century, an interest in pathology began to outweigh concerns about sexual
morality in the biomedical discourses.[14] Weeks comments that "[i]n the great
classificatory zeal that produced the complex definitions and aetiologies and
the new sexual types of the late nineteenth century . . . we can discern the
supplanting of the old, undifferentiated, moral categories of sin, debauchery
and excess, by the new, medical and psychological categories of degeneracy,
mental illness and disease" (*Sex, Politics* 144). The 1890s alone produced a
huge outpouring of publications on sexuality, including some which became
classics in the field, such as Richard Krafft-Ebing's *Psychopathia Sexualis* and
Havelock Ellis's and John Symonds's *Sexual Inversion*.[15] Moreover, although
many of the early sexologists sought to reform and relax attitudes towards sexuality, discussions of "normality" and questions of "nature" and "natural
instinct" tended to reaffirm gender ideology and bourgeois sexual conventions. Krafft-Ebing, for instance, made a clear distinction between pathology
and "vice," stating that "[p]erversion of the sexual instinct, as will be seen
from what follows, is not to be confounded with perversity in the sexual act;
since the latter may be induced by conditions which are not psychopathology.
. . . In order to differentiate between disease (perversion) and vice (perversity),
one must investigate the whole personality of the individual and the original

impulse leading to the perverse act" (56–57). Perverse acts, according to Krafft-Ebing, arose from situations in which the "normal" object choice was not available ("*faute de mieux*" occurrences [*Psychopathia Sexualis* 188]), as when individuals were in boarding schools or imprisoned in jail. Despite a belief that "perverse" acts were abnormal and sometimes even "monstrous," Krafft-Ebing tried to avoid pathologizing all such acts, demonstrating an attitude which was tolerant by conventional standards (56). Yet I would also argue that even this comparatively tolerant attitude towards sexual deviance contributed to the development of a scientific norm which aligned itself with the bourgeois perspective. Krafft-Ebing asserts, for instance, "[w]ith opportunity for the natural satisfaction of the sexual instinct, every expression of it that does not correspond with the purpose of nature,—*i.e.*, propagation,— must be regarded as perverse" (56). Krafft-Ebing walks a fine line here; he wants to avoid pathologizing mere "vice," but he connects even the "perverse" act with biological abnormality. The perverse act is not only abnormal; it is "unnatural" in a biological sense because it does not follow "the purpose of nature." Reproduction here becomes an imperative, the guarantee of "natural" or "normal" sexuality.[16]

Foucault credits the nineteenth century with the creation of perverse sexualities and targets "the setting apart of the 'unnatural' as a specific dimension in the field of sexuality" as a pivotal moment in the history of sexuality, one which has repercussions even to this day (*Sexuality* 39). As he asserts, sexual researchers did not "discover" already-existing behaviors and types, but by drawing attention to sexual activities and establishing an energetic and extensive discourse of perversion, they created an atmosphere in which "peripheral sexualities" flourished (*Sexuality* 42). Moreover, the new sexual "experts" were not confined to the medical realm, but included parents, teachers, and social administrators of all kinds. Tracking, defining, and locating "unnatural" sexualities became the occupation of many self-styled authorities who devised numerous ways of inspecting the sexual behavior of the least powerful members of society. "[W]hat came under scrutiny," Foucault notes, "was the sexuality of children, mad men and women, and criminals; the sensuality of those who did not like the opposite sex" (*Sexuality* 38). In this manner, the sexual deviant became the new outlaw, target of an ever-expanding discourse of perversion. Foucault's rendering of sexual history illustrates the complex and far-reaching ways in which the study of sexuality affected all aspects of cultural life, from the organization of institutional space to the invasion of the most intimate moments of ordinary lives. Despite the desire of many sexual experts to ease social strictures on unconventional sexual behavior, the scientific tendency to catalog, define, and pathologize social and sexual phenomena increased, further expanding an existing biomedical discourse that affected the way the lay community saw itself, both as separate individuals and as a social aggregate.

THE FEMALE BODY AND BIOMEDICAL DISCOURSE

Long before the advent of sexological discourses, the female body and female sexuality were a particular focus of interest for many in the fields of science and medicine. While sexology centered much of its attention on sexual inversion, scientists interested in the female body centered much of their attention on the topic of sexual difference. From about the late eighteenth century through to the end of the nineteenth, the biomedical community laid the groundwork for a theory of radical sexual difference, in effect constructing the female body as profoundly "other" to the male and pathologizing feminine social behavior that did not conform to bourgeois norms. Moreover, traditional beliefs which associated women with nature and the body and men with culture and the mind were underscored and given a biological foundation, thus placing social divisions on a new "objective" footing. Sally Shuttleworth notes, for instance:

> From the late eighteenth century onward, we find that the traditional, rather undefined, associations between woman and the body are strengthened, particularized and codified in medical science. The introduction by Linnaeus of a sexual system of plant classification in the eighteenth century was indicative of a whole shift to a taxonomy of gender that was to emerge in the biological and social sciences in the nineteenth century. Victorian scientists and social theorists increasingly sought out and extolled biological evidence of the sexual division of functions in all forms of life, transforming the interpretive map of both natural and social existence into one continuous chart of gender polarity. (53)

Thus, as various branches of the life and social sciences expanded and developed after the mid-eighteenth century, middle-class beliefs about men's and women's separate spheres were given a scientific justification. Obscured as it was in "impartial" language, biomedical discourse reproduced the terms of bourgeois domestic ideology in a virtually invisible manner.

Underlying late eighteenth- and nineteenth-century scientific appraisals of the female body was an ideological view closely tied to widespread social and economic transformations. As urban society became progressively more industrialized over the course of these centuries, gender relations for the expanding middle classes were fundamentally transformed. Before the existence of a widespread industrial economy, many businesses

were home-based, with fathers, mothers, children, extended family members, and hired employees living and working together in various capacities.
As manufacturing and other businesses became larger and more mechanized,
well-to-do families moved away from the town centers to escape the dirt and
pollution associated with the new factories. Women in these situations
became less involved in the family business, and it became a mark of status
and respectability for a man to be able to afford to support a wife and children in idle comfort. Thus, the physical separation of home and workplace
led to an ideological separation between male and female spheres, imagined
as public and private. In the new economic order, women's sphere was the
home—an idealized space of emotional nurturance and spiritual purity—
while men's sphere was the workplace—the rough and tumble world of business and commerce. Historically, middle-class life was far more varied than
the tenets of domestic ideology would have us believe. Many middle-class
women participated in running the family business, as they would have done
in pre-industrial times, and much other work, as Kathyrn Gleadle points
out, such as "social work, domestic labour, [and] estate management . . . was
unpaid and non-contractual," and therefore unrecognized (51). Yet despite
the very real economic and historical circumstances that allowed many
women to function in non-stereotypical ways, the idealization of home and
hearth appealed to the self-image of the middle classes. "The Angel in the
House," a well-known mid-nineteenth-century poem by Coventry Patmore,
for example, captured the imagination of bourgeois readers with its descriptions of feminine docility, becoming the model of ideal Victorian womanhood for years to come. A decade after its publication, the art critic and
social commentator John Ruskin, in his paean to feminine difference, "Of
Queens' Gardens," praised Patmore's poem lavishly, calling Patmore "that
poet who is distinguished . . . from all others—not by power, but by exqui-
site *rightness*" (87). Like Patmore, Ruskin believed in woman's "majestic
childishness" and "natural tact of love" (Ruskin 89). Yet Ruskin cautioned
that without proper guidance, a girl's sweetness could turn to "hardness"
(88): "She grows as a flower does—she will wither without sun; . . . she may
fall and defile her head in the dust, if you leave her without help at some
moments of her life" (95–96). Paradoxically, then, woman's nature was both
pure and yet always at risk of ruin. Only through judicious instruction and
management could a catastrophe be averted.[17]

Eve Sedgwick's discussion of minoritizing and universalizing discourses
of sexuality can be usefully applied here to illuminate the paradox of such
thinking. As she states in *Epistemology of the Closet*, "issues of modern
homo/heterosexual definition are structured, not by the supersession of one

model [or discourse of sexuality] and the consequent withering away of another, but instead by the relations enabled by the unrationalized coexistence of different models during the times they do coexist" (47). While Sedgwick is referring specifically to discourses of sexuality, a similar coexistence of incongruent discourses is applicable to gender discourses. Thus, the nineteenth century's universalizing discourse of female purity did not merely replace an earlier universalizing discourse of female impurity, but rather was coextensive with and sustained by earlier forms.[18]

The extreme gender differences praised by Ruskin, Patmore, and other champions of domestic ideology were similarly underscored in the developing life and social sciences. Darwin's and Spencer's theories, in particular, were essential to the scientific explanation of radical sexual difference and they supported the gender divisions apparent in the new industrial economy. Both theorists believed in women's inferiority to men and sought scientific explanations to support their beliefs. Russett notes that even before the publication of the *Origin*, Darwin was interested in why certain physical features were present in one sex and not the other.[19] Natural selection alone would not account for such differences; consequently, in the *Origin* Darwin offers a theory of sexual selection—a struggle for possession of the opposite sex—to explain the phenomenon. Thus Darwin reasons:

> [W]hen the males and females of any animal have the same general habits of life, but differ in structure, colour, or ornament, such differences have been mainly caused by sexual selection; that is, individual males have had, in successive generations, some slight advantage over other males, in their weapons, means of defence, or charms; and have transmitted these advantages to their male offspring. (*Origin* 137–38)

Embedded in Darwin's theory of sexual selection was the Lamarckian notion of acquired characteristics; certain traits were enhanced in the male sex not only because they enabled it to survive, as in natural selection, but also because they attracted the female sex, through habit and circumstance, and were passed on to the next generation. A second aspect of Darwin's theory of sexual selection was an assumption that characteristics were passed on from male parent to male offspring, as illustrated in his comment that "individual males . . . have transmitted these advantages to their male offspring" (*Origin* 137–38). Thus, variations in structure and color which have been favored by the female of the species devolve onto the male offspring only.

Both bases of the sexual selection argument—the assumption of acquired characteristics and the passage of traits from male to male—were fundamental to Darwin's later contention that men and women differed markedly in intellectual ability. In *The Descent of Man,* for instance, Darwin asserts that, "The chief distinction in the intellectual powers of the two sexes is shewn by man attaining to a higher eminence, in whatever he takes up, than woman can attain—whether requiring deep thought, reason, or imagination, or merely the use of the senses and hands" (2: 327). Darwin supports his theory of the intellectual superiority of men with a three-pronged argument:

> Now, when two men are put into competition, or a man with a woman, who possess every mental quality in the same perfection, with the exception that the one has higher energy, perseverance, and courage, this one will generally become more eminent, whatever the object may be, and will gain the victory. . . . [T]he higher powers of the imagination and reason . . . will have been developed in man, partly through sexual selection,—that is, through the contest of rival males, and partly through natural selection,—that is, from success in the general struggle for life; and as in both cases the struggle will have been during maturity, the characters thus gained will have been transmitted more fully to the male than to the female offspring. Thus man has ultimately become superior to woman. (2: 328)

Consequently, Darwin's belief in a disparity between male and female intellect depended upon the accuracy of several elements: natural selection, sexual selection, and the transmission of characteristics from male to male. Moreover, acquired characteristics—of the man who gains "ascendancy" over the woman through his perseverance and so develops "higher powers"—were an essential part of the reasoning, providing a crucial support to the theory of sexual selection. Like other scientists of the time, Darwin saw no conflict between a theory of acquired characteristics and one of natural selection—particularly when they supported deeply ingrained beliefs about gender polarity.

Like Darwin, Spencer combined theories of natural selection and acquired characteristics to support the idea of a radical difference between the sexes. Drawing upon both recapitulation theory and the law of the conservation of energy, Spencer theorized that women were smaller physically and possessed a lesser brain function than men because the demands of the reproductive system arrested women's evolutionary development. According to conservation theory (or the First Law of Thermodynamics), as Russett explains, "the energy of a system remains always constant, although its usefulness for work may diminish, because energy can neither be created nor destroyed" (106). Not surprisingly, it was women's reproductive functions which brought mental, physical, and emotional development to a sudden halt; there simply was not enough energy to support both the complex cycle of menstruation and child-bearing along with the development of other more abstract faculties. Thus, in an 1873 article Spencer reasons:

> This rather earlier cessation of individual evolution thus necessitated, showing itself in a rather smaller growth of the nervo-muscular system, so that both the limbs which act and the brain which makes them act are somewhat less, has two results on the mind. The mental manifesta- tions have somewhat less of general power or massiveness; and beyond this there is a perceptible falling-short in those two faculties, intellectual and emotional, which are the latest products of human evolution—the power of abstract reasoning and that most abstract of the emotions, the sentiment of justice—the sentiment which regulates conduct irrespec- tive of personal attachments and the likes or dislikes felt for individuals. ("Study of Sociology" 25)

Spencer's views on the limits of the female mind and the conservation of energy were shared by many others of his generation. Henry Maudsley, a British psychiatrist, put the matter succinctly: "When Nature spends in one direction, she must economise in another direction" ("Sex in Mind" 33).[20] Thus, women could not possess healthy reproductive systems and at the same time engage in strenuous mental activity; injury to either mind or body would be the necessary result. Moreover, Spencer believed that in addition to conservation theory, acquired characteristics worked against women to make them inferior mental and emotional beings. Habits developed in response to social conditions, he speculated, could make women more devious, more intuitive, or more desirous of approval.[21] Although environmentally acquired, Spencer surmised, these traits were enhanced in women through repeated generations of biological inheritance.[22]

The principle of the inheritance of acquired characteristics was revised and challenged by new scientific theories in the 1880s and 1890s, yet social biases about gender roles continued to influence biomedical premises. The publication in English in 1882 of August Weismann's theory on the germ plasm discounted the possibility of environmental causes producing varia- tions in species, yet scientists merely looked for other biological explanations for social and gender inequalities.[23] Even in light of Weismann's findings, the theory of acquired characteristics did not fully erode for some years to come, but instead fueled fears about degeneration through to the end of the cen- tury. Yet as confidence in the theory of the biological inheritance of environ- mental factors waned, other concepts took its place. An 1889 publication entitled *The Evolution of Sex*, in particular, by Patrick Geddes and J. Arthur Thomson, asserted that secondary sexual characteristics were imposed at the cellular level, as a result of metabolic functioning.[24] Russett explains, "[t]he metabolic model conceived of organisms as heat machines engaged in energy transformation, and thus amenable to analysis by physical and chemical methods" (90). According to Geddes and Thomson, the female ovum and male sperm contained vastly different cell structures which resulted in equally vast differences in mental attributes.[25] Interestingly, Geddes and Thomson's view of male and female sexual differences were much more fixed than Darwin's, whose theory of sexual selection left more room for flux and change in sexual characteristics.[26] The upshot of Geddes and Thomson's findings was to keep the theory of radical gender difference firmly in place.

As a result of the emphasis upon gender polarity in the biomedical sciences, women's bodies were increasingly scrutinized over the course of the century. In contrast to the male body, envisioned as normal, the female body was pathological, a deviation requiring close supervision and expert care. The investigation of the female body became an absorbing concern for many medical practitioners, with gynecology constituting a major field of study by the mid-nineteenth century. "It is striking," Ornella Moscucci notes, "that gynaecology developed at the same time as the scientific study of humankind, yet the growth of gynaecology was not paralleled by the evolution of a complementary 'science of masculinity' or 'andrology.'"[27] Originally the purview of midwives, the supervision of childbirth and the treatment of women's diseases were slowly taken over by medical professionals during the eighteenth century.[28] Midwifery was considered a lay craft rather than a medical skill, practiced mostly by women and only occasionally by men.[29] In general, midwives attended normal births, only calling in doctors when problems occurred or were anticipated. Eventually, however, medical professionals expanded their authority, intervening even in routine births and advocating a prolonged period of convalescence after birth.[30] The result was that women were encouraged both to rely on medical expertise for all major or minor health problems and to envision their own bodies as fragile, complex systems comprehensible only to the trained doctor. As Barbara Ehrenreich and Deirdre English remark, "Doctors stressed the pathological nature of childbirth itself—an argument which also was essential to their campaign against midwives" (111). Even for women who enjoyed sound health, pathology was unavoidable.

By far the greatest factor that defined the female body as distinct from the male was the reproductive system. To the nineteenth-century doctor, the female reproductive system was inherently unstable, the key to women's lesser mental and physical capacities and the cause of endless ailments.[31] For most doctors, the primary indicator of reproductive health and the element that touched upon all aspects of physical and mental functioning was menstruation. In an 1861 edition of a textbook on women's medical diseases, for example, Charles West, a London physician, writes:

> You know menstruation to be merely the sign of a more important process going on deeper within the organism. The non-appearance of the discharge, then, or its suppression, suggests at once many important inquiries which must be carefully followed up, till you can return to them a satisfactory reply. Is the system so feeble that, like an ill-thriven plant, its sexual power remains altogether in abeyance? . . . Or, again, your patient suffers from what she conceives to be excessive menstruation, her health is breaking down beneath it? . . . These, and similar inquiries possess a special importance at certain epochs of a woman's life; for when the sexual powers are on the decline, disease is especially liable to be set up, and you therefore regard all menstrual irregularities at that time with closer attention than at any former period. (20–21)

West, like most other doctors at the time, regarded even slight variations in menstruation as ominous indications of ill health. A woman could not be considered healthy, in medical terms, unless all aspects of her menstrual cycle were considered normal. Even more seriously, women's nervous systems were so intertwined with their reproductive function, doctors assumed, that any minor emotional disturbance could upset the menstrual cycle, causing problems ranging from simple fatigue to insanity and even death.[32] Doctors cautioned that the woman with "strong emotions," for instance, could be exhibiting signs of insanity or, at the very least, be at risk of mental breakdown.[33] Given this set of circumstances, it was not surprising that many women's physicians felt that menopause was greatly to be desired, as the cessation of menses, they surmised, decreased the possibility of physical and mental instabilities. Edward Tilt, a London physician, describes the miraculous recoveries of "some forty patients" after menopause, including recovery from conditions such as "dispepsia" and "insanity" (13). To support his case, Tilt relates the comments of another doctor detailing the experiences of female mental patients: "There are many females between the ages of forty and fifty whose recoveries may be expected when the uterus shall have become quiescent, and when the brain shall have lost a fertile source of irritation and disease. Unfortunately it happens that the poor classes are much too unmindful of the health of women at the critical period of life, . . . and therefore insanity is of so frequent an occurrence among women" (qtd. in Tilt 13).

Given the dangers that menstruation visited upon women, it was a wonder that so many escaped serious consequences. Clearly, the connections between the female mind and body were so complex that they required constant medical supervision.

Faulty menstruation and "strong emotions" were only two of the many possible causes of female mental disorders. Both insanity and lesser mental afflictions could be caused by any number of difficulties associated with the reproductive system and the sexual organs. The problem could originate in the ovaries, for example, or be brought on by prohibited habits such as masturbation. In either event, medical interventions could remove the suspect organ and speed the patient on to health. One remedy for treating such emotional and mental problems associated with reproductive disorders was the ovariotomy, which became especially popular after the 1840s when the use of anesthesia enabled the procedure to be done with a minimum of pain.[34] Although there were valid reasons for performing ovariotomies, such as the removal of cysts, Ehrenreich and English point out that the procedure was over-performed. Touted as a cure for social and psychological disorders, the list of problems that could prompt an ovariotomy included "troublesomeness, eating like a ploughman, masturbation, attempted suicide, erotic tendencies, persecution mania, simple 'cussedness,' and dysmenorrhea" (qtd. in Ehrenreich & English 124). A procedure far less common than ovariotomies was the clitoridectomy, which was sometimes performed as a cure for masturbation and the nervous disorders that masturbation was thought to cause.[35] The chief advocate of clitoridectomies in Britain, Isaac Baker Brown, was discredited in 1866, but the operation continued to be used in the U.S. through the early twentieth century.[36] Brown considered the clitoridectomy a cure for a range of maladies, both moral and physical. He was especially concerned with the issue of masturbation, which he felt was a moral vice in both men and women, but particularly problematic for women. Thus, he lists the health problems that result from such an abuse:

> [T]he general disorder of the health which arises from self-induced irritation of the clitoris requires to be particularly noted, as well as certain characteristic appearances of the genital organs. . . .
>
> The patient becomes restless and excited, or melancholy and retiring; listless and indifferent to the social influences of domestic life. She will be fanciful in her food, sometimes express even a distaste for it, and apparently (as her friends will say) live upon nothing. She will always be ailing, and complaining of different affections. At first, perhaps, dyspepsia and sickness will be observed; then pain in the head and

> down the spine; pain, more or less constant, in the lower part of the
> back, or on either side in the lumbar region. (*Some Diseases* 30)

The ailments listed are so wide-ranging as to be almost impossible to avoid throughout an entire lifetime. Moscucci takes issue with the suggestion that clitoridectomies were an example of the medical oppression of women, noting that circumcision also was used as a cure for masturbation in the male.[37] Nonetheless, in my view, such procedures demonstrate the importance of the female reproductive system and female sexual practices in debates about women's diseases. Discursively and ideologically, both clitoridectomies and ovariotomies connected transgressive feminine behavior to medical pathology.

Given the fallibility of women's reproductive systems and the numerous ways that the malfunctioning feminine body could produce mental and emotional disturbances, it is not surprising to learn that many women were diagnosed with nervous disorders. Depression, anxiety, anorexia, nervous exhaustion, and hysteria were all part of a substantial repertoire of potential feminine maladies. Both men and women in the nineteenth century suffered from various nervous complaints, yet the attitude toward the female patient was often very different from that toward the male. Some disorders, such as neurasthenia, had a certain amount of cachet for the male sufferer, but were seen as less desirable in women. The symptoms of neurasthenia were especially wide-ranging, from headaches and insomnia to complete mental collapse.[38] A typical male neurasthenic was educated and successful, pushed to exhaustion by virtue of his driving ambition and hectic way of life. The female sufferer—who was not supposed to be ambitious, educated, or hard-driving—might be elegantly enervated or downright cantankerous, depending on her circumstances and the judgment of her doctor. Other disorders, such as hysteria, were more specifically associated with women and generated a greater amount of social disapproval. F.C. Skey, writing in 1867, asserts: "[Hysteria] notoriously is far more common in women than in men, and in young persons from the age of seventeen to thirty, in the unmarried than in the married. We do not associate hysteric affections with persons of either sex who are characterized by vigor of mind, of strong will, of strength and firmness of character" (*Hysteria* 58). Unlike neurasthenia, which was a fairly genteel form of nervous exhaustion, hysteria crossed the boundary of acceptable behavior. Whereas neurasthenics were thought of as quietly anxious, hysterics were deemed troublesome and uncooperative. Moreover, given the similarity of symptoms, doctors often confused the diseases. An 1899 medical text on nervous diseases explains, for example: "*Hysteria* may be associated with neurasthenia, but has its own stigmata. It is to be kept in mind that disturbances of function in neurasthenia are those of irritable weakness and not of actual loss. Anesthesias, palsies, convulsions, complete loss of self-control, actual amnesias, are not the property of neurasthenia, but are the ear-marks of hysteria" (Church and Peterson 558–59). Symptoms for both diseases included paralyzed limbs, chronic coughs, and speech disorders, while dramatic convulsions or paroxysms would signal hysteria. On the other hand, refusal to eat, rebelliousness, or angry outbursts, might be a sign of either disorder, but more likely would be identified as hysteria. In either situation, woman's biology was presumed to be the cause, and social transgression (female rebelliousness, for example) of any type could point to disease. No matter what the diagnosis, social concepts of correct feminine behavior entered into both the treatment and the identification of the disease.[39]

In some cases, a nervous or intractable woman might be diagnosed with the more serious charge of madness, particularly during the middle decades of the nineteenth century when the system of "moral management" began to gain widespread approval from the medical community and general public.[40] Under this philosophy, the insane were to be handled with respect and compassion rather than physical constraints. This new system of treatment was, in part, a response to public outcries against the inhuman treatment of the insane. Many asylums were, as Porter notes, "riddled with corruption and cruelty, where whips and chains masqueraded as therapeutic" (*Madness* 99). In some cases, protests were launched by former inmates themselves, many complaining that they had been unjustly confined.[41] Moreover, moral management was very much the legacy of Enlightenment principles of reason and equality. Inspired by such principles, Philippe Pinel, an eighteenth-century French psychiatrist, promoted moral therapy in Paris.[42] Explaining his conversion to this approach, he explains, "I . . . discovered, that insanity was curable in many instances, by mildness of treatment and attention to the state of the mind exclusively, and when coercion was indispensible, that it might be very effectually applied without corporal indignity" (Pinel, *Treatise on Insanity* 108). Under the system of moral management, asylums were "modelled on the ideal of bourgeois family life, and restraint was minimized."[43] In contrast to the old procedures, the new standards were an improvement and many professionals embraced the modern philosophy for altruistic reasons.

Yet despite well-meaning motives on the part of many administrators, the moral management system, with its emphasis on bourgeois notions of proper behavior, led to a reconceptualization of social transgression—especially along gender lines—as madness. Self-control, cleanliness, and cheerfulness were high on the list of desirable traits and rebelliousness, eccentricity, or sexual boldness in women were objectionable. In this new context, insanity was redefined as "moral insanity," a concept which covered a much larger territory than earlier definitions. As Showalter explains:

> "Moral insanity," a concept introduced by James Cowles Prichard in 1835, held madness to be "a morbid perversion of the natural feelings, affections, inclinations, temper, habits, moral dispositions, and natural impulses, without any remarkable disorder or defect of the intellect, or knowing and reasoning faculties, and particularly without any insane illusion or hallucination." This definition could be stretched to take in almost any kind of behavior regarded as abnormal or disruptive by community standards. (*Female Malady* 29)

Once the absence of reason or intellect was no longer a requirement for the identification of insanity, doctors had a much greater latitude in imposing the label of madness on the chronically depressed, rebellious, or sexually aberrant individual. However, because of the greater social imperative for women to be docile and virtuous, the designation of insanity was much more likely to be attributed to a woman than to a man. Showalter notes, for instance, that by the mid-nineteenth century women made up the majority of persons institutionalized as insane, completely reversing the situation that existed just a few years before.[44] Moreover, female insanity, as with the more commonplace nervous and psychological disorders of women, was typically associated with reproductive imbalances. Thus, as Moscucci observes, "[b]y the end of the century, medical practitioners were advocating the appointment of gynaecologists to the staff of insane asylums and recommending routine gynaecological examinations in the diagnosis of women's mental disorders" (*Science of Woman* 105). Like nervous disease, mental derangement was further proof of the female body's pathological tendencies.

Because moral insanity could so easily include infractions of social conventions, sexual transgression figured prominently in diagnoses of female madness. Domestic ideology of the mid-nineteenth century pictured women as chaste and sexually unresponsive, channeling their primary emotions into maternal and spiritual devotion. British medical thinking mirrored domestic ideology, with many doctors believing that most "normal" women felt little or no sexual desire.[45] William Acton, a doctor specializing in venereal diseases, expressed the thoughts of many of his medical peers when he wrote in 1875: "[T]he majority of women (happily for society) are not very much troubled with sexual feeling of any kind. What men are habitually, women are only exceptionally" (*Functions and Disorders* 61). Not surprisingly, Acton felt that "immoderate" sexual desire in women could be a sign of madness, and termed nymphomania "a form of insanity that those accustomed to visit lunatic asylums must be fully conversant with" (*Functions and Disorders* 61). For Acton, as for many other nineteenth-century medical professionals, female sexual transgression signified pathology.

Most women who fell outside the bourgeois ideal were not deemed insane, but over the course of the century the socially or sexually transgressive woman increasingly was seen as biologically aberrant rather than merely morally deficient. Moral considerations still continued to inform medical analyses and influence public opinion, but scientific arguments possessed much authority in a culture that was becoming less religious. This increasing reliance on biomedical reasoning to describe female social and sexual transgression was especially apparent in the changing attitude toward prostitution. During the 1830s and 1840s, medical professionals and the general public demonstrated a deepening concern about prostitution which was reflected in an expanding discourse on the subject. In the early part of the century, discourses on prostitution centered mostly on social and moral issues such as crime and vice, while to a lesser extent medical considerations of disease and biological normality were being voiced. Public debate on prostitution began in earnest following the publication in 1836 of a major study of Parisian prostitutes by a French doctor, Alexandre Jean Baptiste Parent-Duchâtelet, which combined the "objective" language of science with the moralistic concerns of a bourgeois populace.[46] Parent-Duchâtelet's *De la prostitution dans la Ville de Paris* connected the prostitute not only with specific venereal diseases, but also with a generalized concept of urban filth metaphorically represented by the Paris sewers. This study was followed in Britain by a number of publications on prostitution in the 1840s.[47] The first British studies of prostitution were by doctors and nonmedical writers influenced by evangelical teachings and concerned with the moral reform of the poor.[48] At the same time, a new type of social science advocated "objective" analysis, using the tools of statistics and empirical research. W.R. Greg's 1850 *Prostitution* provided a link between older evangelical approaches to prostitution and the new project of social analysis, showing concern for the suffering of prostitutes and emphasizing their exile from the refuge of bourgeois family life.[49] Greg's commentary appeared about the same time as Henry Mayhew's reports on prostitutes, originally published in the *Morning Chronicle* in 1849 and 1850 and later republished in an 1861 multi-volume collection.[50] Mayhew's accounts took a harsher sociological and moral perspective more typical of the mid-century, aligning the prostitute with "thieves, swindlers, and beggars" (Poovey, "Speaking of the Body" 31). Like Chadwick's sanitary report, Mayhew's analysis combined medical concerns about sanitation and overcrowding with moral concerns about sexual indiscretion and unprincipled behavior.

Implicit in many of the medical studies of prostitutes was the idea that the body of the sexually transgressive woman was decidedly different from the body of the "normal" woman. Like nineteenth-century medical researchers who sought to find correspondences between the genitalia of African women and white prostitutes, other analysts of prostitution assumed a biological difference between the chaste woman and her sexually transgressive counterpart. Shannon Bell has argued, for instance, that Parent-Duchâtelet has offered contradictory readings on the question, at first countering prevailing medical opinion that the prostitute's body is physically different from the non-prostitute woman's body, and later implying the opposite. Paraphrasing Parent-Duchâtelet, Bell notes that when he asserts, in effect, that "the [prostitute's] sexual organ is prone to labial tumors and abscesses," he suggests that the prostitute's body is indeed different at the physical level (48). Parent-Duchâtelet's contradictory logic is duplicated by William Acton, as Bell observes, in Acton's 1857 *Prostitution,* an examination of prostitution in England. She concludes that "Acton in his early chapters makes a strong link between the prostitute and the 'normal' woman. . . . Yet later, with the same set of words with which he equates the prostitute and mother bodies, he sets the two apart: 'prostitutes . . . become . . . with tarnished bodies and polluted minds, wives and mothers'" (51). Although in the case of both Parent-Duchâtelet and Acton it is not clear whether the prostitute's body is inherently different from the "normal" woman's body or becomes so through her sexual activities, in both instances her social habits mark her body and mind as diseased.

Aside from the physical concerns raised by Parent-Duchâtelet and Acton, the most visible sign of pathology in the prostitute's body was venereal disease. Syphilis, in particular, was both a feared disease and a symbol of the prostitute's connection with "filth," as Parent-Duchâtelet's writings affirm. In the wake of many medical pronouncements on prostitution and disease, a series of acts known as the Contagious Disease Acts were introduced in the 1860s.[51] The purpose of the C.D. Acts was to control the spread of venereal disease among enlisted military men by compelling prostitutes to undergo periodic medical examinations, yet the Acts ignored the responsibility of the soldiers.[52] Public reaction to the C.D. Acts was harsh and divided, with those who felt the Acts would control the spread of venereal disease on one side and those who opposed state control of women's bodies on the other. As Walkowitz observes, the Acts endorsed a double standard, placing an unjust amount of attention on female behavior and virtually ignoring the participation of male clients:

[T]he practical medical goals that underlay the C.D. acts were in fact fused with, and at the same time undermined by, a set of moral and ideological assumptions. In pressuring for the medical inspection of prostitutes without imposing periodic genital examination on the enlisted men who were their clients, architects of the acts obliterated from the start whatever effectiveness as sanitary measures the acts might have had. (3)

The result of the Acts was to weaken the medical basis of regulation and instead punish the women for their sins. Bourgeois moral concerns about proper female behavior could be subsumed under the heading of public health, legitimizing the intrusion of state and local authorities into the private lives of an unwanted underclass. The Acts were eventually repealed in 1886 after a long and contentious campaign,[53] but the lengthy time needed to accomplish the task illustrates the central ideological position that female sexual and social transgression occupied in Victorian culture.

The medical treatment of prostitution focused attention on the supposition that prostitutes were either abnormal or that they posed a health hazard to society. In either case, the prostitute's transgression was not merely a legal, moral, or criminal problem, but something etched on her body or mind. Just as many doctors thought that nymphomania denoted insanity, so too many equated prostitution with physical or mental pathology, in large part because the prostitute was seen as abnormal compared to the bourgeois woman of domestic ideology. In this sense, her gender transgression was just as important as her legal transgression. Thus even though Acton, for instance—in contrast with other medical professionals—was willing to assert that both the prostitute and her customer were "in an unnatural state," it was the prostitute and not her male customer who was the subject of Acton's studies and the many studies of others (*Prostitution* 115). Most importantly, the general conviction that the prostitute was an "unnatural" woman gave scientific validity to social prohibitions, concealing a reliance on bourgeois conventions behind a cloud of "impartial" language.

While social and moral concerns about prostitution gained legitimacy from medical assertions about women's biological nature and threats to public health, general concerns about growing numbers of independent, educated women were supported by similar assertions. Throughout the second half of the nineteenth century and increasingly towards its end, doctors warned against female intellectual exertion and women's ambition in the male sphere specifically because it was against woman's nature and would result in harm to her body or mind. S. Weir Mitchell (1829–1914), an American doctor well known in Britain, cautioned in an 1887 publication, "there comes a time when the matured man certainly surpasses the woman in persistent energy and capacity for unbroken brain-work. If she then matches herself against him, it will be, with some exceptions, at bitter cost" (43). Mitchell later concludes: "The cases I see of breakdown among women between sixteen and nineteen who belong to normal schools or female colleges are out of all proportion larger than the number of like failures among young men of the same ages . . ." (44). The logic here is similar to that pertaining to prostitution: objections to female gender transgression which were basically moral and social in character gained validity through medical pronouncements. The girl or woman who sought to educate herself beyond the norm for her sex was at risk of "breakdown," unlike her male counterpart. Like the prostitute, the educated woman was pathologized for not conforming to gender conventions.

Medical concerns about "over-educated" women continued throughout the 1880s and 1890s as more and more middle-class women took on jobs outside the home and pursued higher education. A changing economic climate, feminist campaigns, and increasing numbers of "redundant" (unmarried) women encouraged many women to seek work in formerly male terrains. During the mid-century, jobs for middle-class women were restricted in the main to those of governess and teacher, both poorly paid occupations with low social status. Towards the end of the century, women took on more remunerative clerical positions and some pursued professions in medicine, as nurses and doctors. At the same time, improved educational opportunities allowed women to receive better instruction at the secondary level and, less frequently, to enter universities. Yet despite advancements in women's education, objections from the general public and the medical establishment meant that concessions to gender ideology were constantly being made. As Gleadle notes:

> In 1884 a Professor of Obstetrics, John Thorburn, argued that courses designed specifically for women were essential to circumvent the grievous effects which he believed the standard course of study would have upon the female constitution. . . . As women gained greater access to employment and education, the popularity of such theories, particularly among the scientific community, intensified. (143)

Ideas about differences between male and female intellect which had gained scientific credence in the middle of the century from Darwin, Spencer, and the medical establishment came back with a vengeance in the 1880s and 1890s, when universities began opening their doors to women. All the old arguments about conflicts between intellectual work and the female reproductive system were asserted.

Some medical professionals, like John Harvey Kellogg (an American physician whose guidebook on women's health went through several editions during the 1880s and 1890s), allowed that women had the same mental capacity as men, but cautioned that women's reproductive systems rendered them more prone than men to nervous collapse when faced with demanding intellectual work. This fine distinction between mental and physical capacity had the same result as arguments about female intellectual inferiority; both theories could be used to support arguments against advanced female education and both pathologized female intellectual exertion. Kellogg was especially concerned about the effects of "overstudy" (204) on the female reproductive system and writes:

> [T]he girl who is approaching puberty . . . is not prepared to sustain any severe tax of either mind or body, and if at this time she is compelled to keep pace with others whose conditions are not such as to demand shorter lessons and less severe mental taxation, the exhaustion of the nervous system which may result may interfere seriously with the proper completion of the approaching changes in her physical system intended to result in the establishment of an important function. (204–5)

Kellogg, like his peers, was primarily concerned that "overstudy" would seriously compromise the "establishment of an important function"—the future childbearing capacity of female students. He goes on to caution that female mental exertion at any time during the reproductive years—especially between "the ages of twelve and eighteen"—could result in "certain dangers" (205) to the reproductive system. For similar reasons, Kellogg warned against the pernicious effects of novel reading for girls, which he felt caused too much excitement and placed excessive stress upon the reproductive system. Doctors such as Kellogg felt that the "wrong" kind of reading and "excessive" intellectual effort would create numerous nervous disorders in women— neurasthenia or hysteria, for instance—and that reproductive problems could result. Thus, although medical evaluations of the female body changed as the century drew to a close, gender transgression and issues of reproductivity remained central.

THE REPRODUCTIVE IMPERATIVE

Medical attitudes about sexuality and the female body took a new direction towards the end of the nineteenth century partly in response to changing gender paradigms and partly in response to sexological discourses. Instead of being a domestic angel whose sexuality was circumscribed by maternal instinct, the "normal" woman of late nineteenth-century biomedical discourse began to be seen as a desiring being in her own right. To a great extent this re-evaluation of female sexual desire proceeded from the assertions of the sexologists. Sexual passion was "natural," although some confusion existed as to just how much desire was normal for women. Krafft-Ebing, for example, confessed to encountering great difficulty in distinguishing pathological female desire from normal. In 1892 he writes: "Since woman has less sexual need than man, a predominating sexual desire in her arouses a suspicion of its pathological significance; and the more, when this expression in desire for adornment, coquetry, or male society, which, passing beyond the limits set by good breeding and manners, becomes quite noticeable" (48). One senses here the traces of an earlier interpretation of female sexual desire as nymphomania or insanity, while at the same time there is an acknowledgment of some degree of acceptable desire.

Rather than considering women passionless creatures, then, doctors began to acknowledge that "normal" women did have sexual desire, but there was a caveat: normal desire, for both men and women, could only be experienced in relation to a normal object choice. For women, that object choice was clear: it was the male subject of bourgeois heteronormativity. Thus, the new medical attitude toward sexuality, although liberating in some respects, was also limiting in others. "Sexuality" became automatically restricted to the confines of what Adrienne Rich has termed "compulsory heterosexuality"—a cultural mandate to engage in heteronormative sexualities and social practices.[54] Rich identifies compulsory heterosexuality as an institution supported by a web of cultural assumptions, from economic and legal inequalities to popular ideas about "sexual liberation" (633). Opposing compulsory heterosexuality are those whom Rich places on the "lesbian continuum"—women who share common experiences in their responses to political and economic conditions but who do not necessarily identify themselves as lesbians or desire sex with another woman (648). She includes, on the lesbian continuum, "such associations as *marriage resistance* and the 'haggard' behavior identified by Mary Daly . . . which have lain out of reach as a consequence of limited, mostly clinical, definitions of 'lesbianism'" (649). Rich's essay addresses social aspects of female experience rather than medical assessments, yet her targeting of compulsory heterosexuality as the unspoken concept that separates socially-permitted from socially-prohibited sex and gender identities captures the essence of the "pathological" label that so many experts resorted to. More particularly, the concept of compulsory heterosexuality locates an important site of ideological formation and draws attention to a significant aspect of my analysis.

With the shift away from a discourse of domestic ideology to one of compulsory heterosexuality, "natural" female maternal desire and passionlessness was redefined as "natural" sexual desire for the heterosexual object choice. Although this was seen by many to be a liberating move, it nonetheless was pathology by a different name. Both "too much" and "too little" desire could be seen as unnatural, just as was the improper sexual object choice.[55] More importantly for my purposes, this narrow space of allotted desire duplicated some crucial aspects of earlier medical formulations by making reproductive sexuality the cornerstone of normality. In an article on sexology and the New Woman, Smith-Rosenberg makes some comments relevant to my study here. Smith-Rosenberg's argument is that sexological discourses affected the way that the New Woman—the emancipated woman of the late nineteenth and early twentieth centuries—was perceived, both by self-identified New Women and those who sought to define them.[56] In Smith-Rosenberg's formulation, there were two phases in which the American New Woman was a recognizable phenomenon. During the first phase, she argues, the New Woman was pathologized by sexologists up through the end of the century and slightly beyond. At this time, she observes, sexologists were shifting their focus from male homosexuality to female homosexuality. The second phase covered the interval after World War I, a period when American lesbians adopted the language of pathology as their own. This second generation of New Women, Smith-Rosenberg contends, was manipulated by the rhetoric of the "New Men"—progressive doctors and intellectuals—who equated female liberation with heterosexual license (272). She states:

> Divorcing women's rights from their political and economic context, they made the daughter's quest for heterosexual pleasures, not the mother's demand for political power, personify female freedom. Linking orgasms to chic fashion and planned motherhood, male sex reformers, psychologists, and physicians promised a future of emotional support and sexual delights to women who accepted heterosexual marriage—and male economic hegemony. (272)

Thus, the new discourse of female sexual freedom supported older concepts of male economic control and re-envisioned bourgeois domestic ideology in a slightly different form. Female "freedom" was the freedom to engage in bourgeois heterosexual practices, while lesbianism—or any activity that opposed heteronormative gender roles—was equated with perversion and an "unnatural" lust for personal and economic autonomy.

Although the scope of Smith-Rosenberg's argument extends beyond the chronological period covered in my analysis, her understanding of the changing discourse of female emancipation both before and after the early twentieth century illuminates the adaptability of biomedical discourse to new social conditions and the persistence of conventional beliefs even in the face of radical social change. Moreover, her formulation demonstrates that discourses of liberation and sexual freedom were, for many women, pathologizing discourses because they classified nonconformance to the heteronormative ideal as abnormal. This idea, and Rich's theory of compulsory heterosexuality, both have a particular relevance to Chapter Four of my study, on *Jude the Obscure,* because I am concerned there with the way that constructions of female sexual deviance coalesced around issues of female reproduction even as gender conventions changed. During the middle years of the nineteenth century, when the theory of domestic ideology was at its zenith, women's reproductive systems identified them as radically different from men and consigned women to a particular kind of gender identification; in later years, as biomedical discourses changed and sexology identified a certain amount of female sexual desire as normal, reproductive *difference* became less important as a defining concept for women than the orientation towards reproductive *sexuality.* In this framework, nineteenth- and early twentieth-century lesbians, "mannish women," intellectual women threatened with sterility, or emancipated women who desired economic autonomy and so rejected marriage, were pathologized specifically because they did not conform to biomedical and bourgeois ideas about female reproductivity. It was not that all women were expected literally to give birth, but that bourgeois culture placed so much importance on the concept of female reproductivity that to fail to conform to what had been deemed the single most important aspect of female social and sexual identity amounted to a rejection of femaleness and thus, a rejection of the cloak of bourgeois convention.

The larger argument I am making in this study is that deviance as envisioned in the nonreproductive or reproductively problematic female body illustrated the very worst that could happen to a biological organism, so that the deviant female body had a certain kind of symbolic value in scientifically-conscious nineteenth-century British culture. Thus, literary representations of the deviant female body allowed the reading public to explore or resolve cultural anxieties about a social domain that was itself imagined in biological terms. As discourses of the life and social sciences became increasingly prominent during the nineteenth century, Victorian society was able to see itself as a biological entity, comprised not merely of individual beings, but of smaller organisms within a larger species. After Darwin, the idea of a species emerging, developing, or declining as a large, interconnected body became imaginable. Within the Darwinian model, reproduction became something more than an individual act; instead, it became something relating not only to the natural world, but also to political, economic, and social realities. Weeks observes, for example, that "[Darwin's] claim that sexual selection (the struggle for partners) acted independently of natural selection (the struggle for existence) [implied] that survival depended upon sexual selection, and the ultimate test of biological success lay in reproduction" (*Sexuality* 67). Healthy reproduction was the guarantee of a vigorous society, and Spencer's biological metaphor underscored this concept, paving the way for a theory of the social domain as social body. Under this formulation, if society really were an organism, then only reproduction would ensure its continuance.

My study locates three separate instances of biological thinking connecting the female body to the social domain within the nineteenth-century English novel. My goal in Chapter Two is to explore biological reasoning in Dickens's *Hard Times* in relation to industrial society and the deviant female body. In this narrative, reproductivity is central, although not obviously so, to the idea of healthy social and sexual relations. The healthy family is defined as the one that not only evidences vigorous reproduction, but also understands—at least on an intuitive level—that human beings are connected to each other in the same way that various plants within a particular species are connected. The larger biological system must be healthy so that the individual components can survive. Thus, *Hard Times* demonstrates that people inhabit a social environment in the same way that plants inhabit a biological environment. In both instances, if the environment is unhealthy, the individual organism may either die or fail to reproduce—and what happens on the individual level can happen to the entire species. In this text, Louisa Gradgrind, the deviant woman of the story, embodies everything that is wrong in the industrial world. She is raised in an environment of disaffected social relationships, has incestuous sexual desires that cannot lead to children, and lives her life childless, as an example to industrial society of the self-destructive habits it generates.

Similar reproductive issues are evident in Rider Haggard's *She,* the subject of Chapter Three. Here my aim is to demonstrate how the diseased African "body"—both a geographical and a physical body—corresponds to the body of Ayesha, the deviant "white" woman of Arabic descent who rules over a community of Africans. Ayesha's deviance is one of unnatural sexual desire; she displays a selfish disregard for the people over whom she rules and an aggressive sexuality. Her deviant character is paralleled by the African landscape which is rendered in terms of a diseased female reproductive system: polluted canals, underground caves packed with dead bodies, all suggest a biological system which cannot reproduce because it is socially, morally, and physically unhealthy.

Chapter Four addresses some of the issues discussed by Smith-Rosenberg about the contradiction between a liberatory discourse of female sexual freedom and a confining one of heteronormative object choice. Even though Smith-Rosenberg classifies these contradictory liberatory sexual discourses as being post-World War I, my study looks at the way in which such contradictions—between sexual freedom and sexual restraint—can be seen in at least one major British novel of the pre-World War I period: Hardy's *Jude the Obscure*. In that narrative, the central female protagonist, Sue Bridehead, is portrayed as both socially liberated and sexually deviant, in the sense that she is repelled by heteronormative sexuality. Her pathology, which is portrayed as both a lack of sexual desire and a nervous constitution, is an exaggerated example of a similar pathology which affects the larger social domain. Both compulsory heterosexuality and late-nineteenth century discourses of neurasthenia are important factors which circumscribe Sue and the "modern society" in which she lives. My argument here is that Sue's problems with reproductivity—evidenced by the death of her children and the birth of her stillborn child—and her reluctance to engage in heteronormative sexual relations are symptomatic of the same difficulties that plague the larger social domain: nervousness and problems with heteronormative sexual desire. Consequently, Sue's reproductive failure is the parallel to the reproductive hazard that threatens "modern society" as it is depicted here.

In a culture concerned about its own survival and its own susceptibility to disease, the deviant female body serves a convenient purpose. The woman who does not conform to the concept of healthy bourgeois heteronormativity and all of its supporting practices and institutions enacts cultural anxieties about reproduction and the future of the social body as a collective species; it is through her body that the larger cultural decline can be imagined and conveniently displaced. Just as the transgressive woman's "disease" is defined as a reproductive failure, so too does she embody the diseased society's fears of reproductive decline. Literary representations of feminine deviance allow society to imagine the abnormal female body as symptomatic of widespread cultural deterioration and, in turn, to project its collective fears onto that body. Thus, larger anxieties about the health of society and the longevity of the species become a question of individual female sexual pathology. In this way, a diagnosis of female sexual perversion appears to be the answer to a cultural mystery; by revealing the "truth" about this perversion, the suggestion is, the larger systemic problem is resolved. The following three chapters trace the changing conception of female deviance in the English novel and culture throughout the second half of the nineteenth century.

Chapter Two

Towards a Discourse of Perversion: Female Deviance, Sibling Incest, and the Bourgeois Family in Dickens's *Hard Times*

At first glance, Charles Dickens's *Hard Times* seems focused primarily on the ills of industrial society; the working poor and middle class alike are burdened by social and economic policies that ignore the non-material needs of human beings. Yet at the center of the industrial drama is the bourgeois family, whose implication in the problems of industrial society is embodied in the figure of the female sexual deviant. The Gradgrind family, with its emphasis on utilitarian education and statistical thinking, is lacking in those affections which join people together in mutual support and shared goals. Thus, disaffected family relationships plague the Gradgrind household, laying the groundwork for a perverse relationship between the elder Gradgrind siblings, Louisa and Tom. Louisa's unhealthy love for her brother is arguably the central problem that holds the various plots together: industrial and domestic, bourgeois and working class. By illustrating a contrast between natural and unnatural family attachments, sibling incest demonstrates the hazards of mechanistic thinking in the social domain.

The basic problem I am examining here is how the deviant female body enters into the delineation of natural and unnatural spheres in *Hard Times*. I am interested in the way that *Hard Times* follows a particular scientific logic apparent in later Victorian novels wherein the pathologized female body becomes identified with the pathologized social body, thereby displacing, eliding, and appearing to solve the problems of the social sphere by revealing a hidden "truth" about female deviance. In later chapters—on Haggard's *She* and Hardy's *Jude the Obscure*—I analyze similar problems having to do with the relationship between female perversion and the social domain.

All three novels make certain connections—between the human body and the social domain, and between the deviant female body and a diseased social sphere—which demonstrate convergences among biomedical and literary discourses and texts. In each of these novels, I trace the varying ways in which representations of the pathologized female body in literary works speak to larger cultural issues. *Hard Times* occupies a unique position in this sequence of novels in that it precedes many of the pertinent scientific publications I discuss in my Introduction—Darwin's *Origin of Species,* Spencer's "The Social Organism," various writings by medical professionals on female sexuality, and later accounts of sexual perversion—yet it also touches upon ideas which these publications address. By including *Hard Times* in my study, I am adopting Foucault's notion of discourse as fluid and multi-directional; thus, I am assuming that literature does not merely follow in the footsteps of other cultural discourses, nor does it bear any fixed relationship to self-consciously "nonfictional" texts and discourses, but instead participates in the formation of those other discourses, both fictional and nonfictional. In order for the *Origin* to reach a cognizant and admiring public, for example, the ideas presented must be within reach of its readership. *Hard Times* is interesting in this respect because it addresses problems having to do with "nature," perversion, and the biological character of the social domain before discourses about those topics had been fully articulated in the public sphere, suggesting that these topics were much more prevalent in the British consciousness than would at first seem likely.

GOOD SCIENCE/BAD SCIENCE: NATURE, PERVERSION, AND THE ORGANIC MODEL

Hard Times has an ongoing dialogue with the scientific premises of its day. On its most visible level, it is antagonistic towards a kind of statistical thinking that was being used in the social sciences: in the Utilitarian philosophy of Jeremy Bentham, particularly, and other social theories which relied on quantitative reasoning, reducing people to numbers and ignoring the needs of the individual. On a less visible level, however, *Hard Times* endorses an alternative view of science that is based on the natural world: the world of plants, of unfettered growth, and of biological relatedness. As the events of the narrative demonstrate, rigid thinking of the kind associated with utilitarianism inhibits and deforms the natural development of living beings.

Historically, utilitarianism was comprised of many contradictory concepts and different social theorists applied its precepts in varying ways; yet the central idea promoted by Bentham can be summed up in a few words: that the rightness or wrongness of a given social action should be judged on whether that action would bring about the greatest happiness for the greatest number of people. This idea is lampooned extensively in *Hard Times,* mainly through the teachings of Thomas Gradgrind (the elder), who sees the social sphere in mere numbers and cares nothing for the sufferings of people on the losing end of the utilitarian yardstick.[1] Gradgrind is aptly described as having "a rule and a pair of scales, and the multiplication table always in his pocket . . . ready to weigh and measure any parcel of human nature, and tell you exactly what it comes to" (10). In his role as schoolteacher and parent alike, Gradgrind's educational philosophy espouses a narrow kind of quantitative thinking. His zealous embrace of statistical thinking is matched only by his ardor for "facts"; both are relegated to a primary position in his philosophy, while "fancy" and anything related to the imagination are denigrated. Gradgrind's closest friend is Josiah Bounderby—the town's main bank manager and factory owner—who enthusiastically supports Gradgrind's version of utilitarian philosophy, at least insofar as it allows him to ignore the difficulties of his employees and further a vision of himself as a hardheaded businessman. While Bounderby provides a bit of comic relief, however, Gradgrind is a somber character whose teachings have an oppressive effect on others: the young students whom he instructs, such as Bitzer, a star pupil whose assimilation of Gradgrind's lessons leads him to become cold and selfish; his wife, Mrs. Gradgrind, who, overwhelmed by her husband's "Ologies," eventually dies drawing "figures of wonderful no-meaning" with her pen (201); and, most conspicuously, his own children—especially Louisa and Tom, the eldest children, whose unnatural affection for each other establishes the novel's logic of perversion.

Hard Times alludes to other social theories along with utilitarianism, grouping together a number of different approaches that share a similar statistical approach to social issues. Two of Gradgrind's younger children, for instance, who do not appear as characters but are referred to in passing, are named, suggestively, Adam Smith and Malthus. The reference to Adam Smith recalls Smith's 1776 publication, *Wealth of Nations,* which advocated a form of noninterference in the marketplace loosely known as *laissez-faire* economics and which purported to "follow nature." According to this logic, the economy is like a biological organism, in that a problem or deficiency in one part of the organism will be compensated for in another part. Thus, some individual entities and people may suffer, but that is all for the good of the whole. In Smith's thinking, in a profit-driven economy, monetary problems will sort themselves out without any interference on the part of the government or other regulating body.[2]

Similarly, Thomas Malthus believed that outside interference would not help problems of overpopulation and that society would be better off by ignoring the difficulties of the poor, who were responsible for their own poverty. According to Malthus, population growth proceeded at a faster pace than food production due to "reckless overbreeding," as Jeffrey Weeks terms it (*Sex, Politics* 123). Like Smith, Malthus assumed that society was self-regulating.[3] Both theorists followed a presumed logic of "nature," whereby individual suffering was negligible in light of the greater good—and in this sense their ideas were aligned with utilitarianism.

Hard Times' approach to these social theories brings up an interesting point, because although Smith and Malthus were assumed to follow a biological model, much in the mold of Herbert Spencer's concept of social Darwinism which followed later, the novel clearly repudiates the idea either that the poor were responsible for their own distress or that poverty was a natural state. In *Hard Times,* the organic model is re-envisioned, very much along the lines of the early Spencer (most of whose writings appear after the publication of *Hard Times*), but without the assumption that some individuals must suffer for the good of the larger social body.[4] While the theories of Smith, Malthus, and Spencer use an organic model to uphold the status quo, *Hard Times* employs an organic model for the opposite reason. In the novel's view, the social body is envisioned not as overriding the concerns of individuals, including the poor and disenfranchised, but as supported by mutual cooperation and the optimal health of each individual organism. By imagining the social sphere as an interconnected biological entity, *Hard Times* rejects the people-as-numbers ethic and looks at the problems of individuals.

Many of the economic issues in the narrative are suggested by a working class plot involving Stephen Blackpool, a factory worker; his estranged, dissipated wife; and Stephen's friend and fellow worker, Rachel. Although Stephen would like to marry Rachel (and we assume she would share his feelings if he were unmarried), he cannot because he is unable to afford a divorce and does not understand the legal issues involved.[5] Stephen and Rachel are destitute, but they are depicted as honest and upright, upholding standards of bourgeois morality and hard work and demonstrating the faulty logic of a Malthus who blames the poor for their poverty or a Smith who would not adjust the economy to aid the needy.

The text's main concern with the social approaches advocated by Smith, Malthus, and Bentham is with the indiscriminate use of statistics, ratios, and quantitative reasoning. Such mechanistic thinking creates disaffected social relations which, in turn, fuel the industrial machine that makes life miserable for those at the bottom. The Bounderbys and the Bitzers keep the machine going, although it appears that no person or entity in particular is responsible for the wretchedness of the poor. The description of Coketown (the home of the factory workers and the town nearest to the Gradgrinds) as a "town of machinery" (28) with its "streets all very like one another" (28) and interchangeable, "grace[less]" (29) buildings emphasizes the systemic nature of this mechanistic thinking. By telling us that "the jail might have been the infirmary, the infirmary might have been the jail, the town-hall might have been either," the narrator suggests that the problem is larger than any one person or economic policy (29).

In *The City of Dickens,* Alexander Welsh locates the systemic concept specifically in Dickens's portrayal of the city. Discussing the role of satire as a mode of representation, Welsh notes that although satire is prominent in Dickens's writing, "[it] becomes historically inadequate for coping with the nineteenth-century city" (11). Instead, Welsh states:

> The nineteenth century developed certain organic metaphors for the city. . . . Dickens, in the description of the fog at the beginning of the third book of *Our Mutual Friend,* concluded that 'the whole metropolis was a heap of vapour charged with muffled sound of wheels, and enfolding a gigantic catarrh.' Such metaphors connote an unpleasant or abnormal living thing, in which something has gone wrong with the system. They mark the beginning of an awareness of the city as a systemic problem, and therefore of a treatment or eventual cure for the city that is scientific rather than satiric. (25)

Although Welsh does not refer here specifically to *Hard Times* or locate the human body within the urban system, his comments nevertheless draw attention to both the element of disease and to the city as an interconnected biological system similar to the human body. In *Hard Times,* it is not only the city of Coketown that is diseased, but also the human beings who inhabit that city; in fact, the industrial city is itself a manifestation of abstract social and economic policies developed by those afflicted human beings.

Hard Times depicts Coketown's sorrows as caused by the collision between "fact" (statistical thinking) and "fancy" (imagination). On the one hand, the novel offers a grim portrayal of Coketown's factory workers, trudging from their meager lodgings to work and back again each day with no time for amusement and no outlet for creative thinking. The workers' misery, the narrative suggests, is due to the imposition of machine culture on their lives and thoughts. In a well-known passage, the novel imagines the steam engine as a sentient being, capable of thought and feeling:

> [Coketown] had a black canal in it, and a river that ran purple with an
> ill-smelling dye, and vast piles of building full of windows where there
> was a rattling and a trembling all day long, and where the piston of the
> steam-engine worked monotonously up and down, like the head of an
> elephant in a state of melancholy madness. (28)

The image of the melancholy-mad elephant turned into a machine dramatizes the plight of Coketown's workers; like the elephant, they too have been
turned into machines, their humanness denied. This concept is central to the
story, because when the people of Coketown are denied qualities which
define them as living creatures, tragic consequences ensue as a result of
nature being thwarted.

On the other hand, the novel offers an image of uninhibited imagination ("fancy") through the portrayal of Sleary's Circus, which exists outside
of bourgeois and industrial society. The circus opposes everything that
machine culture stands for: the performers are disorderly and untidy; some
drink a bit too much; and sexual relationships are unclear, with numerous
children belonging to what seems to be an ever-changing pool of fathers
and mothers. However, although the circus does not match bourgeois culture in its social configurations and personal habits, it does display the elements that the narrative endorses: imagination, creativity, mutual
affection, and cooperation among its members. Accordingly, the opposition between the circus and mechanistic thinking is established early on,
when Louisa and Tom are severely reprimanded by their father for
attempting to peek at the performers through a hole in a fence. "Never
wonder" is a constant injunction of Gradgrind to his children, and the circus is guilty of inspiring such wonder.

The mechanistic thinking propounded by machine culture affects not
only Coketown's laboring people, then, but also the town's ruling elite,
and—most importantly—its children, who will be permanently scarred by
their oppressive upbringing: Bitzer will become indifferent to the feelings of
others; Louisa and Tom will become unhappy and self-centered. Thus, the
narrator makes an express connection between the working classes and the
Gradgrind children, asking at one point "Is it possible, I wonder, that there
was any analogy between the case of the Coketown population and the case
of the little Gradgrinds?" (31). The form of the question is important here,
because the reference to the "little Gradgrinds" demonstrates the novel's concern with growth and development. Gradgrind's children are analogous to
Coketown's workers because the miseries of both are the product of a mechanistic environment that stunts normal growth. Machine culture, the novel

suggests, inhibits the natural growth and physical formation of living beings, whereas the domain of the circus gives free reign to mind and body.

Hard Times' focus on "natural" growth, then, suggests a view of society as an organic entity. Machine culture—the world of "facts"—impedes the natural growth of living beings and stunts their formation. Accordingly, the opening lines of the novel establish the central opposition between the world of "facts" and the organic world of "nature": "'Now, what I want is, Facts. Teach these boys and girls nothing but Facts. Facts alone are wanted in life. Plant nothing else, and root out everything else'" (9). The speaker is Thomas Gradgrind, and the organic metaphor ("plant nothing"/"root out") establishes the pattern which will govern the narrative logic. Coketown's laborers and children—thus, all of industrial society—are compared to the natural world of plants and living entities. Like Spencer's biological metaphor, *Hard Times'* organic metaphor establishes a direct relationship between individual human beings and the larger sphere of nature.[6]

This parallel between people and plants is most obviously apparent in the three book headings: "Sowing," "Reaping" and "Garnering," which suggest an organic pattern of birth, growth, and maturation. Against this natural pattern of development, machine culture imposes its arbitrary limits. Observing the opposition between artificial and natural worlds in *Hard Times,* Kate Flint comments:

> The different worlds of this novel are yoked together by a recurrent emphasis on Dickens's part: that contemporary society, and the forms of its culture, can be classified as either natural or artificial. The former is always to be preferred over the latter: it is persistently characterized by imagery drawn from a vegetative, non-industrial world, suggesting that underlying organic patterns will always win out over human-imposed ones. (xii)

Thus, according to Flint, in the struggle between artificial and "vegetative, non-industrial" spheres, "organic patterns" will eventually prevail. Although Flint does not expand on the "organic patterns" in *Hard Times,* it is my purpose here to bring these patterns to light and explore their implications. Moreover, I am applying the logic of *Hard Times'* organic reasoning to the entire narrative, so that the sphere which opposes the natural world is not merely "artificial," but more precisely, "unnatural." By applying the organic metaphor to the entire narrative—and not just to a portion which represents "nature"—I will demonstrate that sibling incest is not an insignificant theme, but one that directly articulates the problems in the industrial sphere.

Machine-like thinking in the social sphere, the novel demonstrates, creates unnatural, perverted children who, as adults, will be unable to foster healthy relations with others or contribute to the social domain in a constructive way. The effects of impeded growth are seen most prominently in Gradgrind's two oldest children, Louisa and Tom. Gradgrind's educational philosophy contains no room for imagination, play, love, or compassion— only facts, numbers, and material factors. Therefore, Gradgrind refers to Sissy, a student in his class, as "[g]irl number twenty" (14) and Bitzer receives Gradgrind's praise for describing a horse as: "Quadruped. Graminivorous. Forty teeth, namely twenty-four grinders, four eye-teeth, and twelve incisive" (12). *Hard Times* examines the impact of such an educational philosophy on growing children, with the result being that Louisa and Tom are shaped by their educational environment in a particular way: a way that stunts their emotional growth and turns them inward upon each other, unable to care for anyone else in the family or in society. Louisa and Tom are unhappy children, bitter and self-absorbed, lacking a sense of ease and contentment. The novel portrays their relationship as perverted and somewhat incestuous, with the clear inference being that these perverted feelings are the direct result of their father's utilitarian teachings. At one point, Gradgrind himself says that "there are qualities in Louisa which—which have been harshly neglected, and—and a little perverted" (243). At another point, when Tom says "I am sick of my life, Loo. I hate it altogether, and I hate everybody except you," the narrator describes Tom as "the unnatural young Thomas Gradgrind" (55). Tom's "unnatural" disposition is directly related to his hatred of everyone except his sister—a reference to his incestuous feelings. In both cases, then, the children are described not as immoral or intractable, but as "perverted" and "unnatural." In the context of the larger narrative, these terms are not incidental; they point to a vision of a natural, organic pattern from which the two have deviated. Thus, the stunted growth that Louisa and Tom experience is not only a social and moral problem, but also a biological one; they are like plants that have adapted themselves to an unhealthy environment and, although they have survived, they are not healthy specimens and in fact will not produce offspring.[7]

I am asserting, then, that *Hard Times* is governed by organic metaphors of growth, development, and reproduction which place the incest theme in the context of biology. Like the machine culture that is ruining Coketown (and making the elephants mad), Louisa and Tom's perversion is "against nature"; it opposes biological laws which support growth. Healthy growth, the narrative suggests, is fostered by a favorable environment; like plants which need certain types of air and soil, children need an atmosphere that allows them to develop freely in body and mind. The Gradgrind children and Coketown's laborers are like plants struggling to survive in an inhospitable climate. Thus, in a scene in which Louisa accuses her father of stunting her emotional growth, she describes her heart as a desolate garden where nothing grows, crying out and striking her breast, "O father, what have you done, with the garden that should have bloomed once, in this great wilderness here!" (239). In a very different scene, the narrative depicts Sissy—a well-adjusted, happy child who is, significantly, the child of circus performers—as loving flowers and flower patterns, even when Gradgrind ridicules her admiration of a flowered carpet as impractical and illogical: "If you please, sir," Sissy responds to Gradgrind's disparaging remarks, "I am very fond of flowers" (14). Moreover, unlike Louisa, Tom, and Bitzer, Sissy is the only child who will grow up to have children of her own—a topic which I explore in more detail below. Thus, Louisa's barren wilderness and Sissy's blooming garden are metaphors for human sterility on the one hand and unconstrained reproductivity on the other. In the logic of the novel, active reproductivity is the direct result of healthy—natural—human development.

The representation of unfettered growth as natural and right offers a counterpoint to the "bad science" of Gradgrind and his peers and anticipates some of the biological reasoning set forth a few years later by Darwin and Spencer. Spencer's 1860 publication, "The Social Organism," for instance, specifically states that while earlier thinkers envisioned the natural world as machine-like, this vision was faulty; instead, Spencer asserts, both the natural world and the social sphere follow organic patterns of growth and development rather than mechanistic ones. Summarizing his theory succinctly, he declares "society is a growth and not a manufacture" (269). In support of his hypothesis, Spencer describes four main points of similarities between societies and individual organisms, stating that societies, like organisms: (1) begin as "small aggregations" but increase in size tremendously; (2) begin, like seeds, as simple structures, but develop into complex organisms; (3) grow to "acquire a *mutual dependence;* which becomes at last so great, that the activity and life of each part is made possible only by the activity and life of the rest"; and (4) have a more prolonged life than and are independent of "the lives of any of [their] component units" (272; emphasis added). *Hard Times* follows a similar logic, demonstrating that industrial society grows, develops, and becomes interdependent in the same way that biological organisms do. The concept of the "mutual dependence" of organisms is especially important in *Hard Times,* as is apparent in the portrayal of Sleary's Circus, the novel's primary example of social cooperation. Thus, Sissy—the circus child—will have a beneficial effect on others, while Louisa and Tom will not.

In a similar manner, metaphors of individual plant formation in *Hard Times* suggest Darwin's logic regarding plant and animal development. The section on "Correlation of Growth" from the *Origin,* for example, maintains that any change in one part of an organism will result in a corresponding change in another part, thus accounting for variations in species. As Darwin states:

> [T]he whole organisation is so tied together during its growth and development, that when slight variations in any one part occur, and are accumulated through natural selection, other parts become modified. . . . *[A]ny malformation affecting the early embryo, seriously affects the whole organisation of the adult.* (182; emphasis added)

This reasoning works in *Hard Times* both on the individual level and the systemic level. On the individual level, Louisa and Tom are like "malformed" organisms whose future development will be affected by the early distortion of their minds. On the systemic level, the malformation of one of the parts will lead eventually to injury to others, as occurs when Bitzer, Gradgrind's young pupil, refuses to help Gradgrind escape his difficulties towards the end of the story.

Dickens's critique of science in *Hard Times* and other publications has generated much debate among scholars. Some believe that *Hard Times'* "scientists" are not accurate representations and that Dickens does not understand the discipline. These critics argue that Dickens unfairly portrays all science as narrow, unimaginative, and limited to facts and statistics. Martha Nussbaum contends, for instance, that *Hard Times* depicts "a reductive charade of science . . ." (888). D.W. Jefferson is similarly skeptical, commenting that "[n]owhere are we told of any deep involvement with the science and technology of the age . . ." (200).

On the other side, however, are those who assert that Dickens's understanding of science was not shallow or ill-founded. Susan Faye Cannon, for example, states that Dickens contrasts "good science and bad science" (20) in his writings, criticizing those who teach science "without imagination and concrete observation (21). In Cannon's view, "[Dickens] placed the blame for the perversion of science not on a particular science but on a particular kind of adult" (22). Deborah Thomas follows a similar line of thought when she notes that Dickens distinguishes between faulty science and authentic science when he compares Gradgrind to "an astronomer in an observatory without windows, a simile that vividly suggests [Gradgrind's] faulty grasp of what Dickens saw as the genuine scientific method" (71). In Thomas's view, as in mine, *Hard Times* critiques not all science, but only a particular kind of science. Along the same lines, George Levine comments that scientific coverage in the journals *All the Year Round* and *Household Words,* of which Dickens was founder and editor, does not suggest that "scientific thought and experiment were dehumanizing" (126). Instead, Levine states, "[t]aken together the essays show that Dickens was familiar with and sympathetic to the large ideas which, though not strictly anticipations of Darwin's theory, were conditions for it" (126). Paul Schacht finds similar indications in the journals which, he claims, evidence Dickens's interest in scientific investigation, especially of plant life. In particular, Schacht cites articles published in *Household Words* either slightly before or concurrently with the publication of *Hard Times* which explore plant development. An article entitled "Nature's Changes of Dress," for instance, published in the same volume as Chapters Thirteen and Fourteen of *Hard Times,* claims that:

> in every latitude we find plants to which that special territory is assigned as their domain, beyond which their passport will not carry them. . . . The Gulf-stream may carry the tropic seed to the coasts of Norway,— the bird or insect may bear the vegetable germ from Indian woods to plant it in a northern soil; but offended Nature avenges the transgression of her changeless laws. The seed never germinates, but is blighted by the asperities of a new and more rigorous clime. (304; qtd. in Schacht 82–3)[8]

As Schacht comments, "[o]ffended Nature avenges Gradgrind's transgression of her 'changeless laws' with the blighted lives of his own children" (83). Scientific inquiry in itself, then, is not the problem; Gradgrind's utilitarian experiment is simply bad science. Good science, *Hard Times* suggests, respects nature's "laws."

SIBLING INCEST AND THE LITERARY TRADITION

The "bad" science illustrated by Gradgrind's utilitarian philosophy and the machine culture of industrial England has disastrous results which find full expression in the incestuous relationship between Louisa and Tom. "Perversion" is the operative term here, relating both to the elder Gradgrind children and to industrial society as a whole. The theme of sibling incest in *Hard Times* is an interesting one, requiring some discussion of its use as a literary trope in the eighteenth and nineteenth centuries and in Dickens's other works. Sibling incest is an unstable concept, full of legal and moral vagaries. In *Hard Times,* incest is identified in very limited terms; yet perversion, as understood in this text, is defined in opposition to forms of close familial alliances and sibling-like marriages which are standard features of literary sibling incest in eighteenth- and nineteenth-century novels. In other words, although sibling incest historically refers to legally and socially illicit relationships, within the tradition of eighteenth- and nineteenth-century British literature it has followed varying trajectories, suggestive both of social sanction and social prohibition. As I will demonstrate, an understanding of literary configurations of socially acceptable sibling incest is necessary to understand the construction of deviance in *Hard Times.* The portrayal of incest in *Hard Times* comments on and reconfigures this earlier tradition.[9]

Definitions of incest in Britain changed often over the centuries, especially after 1600.[10] By the eighteenth century, marriage to cousins had become legal, yet often was discouraged. Glenda Hudson finds such diminishing but still existing taboos present in Jane Austen's *Mansfield Park,* for example, when the character of Mrs. Norris states "that it is 'morally impossible' (*MP,* p. 6) for Fanny to marry Edmund" (Hudson 11). Marriage between in-laws and step-siblings was also discouraged because, as Hudson explains, "the individuals involved had previously treated each other as consanguineal relatives" (11). Numerous other relationships were actively proscribed by law, with marriage to a deceased wife's sister or a brother's widow being especially scandalous to the middle and upper classes. Marriage to a deceased wife's sister, in particular, was hotly debated in Parliament from 1842 to 1907, when it was finally legalized.[11]

Due to intense public interest and conflicted attitudes, incest found ready expression in much eighteenth- and early nineteenth-century literature. In the eighteenth century, for example, realistic novels such as *Moll Flanders, Joseph Andrews,* or *Evelina* and gothic novels such as *The Monk* or Horace Walpole's *The Mysterious Mother* used incest motifs to titillate, shock, or amuse an eager readership. Over the course of the century, incest in literature appeared with increasing frequency, illustrating a complex array of alliances forbidden by law. Within the gothic genre, parent-child and similar relationships (uncle-niece, guardian-ward) frequently appeared as examples of unspeakable horror. But far more common, especially within the realistic genre, was sibling incest. Incestuous relationships modeled on sibling and sibling-like alliances became a standard motif not only in much eighteenth-century fiction, but also, with certain variations, in Romantic works and in later nineteenth-century fiction.

Sibling incest in eighteenth- and nineteenth-century literature covered a range of possibilities, both licit and illicit. While the eighteenth-century novel tended to employ incest motifs for their shock value or to portray fragmented families and lawless social orders, toward the end of the century bourgeois, socially acceptable models of incest based on supportive sibling alliances began to appear. One trend that affected incest motifs from at least the late eighteenth century on and into the early nineteenth is what Julie Shaffer refers to as "familialization," or the tendency to "[broaden] supportive alliances by turning non-family into family, based in an Enlightenment belief that humankind's innate benevolence and sympathy lead to community building . . ." (67).[12] Sibling familialization, according to Shaffer, often coincided with sibling familialized incest, or marriage to a partner who became like family through long association. Shaffer's point here is that the tendency towards familialization in the novel led inevitably to the portrayal of incest-like relationships and sometimes of legal incest, such as marriage between first cousins. In exploring this trend, Shaffer examines the ways in which sibling familialized incest signalled sympathy and the mutual associations that come with a shared background.

Shaffer's concepts of sibling familialization and sibling familialized incest are important to my analysis because they aid me in demonstrating the extent to which *Hard Times'* model of sibling incest corresponds to and diverges from other models of incest in eighteenth- and nineteenth-century literature. Examples of sibling familialized incest and socially acceptable but legally prohibited sibling incest, with their emphasis on bourgeois heteronormativity, became more frequent within various literary genres in the late eighteenth century, greatly complicating the subject of literary incest as an area of critical inquiry. By examining some of the major trends in literary incest of the eighteenth and nineteenth centuries, I wish to show that the relationship between Louisa and Tom both refers to these earlier models and adapts itself to contemporary views about nature and perversion.

While Shaffer's analysis of sibling familialized incest and sibling familialization focuses directly on portrayals of incest in some late eighteenth- and early nineteenth-century sentimental and gothic novels, many of her conclusions correspond to those of Glenda Hudson, who discusses fraternal love and sibling incest in Jane Austen's work. Hudson sees Austen's fiction as promoting marriages based on similar backgrounds and shared associations, including faintly taboo alliances between close relations. As Hudson explains, "[i]n Austen's novels, incest between cousins and between in-laws, who act towards each other like blood brother and sister, seems to be purposive and is promoted as a way of fortifying the family" (25). Like Shaffer's description of sibling incest, Hudson's model focuses on mutual affinities and a sense of equality between marriage partners that ultimately work to support the family and promote bourgeois social values.

At the same time that eighteenth- and early nineteenth-century novels were exploring sibling and sibling-like relationships, English Romantic poetry pursued themes of sibling incest that both corresponded to and diverged from trends in the novel. On the one hand, while the Romantic version of sibling incest moved toward the kind of fraternal, supportive alliances between similars that Hudson and Shaffer point to, Romantic motifs contained tensions that were not operative in the situations Hudson explores in Austen's work. Alan Richardson comments, for instance, that sibling incest in Romantic poetry usually ends in "a death that divides the siblings, a death related to the consummation—whether physical or spiritual—of their love" ("Dangers" 740). Rather than supporting the family and bringing the lovers into the larger social sphere, as demonstrated in the sibling-like unions discussed by Hudson and Shaffer, Romantic incest isolates the lovers and bars them from social integration. At the same time, however, Romantic poetry's portrayal of incestuous sibling relationships as mutually supportive and sympathetic signalled a break from eighteenth-century treatments which turned on the issue of instinctual sibling attraction. Thus, Richardson observes that in the eighteenth-century novel, the principal issue in the treatment of sibling incest was the "intuitive attraction of a blood tie," while for the Romantic poets "the emphasis [was] on a shared childhood, on experience that unite[d] that couple through countless mutual associations built up during the most idyllic stage of life" ("Dangers" 739). For the Romantic poets, according to Richardson, childhood bonds and shared experiences created deep, sometimes erotic attractions between siblings and sibling-substitutes, whereas in the eighteenth-century novel, the sibling relationship usually was not revealed until after the two were romantically involved, suggesting an instinctual bond rather than one based on shared associations.[13] Wordsworth's expressions of love for his sister Dorothy in "Tintern Abbey," for example, or the actual incest portrayed in Shelley's *Laon and Cythna* and Byron's *Manfred,* are founded upon profound sympathies and a recognition of the other as being almost like the self. Hudson makes a similar distinction between the eighteenth-century English novel and Romantic literature, stating that "[g]enerally speaking, the real [incestuous] relation of the man and woman [in the eighteenth-century novel] is not discovered until after their liaison begins; they are attracted to each other not by a shared childhood and associations but by instinct" (22); in contrast to this trend, Hudson continues, "[t]he attraction of similars held a fascination which deepened as the eighteenth century progressed and which reached a climax during the Romantic period" (22). Thus, although eighteenth- and nineteenth-century treatments of sibling incest differed in many respects among various genres, they coincided towards the end of the eighteenth century in the tendency to portray sibling erotic alliances as based on sympathy and similarity.

The trends discussed by Shaffer, Hudson, and Richardson can be seen not only in literature of the eighteenth and early nineteenth centuries, but also in literature of the middle decades of the nineteenth. In Victorian literature, however, the tendency was to focus on sibling-like alliances—sibling familialization, to borrow Shaffer's term—rather than actual sexual relations between brothers and sisters. While the suggestion of incest still lingered, especially in marriages between first cousins, the trend was to concentrate on the supportive and sympathetic bond established in relationships between similars. As the English novel focused ever more closely on the inner workings of the family, promoting an ideal of familial peace and unity, brother-sister love and sibling-like marriages became a way to express both the harmony of domestic life and the sexuality of female protagonists. As several critics have pointed out, sibling familialization and sibling familialized incest gave writers a way to portray women with strong passions and sexual feelings while still adhering to bourgeois ideas about female sexuality. Both Shaffer and Hudson discuss this aspect of sibling incest in connection with late eighteenth- and early nineteenth-century literature, yet it applies equally to Victorian fiction. Joseph Boone and Deborah Nord, for instance, writing about brother-sister relationships in Dickens, Eliot, and Brontë, state:

> [W]hen consanguinity is used metaphorically to describe actual *lovers* rather than literal *siblings,* it often serves a more covert function: that of disavowing or masking the sexual attraction that underlies that process of socially sanctioned love-making known as courtship. That is, the language of chaste sibling love in particular serves to protect the heroine's reputation by providing her with a coded language for articulating her erotic feelings. . . . (166)

Boone and Nord further comment that "[t]his tendency to fraternalize romantic feeling is not always, or simply, to suppress or defer its sexual contents, however; the rhetoric of sibling identification and/or affection can also serve as a mode of wooing, precisely by clearing a linguistic space for erotic sparring between otherwise undeclared lovers" (166). This last distinction is a crucial one, because it demonstrates that coded language in the Victorian novel is not always about prohibition, but can be a way of presenting an image of socially-sanctioned, "healthy" female sexuality. The language of sibling love can allow the female protagonist to express sexual interest in ways that are acceptable to bourgeois culture and that work to bring the family together.

Certainly not all Victorian models of sibling familialization and sibling familialized incest foster community building and family harmony. George Eliot's *Mill on the Floss* comes to mind as an example of a type of sibling love based on the Romantic pattern: Tom's and Maggie's intense sibling bond ends in an apocalyptic death that is the antithesis of social cohesion. On the other hand, the work of Emily Brontë and Charles Dickens provides clear examples of the kinds of sibling alliances that promote the well being of the family. Emily Brontë's *Wuthering Heights,* for instance, contains erotic alliances between foster-siblings in the first half of the book, while marriage between first cousins in the second half of the book ultimately heals the conflicts of the previous generation and brings the dissenting families together. There are numerous other minor examples of sibling domestic harmony in the Victorian novel, such as Charlotte Brontë's portrayal of St. John Rivers and his sisters, Mary and Diana, in *Jane Eyre,* or examples in which the language of sibling love stands in for erotic love in works by Trollope, Gaskell, and others. Perhaps more often than any other major Victorian writer, however, Dickens turns to sibling love as the ideal for domestic happiness.

To understand the degree to which Louisa's love for her brother, Tom, crosses from lawful into unlawful territory, it is helpful to look briefly at sibling love in some of Dickens's other works and the critical responses which followed. Tom and Ruth Pinch in *Martin Chuzzlewit,* Nicholas and Kate Nickleby in *Nicholas Nickleby,* Redlaw and his sister in *The Haunted Man,* Agnes and David in *David Copperfield,* and John and Harriet Carker or Florence and Paul in *Dombey and Son* all illustrate sibling relationships patterned upon the ideal marriage envisioned by domestic ideology. Not surprisingly, critics have long noted the frequency of the incest theme (both sibling and parent-child) in Dickens's work. Russell Goldfarb pinpoints George Orwell's 1939 essay on Dickens as perhaps the first to recognize the pervasiveness of the topic. An "incestuous atmosphere," Orwell writes, is "perfectly attained in *Nicholas Nickleby, Martin Chuzzlewit,* and *Pickwick,* and . . . is approximated to varying degrees in almost all the others" (qtd. in Russell Goldfarb, 116). Goldfarb, writing in 1970, argues that Dickens's descriptions of orphans and incest are "topical outlets for [Dickens's] repressed sexuality" (138), with incest representing one type of an "inward-looking, intense sexuality," and orphans representing an "outward-looking, enlarging kind of love" (137). Other critics after Orwell who comment upon the incest theme in Dickens include Mark Spilka in the 1960s and Michael Slater in the 1980s. Spilka, for instance, calls "Paul Dombey's affection for his sister . . . bathetic and incestuous" (53), while Slater focuses more particularly on the domestic aspect of the brother-sister incest theme. Referring to

Redlaw and his sister in *The Haunted Man,* Slater comments, "[t]his image of a brother and sister living together in a sort of sexless marriage, supporting each other against the world, is a persistent one in Dickens's fiction, beginning with Nicholas and Kate Nickleby (Ruth and Tom Pinch in *Martin Chuzzlewit* are another example)" (32).[14] A few years later, in an article about brother-sister relationships in *Dombey and Son,* Catherine Waters argues that Dickens's treatment of sibling alliances is not as uniform as Slater's comment would suggest. Waters cites contrasts among such characters as Tom and Ruth Pinch, who are "a source of comedy" (9), Agnes, in *David Copperfield,* who "yearns to be more than a sibling to David" (22), and John and Harriet Carker or Florence and Paul in *Dombey and Son,* whose relationships are more complex and serious. Waters' subsequent analysis of three sibling relationships in *Dombey and Son* demonstrates the diverse and sometimes contradictory treatments Dickens gives to this subject. The relationship between Mr. Dombey and his sister, Mrs. Chick, for instance, is fraught with comedic tensions, while Florence and Paul's relationship exists in an idealized realm of absolute spiritual and emotional harmony.

Yet although, as Waters asserts, Dickens's approach to sibling alliances cannot be reduced to one simple formula, I would suggest that his close sibling alliances draw attention to the virtues of domestic love and play an important role in supporting nineteenth-century domestic ideology. Florence and Paul, for example, are like a family-within-a-family, living in and for each other. This intense sibling bond gives Florence a way to recreate the family bond that she does not have with her father or stepmother, and her subsequent romantic relationship with Walter then mirrors her former relationship with her brother.[15] Similarly, in *The Haunted Man,* Redlaw's memories of his deceased sister provide the only happy remembrances of domestic life that he has, and her loss is a perpetual agony to him. *David Copperfield* presents yet another example, in which the fraternal relationship David has with Agnes grows into a more mature and balanced romantic relationship than the one David shared with Dora.

Sibling alliances such as these, while vastly different in detail, bring together two recurrent themes in Dickens's work: the image of childhood as a time of innocence and marriage as a serene haven from a corrupt world. Dickens's accounts of sibling familialization and sibling familialized incest, in fact, seem dependent upon the convergence of these elements, uniting, on the one hand, a Romantic concept of childhood as a time of imaginative insight and profound sympathy and, on the other, Victorian concepts of domestic ideology. And while both marriage and childhood are often portrayed in Dickens as nightmare versions of the ideal, sibling familialized incest offers a way for characters to escape the world of adult selfishness and greed and return to a time before childhood innocence was threatened. This trend is suggested by Judith Schelly, who sees the connection between sibling incest and childhood innocence in *Dombey and Son* as suggesting a Levi-Straussian model of incest:

> Dickens's attitude toward sibling intimacy becomes comprehensible only in terms of the Levi-Straussian model which sees the desire for incest as a nostalgia for a pre-social Eden. . . . Dickens freely borrows the language of erotic love, but only because he regards the affection of Paul and Florence as a refuge from adult degradation. (qtd. in Waters, "Ambiguous" 17)

Dickens's children maintain a tenuous grasp on their innocence, existing uneasily in a fallen world of adult neglect and egoism. Schelly's prelapsarian model suggests the extent to which the fantasy of childhood innocence shapes sibling familialized incest and, I would add, the idealized marriages in texts like *Dombey and Son* and *David Copperfield*.[16]

Mid-Victorian domestic ideology similarly imagined the home as a refuge from a fallen world of corruption and greed. The distinction between public and private spheres in Victorian thought emphasized this opposition, with the public sphere representing the world of business, manufacturing, and urban squalor, and the home representing a place of moral goodness and calm. Just as the home was a refuge from the crass interests of the market-place and the somber realities of urban living, childhood was imagined as refuge from the same world. Both views, in their emphasis on innocence, illustrate the prelapsarian quality that Schelly mentions. Sibling familialized incest joins the discourses of childhood innocence with those of domestic ideology, thus offering a way to portray adult sexuality in a language accept-able to the Victorian middle classes.

The concepts of sibling familialized incest and sibling familialization apparent in the work of Dickens and other nineteenth-century writers are sig-nificant to my analysis of *Hard Times* because they locate the border between normal and pathological in individual and familial relationships. Perversion in this text is defined in direct relation to these earlier formulations. Rather than being a bourgeois model of brother-sister love idealizing domestic values, Louisa's love for her brother Tom is portrayed as being unnatural and perverse precisely because it does not follow the idealized sibling alliances of Romantic and Victorian literature. Similarly, it differs from eighteenth-century versions which depict romantic couples discovering—to their horror and the reader's titillation—that they are blood relations. Yet at the same time, the suggestion of "normal" brother-sister love here owes much to the literary tradition of sibling incest. Louisa and Tom's abnormality is especially serious because sibling love has been privileged to such a great extent in eighteenth- and nineteenth-century literature. As I will demonstrate below, abnormal sibling love in *Hard Times* is less concerned with actual sexual contact between family members than it is with social cohesion. In this sense, sibling incest refers directly back to models of sibling familialization.

PERVERSION AND SOCIAL RELATIONS

Critical responses to incest in *Hard Times* have been limited, and none address the concept of pathology in a sustained manner. Daniel Deneau, writing in 1964, was the first critic to explore in any detail the problematic aspect of sibling love in *Hard Times*. Although Deneau avoids using the word "incest," he discusses what he characterizes as the "abnormal brother-sister relationship" and comments briefly on several key passages (Deneau 177). One of these passages describes a scene in which James Harthouse—an upper-class rogue who pursues an adulterous relationship with Louisa—takes note of Louisa's singular attachment to her brother. Harthouse wonders if anything will brighten Louisa's usually-dour expression, then answers his own question:

> Yes! By Jupiter, there was something, and here it was, in an unexpected shape! Tom appeared. She changed as the door opened, and broke into a beaming smile.
> . . . She put out her hand—a pretty little soft hand; and her fingers closed upon her brother's, as if she would have carried them to her lips.
> "Ay, ay?" thought the visitor. "This whelp is the only creature she cares for." (135)

Deneau merely comments here that "after [Louisa] sacrifices herself in the marriage to Bounderby . . . her love for Tom seems to become more intense" (175), but Richard Fabrizio's observations are more pointed:

> Such [misused and misdirected] love cannot be experienced verbally. It is expressed by the responses of the body. [Louisa] blushes and becomes animated when Tom enters the room. That Harthouse tries to raise the same blush, stimulate the same animated response indicates that he understands their sexual nature. He wishes to replace her brother as her lover. (76)

As Fabrizio notes, Louisa's blush suggests that her affection for her brother has an erotic component to it. At the very least, she is in a state of excitement never achieved with any other person, including—especially—her husband.

Harthouse's keen observation of the scene, combined with the sexual preda-
toriness of his character, further underscore the erotic connotations of the
passage. These erotic connotations, however, are not limited to Louisa's wayward desires; Harthouse, wishing to put himself in Tom's place as the object
of Louisa's affections, becomes part of a triangular configuration that high-
lights the relationship between Harthouse and Tom as much as that between
Louisa and either male character.

Such triangular configuration recalls Eve Sedgwick's theory of male
homosocial desire and demonstrates one of several examples of perverse
social and sexual relations in this novel. Drawing upon René Girard's theory of erotic triangles and Gayle Rubin's argument on female sexual
exchange, Sedgwick asserts that both the exchange of women between men
and male rivalry for the same woman offer a way for homosocial desire,
including—but not strictly limited to—homosexual desire, to be
expressed. Summarizing Girard's theory, Sedgwick states, "in any erotic
rivalry, the bond that links the two rivals is as intense and potent as the
bond that links either of the rivals to the beloved" (*Between Men* 21). Sedgwick's point here is that in such situations, the woman's role becomes secondary to a very primary emotional investment between men, an
investment tinged with erotic implications. Thus, although Louisa is the
ostensible focus in the Harthouse-Louisa-Tom dynamic, male power and
homosocial desire are the unacknowledged motives. The intense cat-and-
mouse game Harthouse plays with Louisa obscures the equally intense
game of domination and control he plays with Tom. For Harthouse,
Louisa's affection is always seen in relation to Tom's defeat. As the narrator
comments, "Mr. James Harthouse began to think it would be a new sensa-
tion, if the face which changed so beautifully for the whelp, would change
for him" (168). Harthouse's ambition to outdo "the whelp" says as much
about his need to assert power and control over another man as it does
about his desire for Louisa.

While the Harthouse-Louisa-Tom configuration illustrates René
Girard's point about male rivalry, another prominent triangle, Gradgrind-
Louisa-Bounderby, more particularly illustrates Gayle Rubin's argument
about female sexual exchange. Rubin's article centers on the way in which
women are used as symbolic property securing relationships between men.
Although primarily about non-industrial societies, Rubin's study has particular significance for industrial capitalist society, in which female sexual
exchange is commensurate with financial exchange. Louisa's situation is classic because her marriage seals the alliance between two of Coketown's most
powerful men—Bounderby and Gradgrind—while reducing her to a mere

economic function. The triangle becomes further complicated when Tom pressures Louisa to agree to the marriage so that he can gain favor with Bounderby, his employer at the bank. Louisa finally acquiesces to the marriage, not to please her father, but to please her brother, thus providing the same link between Tom and Bounderby as she did between Gradgrind and Bounderby. Sedgwick's comments about triangular exchanges are particularly relevant here:

> Sentient middle-class women of [the nineteenth century] perceive the triangular path of circulation that enforces patriarchal power as being routed through them, but never ending in them—while capitalist man, with his prehensile, precapitalist image of the body, is always deluded about what it is that he pursues, and in whose service. His delusion is, however, often indistinguishable from real empowerment; and indeed it is blindest, and closest to real empowerment, in his triangular transactions through women with other men. (*Between Men* 179)

In Sedgwick's formulation, overt forms of male empowerment are intricately tied to covert forms of male desire. Moreover, the triangular configurations in *Hard Times,* I would note, with their reduction of the female role to an economic equivalent and their emphasis on relationships between men, are figured as counter to the tenets of domestic ideology. This becomes especially apparent when Tom attempts to manipulate his sister into marrying Bounderby (a passage designated by Fabrizio as "Tom's 'marriage proposal'" [76]). Tom preys on Louisa's affections, asking, "You are very fond of me, an't you, Loo?" (97). Louisa agrees, but regrets that she sees him so infrequently. Tom responds, "Well, sister of mine . . . when you say that, you are near my thoughts. We might be so much oftener together—mightn't we? Always together, almost—mightn't we? It would do me a great deal of good if you were to make up your mind to I know what, Loo. It would be a splendid thing for me. It would be uncommonly jolly!" (97–98). Tom's avowals of sibling love merely parody the domestic ideal embodied in sibling familialized incest because they are so clearly self-centered rather than other-centered. Accordingly, by de-emphasizing the female role, the triangular exchange upsets the domestic ideal in which the middle-class angel has a central, visible, and influential role to play. Moreover, by reducing Louisa to an economic function—the kind of pragmatic use that Gradgrind's philosophy endorses—Tom applies the ethic of the economic sphere to the domestic, destroying the ability of the domestic sphere to act as a haven against the world of commerce and public life. It is this intrusion of public-sphere reasoning into private-sphere life that *Hard Times* critiques.[17] Both the capitalist ethic and male homosocial relationships come under attack here because they are seen as impediments to domestic life.

Such triangular configurations, then, although supportive of bourgeois economics and thus common in the Victorian novel, are in *Hard Times* anti-bourgeois to the extent that they disrupt the principles of domestic ideology. More importantly for my analysis, however, this anti-bourgeois behavior is seen as abnormal in the context of the novel because it does not enhance the social whole: it does not foster community-building relationships or lead to the birth of children. In this important sense, it is an attack against the social body as an organic, biological entity. Rather than contributing to the growth or development of industrial society, the novel tells us, such relationships are merely solipsistic. Thus, the "marriage proposal" scene both exposes the mechanics of the profit motive in sexual exchange and deviates from natural, healthy sibling-like relationships apparent in Dickens's other work, such as *Dombey and Son* or *David Copperfield*. Tom employs the language of sibling love by referring to a shared sympathetic bond and domestic harmony which his actions scorn. Fabrizio observes that the scene has three aspects that correlate to an elopement: "1. [The couple] will escape from paternal tyranny; 2. They will establish a new home; 3. They will always be together" (76). However, with seemingly all of the domestic elements of idealized sibling love here, the scene is meant to be understood ironically. Tom is not thinking unselfishly of Louisa, but of himself: "It would do *me* a great deal of good if you were to make up your mind to I know what, Loo. It would be a splendid thing for *me*" (98; emphasis added). Tom, as the reader knows, has learned his father's lessons well: generosity and love are not quantifiable and do not lead to profit, so these considerations do not enter into his calculations. Tom's selfishness and greed demonstrate the failings of Gradgrind's philosophy in a twofold manner: not only is Louisa cheated of a brother's proper affection, but so too is the larger social domain cheated of a useful citizen, as the reader will later learn. As narrative events unfold, Tom will rob Bounderby's bank, thereby disgracing his family and invalidating Bounderby's trust. In this context, then, Tom's selfishness can be seen as a systemic problem, potentially affecting the entire species.

HOUSEHOLD ANGELS AND FALLEN WOMEN

Tom's exploitation of Louisa's affections is just one abuse against Louisa among many—by Harthouse, Bounderby, and most powerfully, Gradgrind. Yet despite a large cast of corrupt characters, Louisa's own failings become the focal point within a larger system of physical and moral decay because she is both the product of this decay and, at the same time, its primary symbol. Rather than being a normative model of healthy fraternal love, Louisa's relationship with her brother is shown to be perverse and abnormal because it refutes the premises of domestic ideology which define sexual behavior and gender roles within the family. The primary problem, the novel demonstrates, is that Louisa is not able to care for anyone other than Tom. This is seen as a perversion because the novel establishes mutual sympathy, community building, and childbearing as natural or conducive to biological "law." Thus, many qualities which correspond to gender ideology also follow the dictates of such law within the terms of nineteenth-century science: marriage, motherhood, and heteronormative sexual relations. Louisa is the product of her father's teachings; the absence of nonquantifiable and impractical qualities such as imagination, love, and compassion for others in her life has caused her to become bitter, unhappy, and hostile towards everyone other than her brother.

The intensity of Louisa's feelings for Tom and her divergence from domestic ideals are perhaps most obvious during a scene in which she visits her brother's bedroom at night, ostensibly to persuade him to confess to the robbery. Wearing a "loose robe," finding her way through "the dark," and "approaching his bed with a noiseless step," Louisa "kneeled down beside [the bed], passed her arm over his neck, and drew his face to hers" (190). She asks Tom if he has anything to tell her, which he denies, but she persists:

"My dear brother:" she laid her head down on his pillow, and her hair flowed over him as if she would hide him from every one but herself: "is there nothing that you have to tell me? Is there nothing you can tell me, if you will? . . . O Tom, tell me the truth!"

"I don't know what you mean, Loo!"

"As you lie here alone, my dear, in the melancholy night, so you must lie somewhere one night, when even I, if I am living then, shall have left you. As I am here beside you, barefoot, unclothed, undistinguishable in darkness, so must I lie through all the night of my decay, until I am dust. In that name of that time, Tom, tell me the truth now!"

"What is it you want to know?"

"You may be certain:" in the energy of her love she took him to her bosom as if he were a child: "that I will not reproach you. You may be certain that I will be compassionate and true to you. You may be certain

that I will save you at whatever cost. O Tom, have you nothing to tell
me? Whisper very softly. Say only 'yes,' and I shall understand you!"
(190–91)

As Deneau, Fabrizio, and others have observed, the erotic overtones of this
passage are marked. The attention drawn to Louisa's "loose robe" and her
own reference to her coming to him "barefoot, unclothed, undistinguishable
in darkness" suggest a sexual vulnerability. The sensual way in which Louisa
lets her hair fall over Tom's face, "as if she would hide him from every one
but herself,"[18] emphasizes the secretiveness of the encounter and, as Fabrizio
comments, "the letting down of the hair [is] an ancient sign of female abasement and sexual availability" (78). Similarly, her urgings to "[w]hisper very
softly. Say only 'yes,' and I shall understand you!" further imply the existence
of a shameful secret shared by the two. Conceivably, the aura of shame is created by the spectre of Tom's robbery, but the combination of Louisa's vulnerability, abasement, and evident state of undress suggest that she too has a
shameful secret.

   Moreover, although Louisa's treatment of Tom "as if he were a child"
illustrates that she is capable of maternal love, this love is misplaced and is,
within the novel's terms, a deviation from the norm. The unnatural quality
of her maternal love for Tom, for example, can be seen in connection with
her other familial relationships. Louisa will not have children of her own
because she chooses to marry a man whom she despises and will later leave.
Further, she does not display maternal love or any kind of affection to her
younger siblings, as is evident later on when her little sister, Jane, prefers
Sissy to Louisa. As Mrs. Gradgrind notes, Louisa "very seldom" sees her
younger sister (200). Louisa, in fact, does not have any of the qualities of the
household angel of domestic ideology. The role of household angel, instead,
goes to Sissy Jupe, foster daughter to the Gradgrinds.

   In contrast to Louisa, Sissy exhibits a generosity of spirit towards everyone around her, thereby providing a model of healthy emotional and moral
development. Although initially with the circus family, Sissy comes to live
with the Gradgrinds when her father leaves the circus and abandons her
because he is no longer able physically to perform his act. There is an interesting contrast between the narrative's two fathers, Jupe and Gradgrind.
Although Sissy's father leaves her, the novel suggests that he does so out of
compassion for her because he can no longer contribute positively to the
group or take care of Sissy. Moreover, he believes that Sissy will get a good
education in Coketown, which is his dearest wish. Thus, although, like Gradgrind, Jupe puts his faith in a faulty educational system, unlike Gradgrind, he

is motivated by generosity and love. Sissy's character is an extension of this kind of generosity. From the beginning, it is apparent that her kindness and moral probity will improve the welfare of all. Where Louisa is sullen and withdrawn, Sissy is caring and thoughtful to others. When Louisa becomes dangerously involved with James Harthouse, for example, Sissy visits Harthouse and convinces him to relinquish his hold on Louisa and leave town. Later, when Tom is discovered to have robbed the bank, Sissy turns to her circus friends to disguise Tom and hide him until he can escape to the colonies. But more importantly, Sissy brings love into the family; she is kind to Mrs. Gradgrind, who is ignored by everyone, and is a model of compassion to the younger children.

Sissy's influence on the family and Louisa's very different capacity become especially apparent in the scene of Mrs. Gradgrind's final illness. Sissy brings Jane into the room and Louisa recognizes that Jane is far more intimate with Sissy than she had ever been with her. Jane holds Sissy's hand, and Louisa "observed her with her arm around Sissy's neck, and she felt the difference of this approach" (200). Louisa also notes that Jane's face

> was a better and brighter face than [Louisa's] had ever been: had seen in it, not without a rising feeling of resentment, even in that place [her mother's deathbed] and at that time, something of the gentleness of the other face in the room: the sweet face with the trusting eyes, made paler than watching and sympathy made it, by the rich dark hair. (200)

Jane's face is a "brighter face" than Louisa's had ever been because Jane's upbringing, unlike Louisa's, has been favored with Sissy's kind example and sympathetic interest; thus, Jane flourishes whereas Louisa becomes diminished emotionally. At this point in the story, when Louisa has attempted to break her pattern of self-destruction, it is a sign of the failure of Gradgrind's educational philosophy that Louisa experiences "a rising feeling of resentment" rather than pleasure over her sister's good fortune.

Moreover, the "watching and sympathy" over Louisa's dying mother which have made Sissy "paler" is a familiar Victorian topos which establishes the domestic woman's earnest—but not indecorously fervent—compassion for others (200). In contrast to Sissy, Louisa is an intruder in this scene, although it is Louisa's mother who is dying. This becomes evident when Mrs. Gradgrind says to Louisa at the beginning of their meeting, "You want to hear of me, my dear? That's something new, I am sure, when anybody wants to hear of me" (199). The enormous divide which separates them is apparent through Mrs. Gradgrind's final pathetic, unsuccessful attempts to communicate with her daughter, which culminate in "figures of wonderful no-meaning [which] she began to trace upon her wrappers" (199). Although Louisa's manner is kindly, there is no bond of sympathy or mutual trust between mother and daughter to foster communication.

Although the scene is a comment on domestic ideology and the role of the household angel, it is important to see it also in the context of the organic metaphor. Sissy, as a young child, was nurtured in the proper way and grows into a healthy adult, like a healthy plant. Louisa's and Tom's experiences are quite different because they did not get adequate nourishment as children. Yet the biological metaphor does not end there, because *Hard Times* views the entire social system as an organic entity. Thus, as is the case with Darwin's "malform[ed] . . . embryo, [which] seriously affects the whole organisation of the adult" Louisa and Tom deplete the larger social body, whereas Sissy replenishes it (*Origin* 182). Not only is Jane a happier, more open person than Louisa as a result of Sissy's influence, but she presumably will be more able to establish the kind of supportive relationships that Louisa is unable to establish.

The constructive effects on others and contribution to social cohesion that Sissy brings about contrast with Louisa's very exclusive and isolated attachment to Tom. The model of sibling familialization is significant here because it applies the ethic of brother-sister love to marital love, thereby bringing others into the inner circle of the family. According to the logic of sibling familialization, the siblings or sibling substitutes establish a bond of mutual understanding which later acts as a template for sexual love. The lovers are able to enter successfully into the larger social sphere because their compassion expands outward, towards others, and thus works to sustain family and community. Louisa's alliance with Tom, however, does not cause her to look for fraternal qualities in a mate. Instead, she allows herself to be shackled to Bounderby, who is insensitive to her thoughts and feelings. Her passive compliance demonstrates the extent of her estrangement both from others (except for Tom) and from herself. The novel is hard on Louisa in this respect, making her more responsible for her actions than Tom is for his. Although Tom is a selfish creature, we know far more about Louisa's internal thoughts and motivations than we do about his; Louisa is more complex, more deeply wounded, and more aware of her shortcomings—and thus, far more capable of making ethical choices in her life. While Louisa is capable of compassion—towards her dying mother, for instance, or towards Stephen Blackpool—she lacks the moral conviction, the narrative suggests, necessary to be an effective member of the family and community. By marrying Bounderby even though she openly disdains him, Louisa seems to condone his selfish speech and actions. Unlike Tom, Louisa seems cognizant of Bounderby's contemptible nature; a principled woman would reject marriage to such a man, and thus her marriage to him signals the beginning of a moral decline. Most importantly, moreover, within the context of domestic ideology, Louisa's failings are egregious, whereas Tom's are merely naughty. The Victorian man can lie, cheat, or engage in immoral acts, but the domestic angel has far less latitude.

It is not until later, after Louisa witnesses Bounderby's hurtful behavior towards Stephen Blackpool, that she begins to display the beginnings of a conscience and attempts to extricate herself from the cycle of social indifference she has been drawn into. The moral apathy which Louisa initially displays towards Bounderby is actually a symptom of the larger problem of social disaffection which *Hard Times* pursues. The erotic component of Louisa's love for Tom is a much smaller factor in the construction of her perversion than is her alienation from others. Rather than leading her closer to social cohesion, as does sibling familialized incest, sibling love has led her away from it. Louisa's incestuous love for her brother merely parodies the bourgeois domesticity of sibling familialized incest in that it underscores her inability to care for anyone else.

Despite Louisa's attempts to escape the oppressive weight of her father's utilitarian legacy, she exhibits the consequences that such a legacy confers. Her social disaffection and moral apathy are linked to sexual transgression in a manner that Victorian readers would immediately recognize. In fictional and nonfictional writing alike, the morally ambiguous woman—the non-maternal mother, the petty criminal, the secret drinker—was often construed as sexually transgressive or fallen. The non-maternal mother may veer towards adultery and then prostitution, for instance; the teenage girl who is sullen and contrary towards her family may be found to be a masturbator. Similarly, Louisa's social disaffection and general air of dejection culminate with the threat of sexual fallenness. Her near-adultery with James Harthouse is the overt corollary to the more covert form of sexual and moral perversion she displays in her relationship with Tom. Although she does not actually run away with Harthouse but merely listens—mildly reproachful—to his avowals of love, simply by listening to his declarations and not clearly rejecting him she enters into the realm of sexual transgression. A woman with the correct moral principles, the narrative suggests, would reject outright the improper attentions of Bounderby's supposed friend. When Harthouse begs her to leave Bounderby and run away with him, instead of clearly refusing his offer and removing herself from his company, Louisa appears to go along with his plan and, in fact, lets him put his arm around her, thus violating bourgeois principles. They part, and Louisa does, in fact, leave Bounderby, but she goes to her father's home instead of to Harthouse. Yet within the terms of the novel, Louisa's decision to leave her husband is a serious transgression. At the time of the novel's original publication in the 1850s, British law would have judged this a desertion, and Louisa would have given up all rights to any children and any personal property or money she had possessed, in addition to becoming socially disgraced.[19] The text is thus far more concerned with Louisa's violation of the principles of domestic ideology than it is with Harthouse's corruption. This is well illustrated by a series of references to an imaginary staircase envisioned by Mrs. Sparsit, Bounderby's middle-aged housekeeper. Believing that she will have Bounderby to herself once more, as she did before his marriage, Mrs. Sparsit looks forward to Louisa's moral downfall, picturing Louisa "always gliding down, down" the staircase (205). Appropriately, the last three chapter headings of the second book outline Louisa's "downfall": "Mrs. Sparsit's Staircase," "Lower and Lower," and finally, "Down," which ends with Louisa's desertion of Bounderby and return to her father. Her mental turmoil and moral disgrace are apparent in her words to Gradgrind upon her return: "'I shall die if you hold me! Let me fall upon the ground!' And he laid her down there, and saw the pride of his heart and the triumph of his system, lying, an insensible heap, at his feet" (219). Although not completely dishonored, within the iconography of the Victorian novel, Louisa is a fallen woman.[20]

Louisa's sexual fallenness is further amplified by her metaphoric link to Mrs. Blackpool, Stephen's "debauched" wife, who deserts Stephen early on but returns from time to time to filch his possessions and sell them for drink (*Hard Times* 91). The suggestion is that both women have transgressed, and that if Louisa is not careful, she will sink to the level of her less affluent counterpart. Mrs. Blackpool makes Stephen's life miserable, but since he cannot afford to divorce her and marry the virtuous Rachel, there seems to be no remedy. Thus, the narrative presents Sissy and Rachel, the domestic angels, as foils to Louisa and Mrs. Blackpool, the fallen women. The lives of these working-class women intersect in a manner similar to those of the middle-class women (although Sissy does not have middle-class roots, she adopts the language and behavior of the middle-class and comes to represent its ideals) and demonstrate the novel's vision of moral transgression—or deviance—as debilitating to the social whole.

As the domestic angel, Rachel's sexual virtue is unquestioned; although she and Stephen are deeply attached to one another, Rachel clearly maintains that Stephen's marital status makes it impossible for the two of them to have the kind of intimacy he would like. Similarly, Rachel's domestic virtues are demonstrated in the clean, orderly, and cheerful aspect she brings to the household. When Stephen comes home from work to find Rachel caring for his dissolute wife, "[e]verything was in its place and order as he had always kept it, the little fire was newly trimmed, and the hearth was freshly swept" (86). With Rachel tending the home, "[q]uiet and peace were there" (86). Rachel is also shown, like Sissy, in the familiar posture of the ministering angel: "She sat by the bed, watching and tending [Stephen's] wife" (86); "[s]he turned again towards the bed, and satisfying herself that all was quiet there, spoke in a low, calm cheerful voice" (86). Like Sissy, Rachel's patience, calmness, and compassion all testify to the idealized type of domestic angel.

The similarities between this scene and the scene in which Sissy watches over Louisa, as she had watched over Louisa's mother, are striking. Like Mrs. Blackpool, Louisa has arrived at the home of the patriarch (however disenfranchised, Stephen is still the patriarch in relation to his wife) in a state of disgrace. The morning after Louisa collapses at her father's feet, she awakens and asks her little sister, Jane, how she got to the room. Jane tells her that she thinks Sissy brought her there, and when Louisa asks why she believes this, Jane replies that the next morning Sissy was not in her own room, but "taking care of [Louisa] and cooling [her] head" (223). To Louisa's annoyance, Jane is full of praise for Sissy. When Louisa tells Jane, "What a beaming face you have," Jane replies, "I am sure it must be Sissy's doing" (223). Later, brightened by Jane's presence, Louisa ventures, "[i]t was you who made my room so cheerful, and gave it this look of welcome?" and Jane replies, "Oh no, Louisa, it was done before I came. It was—"; but Louisa stops listening at this point because she knows that Sissy ornamented the room and she resents Sissy's moral superiority (224). Louisa is jealous of Sissy, who has assumed a position of importance in the household that Louisa knows she herself should have assumed, but did not. The two scenes are almost mirror images of each other. Whereas Sissy "cool[s] [Louisa's] head" (223), Rachel attends to Mrs. Blackpool's "wounds": "[Rachel] steeped a piece of linen in a basin, into which she poured some liquid from a bottle, and laid it with a gentle hand upon the sore" (87). Rachel and Sissy are linked through their modest and cheerful conduct, their small attentions to the home, and their ministrations to the sick and the fallen.

The parallel between Sissy and Rachel and their relationship to outcast women intensifies the parallel between Louisa and Mrs. Blackpool; both relationships emphasize the contrast between household angel and fallen woman. As with Louisa's character, Mrs. Blackpool's social transgressions are subtly connected to sexual ones. The overt indication is that Mrs. Blackpool is an alcoholic; she is a "degraded, drunken wretch" (297) with "debauched features" (91) and is insensible, possibly from illness but most likely from drink. Covertly, however, she also bears the signs of the prostitute or adulteress; she is a "self-made outcast" (87) wearing "disgraceful garments" (86). Most importantly, Mrs. Blackpool's sores suggest that she has syphilis, further evidencing her adultery. This line of reasoning is delineated convincingly by John Baird, who notes that Rachel, while cautioning Stephen not to be too hard on his wife, "quotes . . . Christ's words (John 8:7) on the woman taken in adultery" (Baird 408): "'Thou knowest who said, 'Let him who is without sin among you, cast the first stone at her!' There have been plenty to do that" (*Hard Times* 87). Even more telling, however, is the nature of the "wounds . . . about the neck of the self-made outcast," which strongly suggest the marks of syphilis (*Hard Times* 87). The "liquid from a bottle" which Rachel pours to treat the "sore" (*Hard Times* 87), Baird surmises, is probably perchloride of mercury, a common medicine for syphilis.[21] Baird's conjecture would also explain Stephen's extreme reaction to the bottle's label: "It was not so far off, but that Stephen, following her hands with his eyes, could read what was printed on it, in large letters. He turned of a deadly hue, and a sudden horror seemed to fall upon him" (87–88). Clearly, the bottle triggers a very deep revulsion and fear in Stephen. Later Stephen will blame himself because he does not stop his wife from taking what would be a deadly overdose of the medication (which Rachel's timely awakening prevents from happening), but the suddenness with which Stephen reacts to the label suggests that it reveals something more than his own wish to be free of his wife; much more likely is the recognition that his wife is suffering from syphilis, and so has moved from alcoholism to adultery or prostitution. As Baird observes, "drunkenness is both the symptom and the symbol of complete moral abandonment. It is an outward and visible sign of inward spiritual disorder and moral corruption which can be elaborated in respectable middle-class fiction, whereas its congener, adultery, cannot" (408). Although I would modify Baird's assertion that adultery cannot be elaborated in Victorian middle-class fiction—though often obscured by ambiguous language, adultery is referred to fairly openly in the work of Dickens and others—his observation that drunkenness can signal sexual indiscretion is certainly accurate. Social improprieties such as alcoholism can act as coding for sexual improprieties specifically because nineteenth-century medical discourse saw sexual and social transgressions as distinctly interrelated. Female sexual transgression, particularly prostitution, was seen as being closely related to social problems such as poverty, overcrowding, poor sanitation, or drunkenness. Mrs. Blackpool's physical wounds are those of the adulteress; they are the counterpart to the psychological wounds that Sissy recognizes in Louisa.

Admittedly, Mrs. Blackpool's transgressions are far more serious than Louisa's, but Mrs. Blackpool exists as the spectre of what Louisa is in danger of becoming before she returns to her father's home. After all, Stephen's wife does not begin life debauched, but becomes so by degrees. At one point Stephen thinks: "But that he had seen her come to this by inches, he never could have believed her to be the same" (91). Louisa begins life in a similar state of what we assume to be childhood innocence before her father's teachings cause her to become socially disaffected and finally sexually transgressive. The reasoning set forth here is that environmental conditions—Louisa's utilitarian education—have made her a "sick" human being, in the double meaning of moral and physical sickness. Louisa is not only morally corrupt, but biologically sick—or "perverted," as Gradgrind himself admits to Bounderby after Louisa returns home ("there are qualities in Louisa which—which have been harshly neglected, and—and a little perverted" [243]). Although Gradgrind is not using the word in the medical sense that late-nineteenth-century sexologists would, he implies nonetheless a turning away from something "natural" (specifically defined here as bourgeois heteronormativity); Louisa has begun life as a healthy organism but has become, by degrees, diseased.[22] Tom is similarly referred to as "unnatural" ostensibly for his hatred of everyone except Louisa, but also because the extent of his self-absorption prevents him from marrying and becoming a productive member of industrial society.

REPRODUCTION, THE FAMILY, AND THE CIRCUS

Sissy's unselfish compassion and Louisa and Tom's antisocial behavior, I am arguing, are more than social or moral issues; they directly affect the health and longevity of industrial society. That society is figured in a specifically organic way: each part is related to the whole in the same manner that Spencer imagines the "mutual dependence" of individual organisms, both social and biological ("Social Organism" 272). Yet the perversion of social and sexual relations within this larger system results not only in disaffected human relationships, but also—significantly—in a compromised reproductive capacity. *Hard Times,* I am asserting, posits reproduction as evidence of the healthy system. This theme can be seen in the distinction between two groups of characters: Louisa, Tom, and Bitzer, who, because of their self-centeredness, do not establish solid bourgeois marriages that result in children; and Sissy and the circus performers, who illustrate fecundity through their masses of children. The nonreproductivity of the first group and the hyper-reproductivity of the second are directly proportional to what the novel constructs as hostility and alienation on the one hand and goodness and compassion on the other.

Louisa's emotional sterility, as mentioned earlier, is connected with bio-logical sterility in the image of the barren garden ("O father . . . what have you done, with the garden that should have bloomed once, in this great wilderness here!" [239]). Louisa cannot "bloom" in any sense; she will not bear children or engage in any fruitful activities, as the final chapters make clear: "[Louisa] again a wife—a mother—lovingly watchful of her children, ever careful that they should have a childhood of the mind no less than a childhood of the body. . . . Did Louisa see this? Such a thing was never to be" (297). The suggestion here is that although Louisa has tried to remedy her failings to some extent, she has been spoiled "at the root" and can never be completely rehabilitated. Sissy, in contrast, is connected with flowering from the beginning of the story, when she argues for a flowered carpet ("If you please, sir . . . I am very fond of flowers" [14]), to the ending, when we learn that she will bear many happy children ("happy Sissy's happy children loving her; all children loving her" [297]). Thus, Sissy completes the bourgeois pic-ture of contented wife and mother, while Louisa's discontent with the world cannot be completely erased. Successful reproduction here is evidence of bio-logical health.

Moreover, Tom and Bitzer extend this biological reasoning by their own failure to reproduce. Both products of a Gradgrindian education, they are shown to have perverted affections through their lack of compassion for others and the rejection of a heterosexual mandate. Deneau observes in a footnote that "[t]he two male products of the system show no signs of being attracted by members of the opposite sex" (174), and offers some examples, but does not go into any analysis on the subject. In support of his point, Deneau notes that "when Harthouse facetiously questions Tom about carv-ing a girl's name on a tree, Tom's thoughts immediately turn to a 'slashing fortune,' for which he would be willing to sell himself" (174) and also that Dickens refers ambiguously to Tom's "grovelling sensualities" (136). Bitzer similarly dismisses any sexual interest in women when he tells Mrs. Sparsit, "I don't want a wife and family" (122). Both scenes, in my view, are signifi-cant because they show Tom and Bitzer to be sexually deviant in the sense that they do not engage in reproductive, heteronormative sexuality. The other principal adult male characters—Gradgrind, Bounderby, Harthouse, and Stephen—are clearly heterosexual (if not actually fathers, they are mar-ried or sexually interested in women), as are all members of Sleary's Circus. Within this context, Tom's and Bitzer's rejections of heterosexual alliances are conspicuous; in shunning such alliances they repudiate bourgeois notions of family and sexuality, particularly with regard to sexual reproduction. As with

Louisa (and the same could be said of Mrs. Blackpool), biological sterility is the end result of moral corruption and social alienation.

Tom's and Bitzer's rejections of heterosexual relationships is only one aspect of their perverted affections; they also show a marked lack of compassion for others. Although Tom claims to be attached to his sister, his actions show otherwise. He encourages Louisa to marry Bounderby, whom she despises, so that he can get ahead at the bank. He rarely visits Louisa after the marriage and denounces her completely when they meet at Sleary's circus, saying petulantly: "I don't want to have anything to say to you!" (285) and "You never cared for me" (285). The robbery proves Tom to be a criminal, but his lack of concern for Louisa is more serious because it shows him to be without "natural" affections. In this regard, Deneau comments, "[Tom] becomes for the first time something near an emotionally and morally healthy human being . . . through his expression of genuine love for Louisa" at the novel's close (174). Yet Tom's change of heart occurs offstage and just before his death, so rather than alleviating the effects of a wasted life, his transformation tends to underscore the tragic consequences of the Gradgrind philosophy. Similarly, Bitzer, we are told, has "no affections or passions. All his proceedings were the result of the nicest and coldest calculation" (*Hard Times* 120). In *Hard Times,* then, social disaffection is both the sign and symptom of biological and emotional sterility. The problem is not so much that Tom and Bitzer are marked as "homosexual," but that through their repudiation of heteronormative sexuality they are marked as asocial and non-reproductive, and thus a threat to the survival of the bourgeois family. Perversion here is defined as a sort of biological or evolutionary suicide, corrupting the self and destroying family and society in the process.

At the other end of *Hard Times'* reproductive spectrum is Sleary's Circus, a phantasmatic mirror of the bourgeois family. In contrast to Louisa and Tom's biological sterility, the members of the circus are able to reproduce themselves endlessly in scores of children: "There were two or three handsome young women among them, with their two or three husbands, and their two or three mothers, and their eight or nine little children . . ." (41). Added to this confusing mix of fathers, mothers, and children, are visibly pregnant women, such as "the most accomplished tight-rope lady (herself in the family way)" (42). Sleary's Circus provides a spectacle of hyper-reproductivity: rather than an orderly ratio of one father and one mother to a specific number of children, as is customary in the bourgeois family, we have any number of fathers, mothers, children, and mothers-to-be, in uncertain relation to one another, with every indication of future exponential growth.

Bourgeois sexual conventions seem not to apply here, including taboos against incestuous relationships. As Richard Fabrizio observes, "[m]arriage here is endogamous, slightly incestuous by the nature of the tightly-knit circus world" (86): "Jupe marries a circus dancer. E.W.B. Childers marries Josephine Sleary. The diminutive, child-like Little Kidderminster . . . marries a widow, once a tightrope walker . . . 'old enough to be hith mother'" (86).

Yet I would argue that the endogamous, "slightly incestuous" relationships of the circus people are in category a very different from the incestuous relationship depicted between Louisa and Tom. While the circus members are "not at all orderly in their domestic arrangements," there is "a remarkable gentleness and childishness about these people, a special inaptitude for any kind of sharp practice, and an untiring readiness to help and pity one another, deserving, often of as much respect, and always of as much generous construction, as the everyday virtues of any class of people in the world" (*Hard Times* 41). In this way, although the chaotic sexual relations portrayed among the circus people seem to be completely opposed to bourgeois notions of the family, Sleary's performers exemplify bourgeois ideals of family and home through the mutual support and sympathy they offer one another. The "slightly incestuous" aspect of young Master Kidderminster marrying a woman "old enough to be hith mother" thus attains the bourgeois social value accorded sibling familialized incest in its tendency toward community building and social cohesion (*Hard Times* 280). Consequently, in the circus community, actual sexual relations between members of the same "family" are not problematic or deviant; what matters here is that the circus family follows the pattern of sibling familialization and sibling familialized incest, emphasizing mutual sympathy and social cooperation in their relationships.

Most importantly, the social cohesion illustrated in the circus family and suggested by Victorian models of sibling familialization provides the foundation for other supportive social and sexual relationships in the community. In this sense, the circus bolsters the tenets of bourgeois domesticity and the organic social model *Hard Times* endorses. The adults in the circus family act as role models for the younger children, who in turn learn from their elders. Sissy learns the value of compassion, for example, when a kindly mother-to-be comforts her after her father disappears:

> [W]hen [Sissy] saw them all assembled, and saw their looks, and saw no father there, she broke into a most deplorable cry, and took refuge on the bosom of the most accomplished tight-rope lady (herself in the family way), who knelt down on the floor to nurse her and to weep over her. (42)

As with sibling familialization in the Victorian novel, which connects mutual compassion with marriage, the pregnant performer's sympathetic "weep[ing]" and "nurs[ing]" connect the "gentleness and childishness" of the circus people to conventions of bourgeois motherhood and reproductive sexuality. "Natural" social and sexual relationships, the text suggests, result in children, which in turn improves the social whole by expanding it and by providing supportive members of society. Thus Sissy learns, through example, how to nurture others and contribute to their growth and development. At its most simple level, *Hard Times* meditates on the raising of children, eventually demonstrating that if children are nurtured in the proper way and allowed to grow freely, they will in turn nurture others in society: their own children, other family members, and others in the larger social domain. Within the context of the novel, having children and helping the social whole go hand in hand.

Thus, although the sexual configurations of the circus are somewhat unclear and even incestuous, these unconventional sexual relationships do not result in antisocial or nonreproductive cultural practices. A portrait of "natural" or "healthy" female sexuality thus emerges, intimately bound up with bourgeois visions of loving motherhood and active reproduction. The tightrope walker possesses the socially-approved emotional qualities of bourgeois womanhood which she then passes on to Sissy, who has adapted to bourgeois society; and it is Sissy, with her numerous foster mothers, who grows up to have "many happy children" and to love even the outcast and fallen of the world. As such, the incestuous atmosphere of the circus family carries with it the socially beneficial elements of sibling familialization as it appears in the Victorian novel: close sibling-like alliances within the circus act as patterns for other relationships, both sexual and non-sexual, and through example contribute to the benefit of the community. The children of the circus family will not grow up to be useless members of society, like Louisa, Tom, and Bitzer, but will nurture others and encourage the healthy development of the social whole.

In addition to vigorous reproduction and emotional nourishment, the circus family displays a sense of mutual cooperation and social cohesiveness which the novel endorses and which implies the healthy functioning of an interdependent organic system. The social cohesiveness of the circus family is demonstrated in several ways: by the communal sense of child-bearing and child-rearing suggested in their disorderly social and sexual relationships, by their desire to raise Sissy after her father leaves, and by their willingness to defy the law and hide Tom after the bank robbery solely because he is connected to Sissy. In each case, there is the assumption that all members of the circus community are connected, an assumption metaphorically reflected in an image of gymnastic interdependence:

> The father of one of the families was in the habit of balancing the father of another of the families on the top of a great pole; the father of a third family often made a pyramid of both those fathers, with Master Kidder-minster for the apex, and [Mr. Childers] for the base. (41)

Each father (representing at least one or more familial configuration) is dependent upon the other fathers to support him; it is a position requiring absolute trust and an understanding that they must all work together—or fall together. The pyramid neatly illustrates the mutual trust and interde-pendence characteristic of the social structure of the circus: it is a large, close-knit "family" made up of other families who support one another. This close-knit, mutually supportive circus community embodies all that is miss-ing from Coketown's populace, from its industrial workers to its middle-class families, children, and employers. Moreover, the image suggests a biological entity in that each of the parts is related to the whole like the organic system Darwin describes. The scores of children and potential future births depicted in the community indicate that it is a well-functioning system, unlike the social aggregate of machine culture. By allowing the free play of thought and spirit, the community encourages each separate organism to achieve healthy maturity and fulfill its role within the larger biological system. The circus, then, is the natural environment as it should be: nourishing, collaborative, and reproductive.

　　Yet the image of the circus is not unproblematic. Some critics, such as Gallagher, see the circus as "too mobile and too morally ambiguous to serve as an enduring reformist model for industrial society" ("Hard Times" 77). However, while I would agree that Sleary and his group do not constitute a viable reformist model, they nonetheless possess virtues missing from Coke-town which the text nostalgically mourns. Sleary's circus restores the losses of childhood brought about by a mechanistic view of human life: the loss of childish pleasures and imaginative scope, of leisure and the freedom from adult worries, of spontaneous love and sympathy. From these shared losses the text draws its central analogy between the bourgeois family and larger society and causes the narrator to ask: "Is it possible, I wonder, that there was any analogy between the case of the Coketown population and the case of the little Gradgrinds?" (31). As Gallagher explains, "Gradgrind's children and Coketown's workers are both denied 'Fancy' and hence the narrator establishes structural symmetry between the bourgeois family and all of industrial society" (75). Not only are family and society linked through shared losses (the loss of childhood pleasures, such as fancy) but, as Gallagher later observes, they are linked through the then-popular model of social paternalism, which maintained that industrial society would benefit by being patterned on the family. Gallagher also argues, however, that the narrative does not fulfill its promise. "Despite some attempt to reintroduce social themes in the last chapter," she asserts, "Dickens fails to show how modern industrial society might become like a large family" (83). The lives of Coketown workers are not changed by Sissy's goodheartedness or Louisa's or Gradgrind's newly found compassion, for instance. Gradgrind becomes less effective as a civic leader as he becomes more empathic as a family man.[23] The reformed bourgeois family does not provide a useful social or economic model for Coketown's problems.

The argument outlined by Gallagher brings up a significant dilemma that *Hard Times* contains: Although the problems of industrial society seem to be a major concern, the novel appears to lack a clear solution to those problems. According to Gallagher, there are two primary examples of this dilemma: First, the circus is unable to function as a viable reformist model; and second, the domestic plot is unable to account for improvement in the economic sphere. However, I would argue that in the context of the biological metaphor, some issues become clearer. As an exemplary model of nature, the circus demonstrates a kind of excess that cannot be imagined in the bourgeois sphere. In this regard, it is not sufficient to say that the circus either succeeds or does not succeed as a viable model because each line of reasoning leaves out elements that are important to the narrative. On the one hand, if you discount the circus as a functional model, then you fail to see how important it is as an ideal model of nature. If you assert, on the other hand, that it does act as a model, then you fail to see how deeply the novel respects the more restrictive aspects of bourgeois ideology (such as neatness, temperance, and sexual propriety). Thus, there is a conflict here between the conventions of bourgeois ideology and the unobstructed freedom of the circus. This conflict is important because it illustrates the way the novel imagines biological growth: as uncontainable, messy, and powerful; so powerful, in fact, that to ignore its strength is to risk destroying an organism's entire life cycle.

I would assert, then, that the circus community is an excess that the novel cannot contain; it is something that the narrative deeply desires but cannot account for in its own terms. Quite simply, *Hard Times* opens up more than it can handle (but that is part of it richness), yet it appears to resolve everything by producing Louisa as the fallen character and Sissy as the redemptive one. Sissy is a hybrid, simultaneously of both worlds: circus and bourgeois. She brings the positive values of the circus to industrial society and enacts them within bourgeois limitations. Accordingly, although she demonstrates the circus community's positive values of compassion and social collaboration, she does not engage in their anti-bourgeois habits: she is not untidy in her dress or inclined to indulge in drink; and given the speed with which she banishes Harthouse from Louisa's life, it is plain that she will not engage in unconventional sexual relationships. Thus, she appears to solve the problems that the novel sets up, especially in relation to Louisa. Despite the problems in the bourgeois sphere which the novel critiques, that sphere cannot be simply replaced with the circus model; it requires a hybrid character like Sissy who can act in one sphere, but invoke the memory of the other. Consequently, the novel wants two things at the same time: the disorder of the circus, and the order of bourgeois society as it could be, if all were like Sissy.

Thus, we are left with another dilemma, because while the circus cannot literally solve the problems in the bourgeois sphere—it can only point it in a certain direction—neither can it solve the problems of the industrial sphere. Yet the parallel between the two plots, domestic and economic, suggests that the one can be solved in the same manner as the other. And this is where a narrative elision takes place, because while it appears that the problems of the domestic sphere have been solved by Sissy's magical presence, the contradictory thematics that she represents—bourgeois and organic—nullify the logic of a resolution here. Instead, the narrative offers us a series of displacements which take us from a mechanistic industrial world, to a harsh economic realm (the realm of Bounderby's bank), and finally to the troubled bourgeois family, where most of the blame settles on Louisa and a diagnosis of sexual pathology. The problems in the industrial and economic spheres cannot be resolved, but they can be conveniently ignored and replaced by other more intriguing dilemmas more amenable to resolution, at least as they are depicted. By substituting a diagnosis of female sexual deviance for troubling cultural issues, the novel simply sidesteps the problems of the pathologized social sphere.

In highlighting the theme of sibling incest, I wish to demonstrate both the biological reasoning of the narrative and the way in which female sexual deviance comes to stand in for the diseased social sphere. All of the problems in this narrative, I would argue, in both society and the family, stem from perversion of some sort; except for the circus people, all characters are affected by the abnormal constraints of mechanistic thinking. The stunted dispositions of Bitzer, Louisa and Tom affect others in the community and the larger social sphere: Bounderby loses both his wife and his money; Stephen is rejected by his peers and later dies; the entire Gradgrind family is made unhappy by Louisa and Tom. Almost everyone in the novel except Sissy and the circus community experiences the deleterious effects of social disaffection and impeded mental and emotional growth. It is possible, then, to see the incestuous relationship between Louisa and Tom as both metonymically and metaphorically related to the perversions of industrial society. Their relationship is examined more closely than any other issue in the novel and in this way diverts awareness from the problems of machine culture.

More importantly for my argument, however, Louisa's deviation is at the center of the novel, thus diminishing the other problems. Her difficulties take up the majority of the narrative's attentions; Tom's bank robbery and Stephen's travails are merely subplots. In fact, her character is more fully delineated than is any other character's, including Gradgrind's, Tom's, and Sissy's. We know Louisa's inner thoughts and conflicts; we experience her despair; we see her attempting to understand her problems and influence Tom for the better. Thus, ultimately, her deviance stands in for all others, and displaces other problems in the novel. The problems of the economic sphere are not solved in any visible manner, but by placing Louisa's perversion next to Sissy's health, the text presents only one problem (Louisa's abnormality) and one solution (to let children grow in an unfettered, organic way). The other problems are forgotten. Louisa's deformity becomes the issue that displaces all others, seemingly solving them through the many suggested parallels.

CONCLUSION

My overriding concern here is with the way in which the body of the female deviant stands in for the problems of the diseased social sphere, and that is accomplished through *Hard Times'* participation in emergent discourses of science, the body, and the environment. A concept of unnatural, sick, or perverted behavior arises through a biological line of reasoning suggested through references to plant development and human reproduction. Thus, social and moral behavior is seen in developmental terms: adult behavior is determined by childhood environment, so that if the child is stunted early on, he or she will grow up in a deformed manner. The older Gradgrind children are perverted because their father's philosophy advocates ultra-rational thinking and discounts non-quantifiable emotional needs. Louisa and Tom experience profound social disaffection because, like unhealthy plants, they lack the proper nourishment to thrive. As the novel illustrates, the antisocial behavior demonstrated by Louisa, Tom, and Bitzer, will eventually affect others and poison the larger social sphere.

Yet despite being surrounded by a number of emotionally and morally defective human beings, Louisa's imperfections become the focal point of the story. This arises, in part, because of the way that deviance is constructed here—as a divergence from the "natural" sibling affections idealized in narratives of sibling familialization and sibling familialized incest. Moreover, such narratives of idealized sibling love are, of course, themselves deeply embedded within a discourse of bourgeois ideology and given sustenance by a scientific inscription of radical sexual difference upon the female body. *Hard Times* participates in these scientific inscriptions through its rendition of industrial pathology as female sexual pathology. The suggestion is that as a result of disaffected social and sexual relations, industrial society is at risk of reproductive decline, a decline that Louisa represents through her unnatural attachment to her brother. Accordingly, although Louisa attempts to reverse the course of pathology within her own family, confronting her father with his failings and extricating herself from unhealthy relationships, she nonetheless embodies the threat to the bourgeois family and industrial society posed by social disaffection. In the final analysis, then, it is the female sexual deviant who is both sign and symptom of the diseased bourgeois family, the family threatened with extinction. Only by locating and ostensibly "solving" the problem of her pathology through its revelation and diagnosis can the family—and the social organism—thrive.

Chapter Three

Women, Savages, and the Body of Africa: Rider Haggard's *She* as Biological Narrative

Nineteenth-century discourses of health and pathology are fundamental to the logic of Rider Haggard's *She,* a narrative of colonial exploration and masculine adventure. *She*'s circulating racial and sexual metaphors connect the female body to the African body and African landscape, demonstrating late-Victorian scientific assumptions about gender, sexuality, and racial difference. By depicting both non-heteronormative female sexuality and the African landscape and people as diseased and abnormal, Haggard creates a conceptual border separating the white male subject from its racial and sexual others. *She* is, in my reading, a biological narrative that pathologizes women and non-white races, equating the abnormal female body with the pathologized African social body. The social body of Africa is imagined here as both a diseased landscape and a debased civilization which reflect the gender deviance of the central female protagonist. Most importantly, for my reading, the female body stands in for and displaces the problems of a diseased social sphere, here imagined in colonial terms. While many critics have noted the obvious correspondences between *She*'s African landscape and the female body, no extended analysis has been done of the ways in which scientific models of pathology inform the text's construction of gender and race.[1] In brief, I am arguing that metaphors of feminine monstrosity connecting gender deviance with African disease and abnormality are enabled through biomedical and colonial discourses about women and racial others. In this connection, I examine discourses of racial science and colonial possession in relation to nineteenth-century gender ideology about chaste womanhood and maternal devotion. This chapter thus analyzes how these cultural metaphors about feminine monstrosity work and what ideologies they support.

One of the main assertions I am making in this chapter is that *She* does not merely reproduce cultural stereotypes about Africa and Africans, but embeds those stereotypes in nineteenth-century scientific reasoning that links the deviant female body to racial alterity. Thus, there are two main lines of thought I am tracing: the first is the way that Africa and Africans were defined in terms of disease and abnormality in the nineteenth century, and the second is the association between women—especially deviant women—and racial otherness in both biomedical and cultural thinking. By way of introduction, the first section will situate *She* in the context of colonial exploration and the British adventure story, analyzing the masculinist and racial assumptions associated with the white male protagonists of the story. The next two sections will address, respectively, the pathologization of Africa and Africans, and the correlation between the female body and African "savagery." The final two sections will present my argument about women, nonreproductive sexuality, and racial difference.

MASCULINITY, IMPERIAL ROMANCE, AND THE WHITE MALE BODY

She has been categorized variously as imperial gothic, imperial romance, and late-Victorian male romance.[2] These definitions are mobile, but all refer to a type of male-centered narrative popular in the late nineteenth century which contained an adventure or quest as its primary focus. Some critics have suggested that such narratives responded to a perceived crisis of masculinity, relating to changes occurring in the social and economic structure of Britain in the latter decades of the century. Redefinitions of the family, of women's roles, and of class affiliations necessarily led to redefinitions of bourgeois masculinity. Stephen Arata, for example, sees the male romance as a specific response to male uneasiness about cultural changes, noting that "the theory and practice of the male romance reveals an array of anxieties at once personal, 'racial,' political, and aesthetic: anxieties concerning the dissolution of masculine identity, the degeneration of the British 'race,' the moral collapse of imperial ideology, and the decline of the great tradition of English letters" (89). The late-Victorian romance offered a remedy to such anxieties, with male protagonists undergoing tests of physical and mental endurance and succeeding over all odds.

Not surprisingly, these adventure stories often took place in remote locations, where inroads had been made by colonial exploration. British colonies or potential colonies offered a number of possibilities for male self-renewal: disease, difficult terrain, and hostile strangers all could be overcome by a sharp-witted Englishman and an ample supply of quinine. Edward Said observes that late nineteenth-century travel narratives and works of colonial exploration, such as Haggard's *She*, rather than expressing disillusionment as so many realistic novels of the period do, depict "a new narrative progression and triumphalism" (*Culture and Imperialism* 187). As Said explains:

> Almost without exception these narratives, and literally hundreds like them based on the exhilaration and interest of adventure in the colonial world, far from casting doubt on the imperial undertaking, serve to confirm and celebrate its success. Explorers find what they are looking for, adventurers return home safe and wealthier. . . . (*Culture and Imperialism* 187–188)

The colonial territories provided an arena within which fantasies of male valor and accomplishment could be envisioned. Boys left home immature youngsters and came back men, ready to assume their proper roles as leaders of society.

These narratives of male bravery in the colonial context evolved in response to a number of books and articles by Victorian explorers of "uncharted" regions, with Africa getting a large share of the attention. Patrick Brantlinger observes that African expeditions began in earnest in the late 1850s, assisted by the discovery of quinine as a protection against malaria (*Rule of Darkness* 179).[3] As the "scramble for Africa" accelerated in the second half of the nineteenth century, an endless stream of lectures, articles, interviews, books, and cartoons flooded the marketplace, finding an eager readership ready and waiting. The names and endeavors of explorers such as Richard Burton, David Livingstone, and Henry Stanley became well known to the English and others in the western world, while their reports helped create views of Africa and the Africans which became commonplace.[4] Haggard's *She* draws upon these various sources, both fictional and the reportedly nonfictional, contributing in its own turn to the development of what Brantlinger calls "the myth of the dark continent" ("Victorians and Africans").

Although extremely popular at the time it was published, *She* is rarely read now, and so a brief outline of the plot follows. The story traces the adventures of two Englishmen from Cambridge who journey into central Africa to find the secret of eternal life; in so doing, they encounter Ayesha, a "white" woman (of Arabic ancestry, according to the text) ruling over a community of African people of mixed descent, and engage in a struggle for knowledge and power. Like the typical male romance, events are improbable and often absurd, but are given credence by the authoritative tone of the narrator, Horace Holly. Holly is a Cambridge professor who becomes the guardian of a young boy, Leo Vincey, the child of a deceased male friend. Before the friend dies, he leaves Holly with a mysterious iron box which Leo is to open on his twenty-fifth birthday. The box turns out to contain documents tracing Leo's ancestry back about 2,000 years, to an Egyptian princess and a Greek priest, Kallikrates, who breaks his vows of celibacy, so the story goes, to marry the princess. As the documents reveal, tragedy strikes when a ruthless African queen with magical powers becomes smitten with Kallikrates; she offers to give him the secret of eternal life, which she possesses, if he will kill his wife and marry her. When Kallikrates refuses, the African woman kills him, and the Egyptian princess escapes and soon after bears a male child, Kallikrates' son. Along with manuscripts which follow the line of descent from Kallikrates's son through to the Vincey line are two letters: one from the Egyptian princess to her son asking him to kill the African sorceress and discover the secret of eternal life, and one from Leo's father asking him to solve "the greatest mystery in the world" if he is so inclined (29). For Leo, the decision to pursue the mystery through to its conclusion is immediate.

The rest of the narrative follows Leo and Holly's exploits in Africa. They bring their male servant, Job, along with them, and eventually locate the African queen (now 2,000 years old and lovely as ever), whose name is Ayesha, or "She-who-must-be-obeyed." Ayesha is both brutal and seductive, described as a "beautiful white woman" (28) of Arabic descent who rules over a tribe of Africans called the Amahagger (28). The Amahagger are a racially-mixed people living within a vaguely matriarchal social structure. Although the text describes two members of the tribe in favorable terms—Ustane, a woman who marries Leo in a tribal ceremony and Billali, the patriarch of the tribe—the rest of the Amahagger are shown to be treacherous, engaging in cannibalistic practices and ominous rites. Physically, they are described as dark-skinned and "yellowish" (76), but not black; they speak a "bastard Arabic," and yet are "not Arabs" (77). In contrast, Ayesha speaks many languages, including her main language: a very "pure" and "classical" form of Arabic (142). After being courted by Ayesha (who believes that Leo is Kallikrates, returned to her after two millennia) and nearly killed by the Amahagger, Leo and Holly eventually encounter the "flame of life" (291), the final goal of their quest. But rather than granting Ayesha a further extension of her long life, the flame mysteriously malfunctions; in the process of dying, "She" undergoes a physical regression of more than 2,000 years, ending in a pre-human, monkey-like state. In the final pages, Job dies, his nerves "shattered by all he had seen and undergone," and Holly and Leo return to Cambridge, revitalized and wiser than when they began (296).

She focuses much attention on questions of race and lineage. Ayesha, the Amahagger, and the two male protagonists (Job is ignored in this respect), for instance, are described in very specific physical and genealogical terms. The first thing we learn about Holly and Leo is that they are particular physical types, very different from each other but quintessential examples of masculine beauty or strength. In the opening pages, the fictional editor of *She* describes Holly and Leo in minute—even lingering—detail. He states that Leo is

> without exception, the handsomest young fellow I have ever seen. He
> was very tall, very broad, and had a look of power and a grace of bearing
> that seemed as native to him as it is to a wild stag. In addition, his face
> was almost without flaw—a good face as well as a beautiful one, and
> when he lifted his hat . . . I saw that his head was covered with little
> golden curls growing close to his scalp. (1)

The editor dwells on Leo's beauty, grace, vigor—and "native" power. He tells us further that people say Leo looks like "a statue of Apollo" (1) and that his friends call him "the Greek God" (2). The reference to Greek beauty, as we learn later, is borne out in Leo's lineage, for he is the physical descendant of Kallikrates, the Greek priest. Moreover, Leo's beauty is grounded in virtue and integrity, unlike Ayesha's beauty, which conceals a ruthless nature. Accordingly, the editor tells us that Leo's face is "a good face as well as a beautiful one" (1). Leo's moral and physical perfection are matched, as we later discover, by courage, loyalty, and kindness. Thus, race and heritage merge in Leo to portray an image of nobility: powerful, beautiful, and seemingly born to rule. Leo's "native" power and aristocratic lineage suggest that his supremacy is in the blood; it is his by birth.

Holly contrasts vividly with Leo in terms of beauty, but shares Leo's moral rectitude. Where Leo is beautiful, Holly is ugly, "as ugly as his companion was handsome" (2), the editor tells us. Holly is described in simian terms as

> shortish, rather bow-legged, very deep chested, and with unusually long
> arms. He had dark hair and small eyes, and the hair grew right down on
> his forehead, and his whiskers grew right up to his hair, so that there was
> uncommonly little of his countenance to be seen. Altogether he
> reminded me forcibly of a gorilla, and yet there was something very
> pleasing and genial about the man's eye. (2)

Holly's "gorilla" appearance is so marked, in fact, that it prompts Billali to call him the "Baboon" as a term of respect (110). The references to Holly's apishness are extensive and at the same time meant to refer ironically to Darwin's theory of human evolution. (Darwin's *Descent of Man* was published in 1871.) Holly overhears one woman saying, for instance, that his simian looks had converted her "to the monkey theory" (8). However, at the same time that the text asserts Holly's apishness, it also attests to his finer qualities: the editor sees something "pleasing and genial about him" in spite of his unattractive appearance. Holly makes this combination of physical unattractiveness and other compensating factors explicit in his own narration, stating that although he is "abnormal[ly] ugl[y]," he is "gifted by Nature with iron and abnormal strength and considerable intellectual powers" (8). Moreover, Holly asserts his intellectual superiority through the power of his narration: he describes the journey, the African land and its people with clinical expertise and judicious reasoning. Holly's discerning way of observing the world, coupled with his status as university professor, grant him an authority that justifies his roles as narrator, guardian, and guide.

Holly's apish description is meant to be both humorous and ironic because the narrative purports to establish the Africans as the apes, not Holly. Rebecca Stott makes this latter point in reference to Ayesha (but not the Amahagger, whom I analyze below), discussing two significant scenes: one in which Holly refuses to prostrate himself before Ayesha, as Billali does, and another later scene in which Holly falls in confused terror at her feet. In the first instance, Holly remarks defiantly, "I was an Englishman, and why, I asked myself, should I creep into the presence of some savage woman as though I were a *monkey* . . . ? [I]t would have been a patent acknowledgement of my inferiority" (*She* 140; emphasis added). In the second instance, Ayesha has taken off the veil she usually wears in public (so that others will not go mad with desire), then lashes out in anger at Holly when she sees he is wearing a sacred ornament (a scarab). Holly, dazzled by her beauty and power, falls "on the ground before her, babbling confusedly in [his] terror" (*She* 157). Stott remarks that:

> [I]n this . . . debasement, [Holly] implicitly acknowledges her superiority [and] [f]rom this point [his] investigations are directed towards reversing this humiliating defeat, directed towards proving her inferiority by demonstrating her savagery and barbarism, demonstrating that it is Ayesha who is the "monkey" rather than himself. (*Femme Fatale* 106)

Accordingly, then, although Holly is continuously presented as the "monkey," Ayesha is proved to be so during her final regression to her monkey-like form. As I will argue in the final sections of this chapter, Ayesha is associated with the Amahagger and "savage" Africa, so that her final debasement is a debasement that extends to all Africa.

I would also note here that the narrative stages a continuous dialogue between "primitive" and "civilized," so that in its preoccupation with powerful masculinity, supposed "primitive" qualities (strength, bravery, stamina) are valorized and "civilization" takes an occasional beating. Thus, Holly describes his academic brethren as "fossilised" and exults in his new adventures and increased intellectual scope:

> For half an hour I lay still, reflecting on the very remarkable experiences that we were going through, and wondering if any of my eminently respectable fossil friends down at Cambridge would believe me if I were to be miraculously set at the familiar dinner-table for the purpose of relating them. I don't want to convey any disrespectful notion or slight when I call those good and learned men fossils, but my experience is that people are apt to fossilise even at a University if they follow the same paths too persistently. I was getting fossilised myself, but of late my stock of ideas has been very much enlarged. (76)

Holly's portrayal of Cambridge as a place of intellectual exhaustion contrasts with his own intellectual vigor, made possible by the new experiences and ideas gleaned on his African journey. The antidote to male intellectual enervation offered here is the development of skills associated with primitive man: hunting, fighting, and the endurance of physical hardships. Holly and Leo are, of course, ideally suited for this mission; before they ever set foot outside of Cambridge they are shown to be specimens of an innate masculine vigor that presumably resides beneath the veneer of civilization. Besides being unusually strong or powerful, for instance, they are skilled hunters, pursuing game in the wild locales of Scotland, Norway, and Russia rather than the landscaped grounds of country houses (*She* 21). In this sense, they are examples of primitive, "natural" man, with an irrefutable masculinity deeply rooted in the body. This masculinity is, moreover, a specific rendering of English male vigor as "health," a rendering that contrasts markedly with the "unhealthy" African people, as I discuss in the next section.[5]

Yet, significantly, Holly and Leo's virile masculinity is offset by their very marked differences from the "primitive" Africans they encounter. Both men are smarter than the Africans (except Ayesha, who has supernatural intellectual abilities) and, of course, they do not engage in the torture, brutality, and cannibalism associated with the Amahagger, thus identifying

Holly and Leo as "civilized" in these aspects. Maria Iglesia observes this conflict between admiration for "savage virtues" and scorn for the "politeness" of contemporary Britain in Haggard's writing and remarks:

> On the one hand, there was an obsessive fear of regression towards the barbarism those [non-European] cultures were held to represent; on the other, there was a marked tendency to admire and praise the "savage virtues" of certain groups, in contrast with "this polite age of melamite and torpedoes," as Haggard puts it in his introduction to *Nada*. (42)

As Iglesia explains, the contradiction between fear of and admiration for primitive cultures was an impulse of late-Victorian culture that Haggard taps into. I would note also that this contradiction is further exhibited in *She* through sympathetic portrayals of Ustane (who dies trying to save Leo) and Billali (depicted as a noble patriarch) which are set against descriptions of the Amahagger's vicious cruelty.

Moreover, I would assert that *She*'s oscillation between admiration and disgust for the "savage" demonstrates its preoccupation with a specifically English manhood that it attempts to portray: one that is both as hardy as the "savage" races and as "enlightened" as the European. The combination of Leo's "native" power (1) and noble lineage, along with Holly's intellectual authority and physical manliness, links English superiority with bodily attributes. Accordingly, Holly's avowal not to crawl before Ayesha because he is "an Englishman" takes on a particular significance when that avowal is discredited and then reasserted through her final debasement (140). This account of assertion, loss, and reclamation demonstrates that what is at stake in the novel is not eternal life, but a particular kind of white, male, English supremacy. Thus, although I address these issues separately to a certain extent, I would argue that masculinity, femininity, imperial domination, and race cannot be separated in this text because each term is connected to the other in some way.

Holly and Leo's racial superiority gains definition and distinction, then, in relation to both the Amahagger and Ayesha. Like the Englishmen's "civilized" behavior, the brutality displayed by Ayesha and her followers is racially inflected. The Amahagger, however, are depicted in very different ways than their feminine ruler. In stereotypical terms, Ayesha is an Oriental despot, and her dark-skinned followers are a debased and savage race.[6] Moreover, questions of race are intimately bound up with questions of evolution, degeneration, and the notion of "true" origins. Thus, the text contrasts the "extraordinary antiquity of [Leo's] race" with the less glorious past of the

Amahagger (27). At one point Holly muses, "[a]t first we were much puzzled as to the origin and constitution of this extraordinary race [the Amahagger]," and Ustane claims that they have no "origin," as far as she is aware (89); but the narrative will determine otherwise: that the Amahagger are the remnants of an ancient, extinct civilization which descended into depravity and miscegenation. The following section examines the cultural, scientific, and biomedical contexts which support *She*'s vision of African savagery.

PATHOLOGICAL ANATOMY AND THE PRIMITIVE BODY

Racist attitudes of white Europeans towards black and other nonwhite peoples were not new in the nineteenth century, but what did change was that the concept of racial difference gained a much stronger biological footing than had previously existed.[7] Ania Loomba notes, for instance, that in the premodern period the concept of "race" was only nominally biological. Quoting from Robert Bartlett she states "'the language of race—*gens, natio,* "blood," "stock" etc.—is biological' but 'its reality was almost entirely cultural'" (Loomba 37). Loomba further explains that "[i]n practice, races were defined more in social terms of customs, language and law, and all of these could be acquired or changed; premodern understandings of ethnic differentiation were less rigid than their later counterparts" (37). Nineteenth-century discourses contained many of the same cultural biases as existed in earlier centuries, but with increased attention to scientific logic. Thus, along with the move to seek biological causes for the inferiority of women came a drive to seek similar causes for the inferiority of nonwhite bodies. Scientific reasoning linking biological difference to social inferiority eventually led to claims about the abnormality of racial others, often reducing such others to the status of pathological deviants.

Among the many nineteenth-century figures who pursued such lines of thought, Arthur de Gobineau—historian, novelist, and self-styled "Orientalist"—was a leading figure in the development of European ideas about racial difference.[8] Gobineau believed that there were three races—"the black, the yellow, and the white"—with "[t]he negroid variety [being] the lowest" and the whites being superior in all ways (Gobineau 205). Especially pertinent to my analysis is the way in which Gobineau connected cultural stereotypes to the physical body. Writing in 1853, Gobineau carefully delineates the physical characteristics of the different races, claiming that "[t]he animal character, *that appears in the shape of the pelvis, is stamped on the negro from birth,* and foreshadows his destiny" (205; emphasis added). In the case of the "yellow race," Gobineau declares that "[t]he skull points forward, not backward

[,] [t]he forehead is wide and bony, . . . [and] [h]e tends to mediocrity in everything" (206). In contrast, Gobineau does not describe the "white races" with such attention to physical detail, but portrays them as "gifted with reflective energy, or rather with an energetic intelligence . . . [and] a remarkable . . . love of liberty" (207). Thus, he positions blacks at the bottom of the social and biological hierarchy, with the "yellow" race in the middle, and the white race at the top. Moreover, the differences Gobineau outlines—in body and character—are permanent; the "savage" races will always be inferior to the white race. In this regard, he complains at length about "friends of equality" who argue that individual Africans they have met ("Kaffir[s]," "Hottentot[s]," or "Bambara[s]," for example) are skilled in various ways, and declares that although they may indeed be adept at certain activities, they will nevertheless never rise above a level comparable to "our peasants, or even . . . the average specimens of our half-educated middle class" (180).[9]

Gobineau's belief in the inferiority of nonwhite races was shared by many in the second half of the nineteenth century. Cesare Lombroso, for example, merged the nascent field of criminal anthropology with concepts of racial difference.[10] Lombroso's theory of criminal atavism, in particular, joined ideas about evolution, degeneration, criminal behavior, and nonwhite races. According to Lombroso, certain individuals were physically disposed towards crime. This disposition could be determined in the shape of the skull, the pigmentation of the skin, or the texture of the hair—characteristics especially visible in what Lombroso calls the "savage races." As he asserts:

> [M]any of the characteristics presented by *savage races* are very often found among *born criminals*. Such, for example, are: the slight development of the pilar system; low cranial capacity; retreating forehead; . . . thickness of the bones of the skull; . . . greater pigmentation of the skin; tufted and crispy hair; and large ears. To these we may add . . . great agility; relative insensibility to pain; dullness of the sense of touch; great visual acuteness; ability to recover quickly from wounds; [and] blunted affections. . . . (*Crime* 365; emphasis added)

In aligning the "born criminal" with the "savage races," Lombroso implies that black Africans and others living in presumably primitive societies are corrupt and dishonest, while at the same time asserting that modern criminals resemble these primitive beings. Thus, in Lombroso's formulation, the criminal was an atavistic throwback to an earlier form of life, biologically connected to physical types that were predisposed to illicit behavior.

As several scholars have noted, Lombroso's work was from the start focused on the question of racial difference. Even before the appearance of the first edition of *Criminal Man* (published in 1876 as *Uomo Delinquente*), Lombroso demonstrated an interest in defining race according to terms which joined biological, moral, and intellectual characteristics. Daniel Pick notes, for instance, that Lombroso's *The White Man and the Coloured Man* argues unambiguously for white superiority.[11] In this publication Lombroso states that "Only we White people . . . have reached the most perfect symmetry of bodily form. . . . Only we [have bestowed] . . . the human right to life, respect for old age, women, and the weak" (qtd. in Pick 126). Pick comments that "[t]he white races represented the triumph of the human species, its hitherto most perfect advancement. But then inside the triumphant whiteness, there remained a certain blackness" (126). The logic of criminal atavism, then, explained how the "superior" white races could produce beings who violated legal and moral laws of conduct. Only by classifying criminals as a degenerate, backward race biologically aligned with the "inferior" black races could this be accomplished.

Lombroso's later works returned to the same ideas about racial others. In *Crime: Its Causes and Remedies*,[12] he summarizes many of his earlier theories:

> We may add that the atavism of the criminal, when he lacks absolutely every trace of shame and pity, may go back far beyond the savage, even to the brutes themselves. *Pathological anatomy helps prove our position* by showing in the case of the criminal a greater development of the cerebellum, . . . and especially the histological anomalies discovered by Roncoroni in the cortex of the cerebrum of criminals. . . . (368; emphasis added)

Lombroso continues at this point with his cataloging of various physical anomalies which define both criminals and "savages" in terms of "pathological anatomy." According to Lombroso, nonwhites and criminals are not only morally and intellectually inferior, but also physically abnormal; they are born into a diseased state and cannot escape the consequences of their heritage.

One of the issues that concerned many scientists and doctors who believed that the races were morally, intellectually, and biologically different from one another was that of hybridity or interbreeding.[13] Within the context of late-Victorian racial anthropology, the "half-breed" was portrayed as an aberration or biological abnormality. Discussing the image of the half-breed in nineteenth-century Britain, H.L. Malchow comments:

> [E]volutionary discourse about "missing links" and surviving anomalies that straddled the boundaries of species worked its way well down into

popular culture, and the half-breed absorbed a new resonance, which
was strikingly negative. Whatever eighteenth-century associations there
may have been with breeding up (and these would have been weak and
ambiguous in any event), after the 1860s, the associations most available became either the "dead ends" found in the fossil record or creatures like flightless birds or the duck-billed platypus that seemed to be
obsolescent half-species doomed to die out or to survive merely as ludi-
crous evidence of nature's confusion, of experiments gone wrong. It was
not only in the work of the racist propagandist Robert Knox that the
"human hybrid" was now seen as a "degradation of humanity . . .
rejected by nature." (183–84)

The concept of the half-breed gained a new dimension. Rather than there being
a possibility of "improving the stock," the emphasis was on the abnormality of
mixed species or races. Many who supported such thinking at this time agreed
with Gobineau, who stated, "[it is] impossible . . . that the civilizations belonging to racially distinct groups should ever be fused together. . . . [T]he European
cannot hope to civilize the negro, and manages to transmit to the mulatto only
a very few of his own characteristics . . ." (Gobineau 179). In Gobineau's reasoning, interbreeding between races was especially problematic when the more "civilized" European races merged with the less "civilized" negro.

Gobineau's logic was reproduced among many scientists, doctors, and
anthropologists who supported racist thinking in the second half of the nineteenth century. These specialists argued stridently against racial mixing on
the grounds that mixing resulted in debased or monstrous human beings.
Louis Agassiz, a Swiss scientist who immigrated to the United States in the
1840s, was one such person who believed that racial mixing was a crime
against nature.[14] He believed, like many others working in similar fields, that
the races were biologically distinct and that the white race was superior to
other races. Accordingly, for Agassiz, interbreeding between races (known as
"amalgamation" before 1864, when the term "miscegenation" was coined[15])
was troubling. Agassiz expresses the thoughts of many others when he writes:

> The production of half-breeds is as much a sin against nature, as incest
> in a civilized community is a sin against purity of character. . . . Far
> from presenting to me a natural solution of our difficulties, the idea of
> amalgamation is most repugnant to my feelings, I hold it to be a *perver-
> sion* of every natural sentiment. (qtd. in Gould 48;[16] emphasis added)

The half-breed, then, was a "perversion": a deviation from the normal, and
something that interfered with the healthy development of a species or
which could lead to the degeneration of body and mind.

This view of racial hybridity as pathological and perverse speaks directly to the narrative of *She,* which concerns itself with the degeneration that results from racial mingling. Although both Ayesha and the Amahagger are depicted as brutal, the racial profiles of each are quite distinct. On the one hand, Ayesha is of a "pure" race, while the Amahagger are of mixed origins. The Amahagger's racial mixture has received almost no attention from literary critics; the exception is Laura Chrisman, whom I discuss below. A few critics have mentioned the degeneration or debasement of the Amahagger in passing, but none extend their discussions on this topic, nor do they connect degeneracy to racial hybridity, as I am doing. For example, Stott comments that "Ayesha . . . is shown through anthropological comparison with the Armahaggers to share a kinship with her people of sexual cruelty and degeneration," but Stott does not expand on this subject (*Femme Fatale* 105). Similarly, David Bunn describes the Amahagger as a "degraded race," but does not analyze their specific racial composition or extend his discussion further in this direction. In contrast to these writers, I am asserting that the Amahagger's degeneration is the direct result of their racial hybridity. Moreover, I see their hybridity in very specific terms: as between a civilized race and an uncivilized one, as nineteenth-century racial theorists, such as Gobineau, objected to. Finally, in the closing pages of this chapter, I will argue that Ayesha's character embodies this degeneration.

The narrative depicts the Amahagger as being descended from a once-great civilization but becoming debased through their interbreeding with other races. In tracing for Holly the history of Kôr's original inhabitants and their eventual transformation into the modern Amahagger tribe, Ayesha explains that a plague devastated the city, leaving only a few people alive. All that is left of the original civilization are the remains of the ancient city of Kôr, which consists of large underground caves filled with the bodies of the dead. Ayesha surmises that after the devastation the few remaining people intermarried with other races. As she explains, "[t]he barbarians from the south, or perchance my people, the Arabs, came down upon them, and took their women to wife, and the race of the Amahagger that is now is a *bastard brood* of the mighty sons of Kôr . . ." (181; emphasis added). That the Amahagger are a "bastard brood" rather than a "pure" race is emphasized further by *She*'s fictional editor (who publishes Holly's narrative) in a footnote:

> The name of the race Ama-hagger would seem to indicate a *curious mingling of races* such as might easily have occurred in the neighbourhood of

the Zambesi. The prefix "Ama" is common to *the Zulu and kindred races,* and signifies "people," while "hagger" is an Arabic word meaning a stone. (181; emphasis added)

Thus, the fictional editor suggests that the original inhabitants of Kôr— whom Ayesha calls a "great people" (181)—married black-skinned people such as the Zulu. (The mention of "hagger" as "stone" refers to Kôr's large cliffs and boulders.) The result is that the modern Amahagger tribe, because of their intermixing with another race, are a savage—and deviant—form of humanity.

In addition to this explicit reference to hybridity, the name "Ama-hagger" connotes hybridity in another manner, in that it is suggestive of the combined names "Abraham" and "Hagar" from the biblical story. As Daniel Karlin observes, the biblical account indicates that Hagar was cast out into the wilderness with the son she had conceived by Abraham when Abraham's wife, Sarah, complained about her.[17] *She's* fictional editor alludes to this story:

> In speaking of herself as "al Arab al Ariba," [Ayesha] no doubt meant to convey that she was of the true Arab blood as distinguished from the naturalised Arabs, the descendants of Ishmael, the son of Abraham and Hagar. . . . (146)

Unlike Abraham, Hagar was Egyptian, so their child was of mixed race. The text thus distinguishes between Ayesha's bloodline and that of the "naturalised" (or mixed-race) Arabs. It is worth noting that Leo's distant ancestor was Egyptian, like Hagar, and she married a Greek; but presumably these races are meant to be read in exemplary terms, unlike dark-skinned races such as the Zulu, for instance.

This intermixing, I am suggesting, is not random but is that of a "greater" race with a "lesser" one, so that the Amahagger are debased not only through the mixing of two races, but also because one is a more "civilized" race. The precise racial designation of Kôr's original people is not mentioned, but they are clearly not black. Holly explains, for instance, that Kôr's mixed descendants, the Amahagger, are "yellowish in colour" (76–77) yet similar in appearance to the "East African Somali, only their hair was not frizzed up" (77). On the one hand, then, the Amahagger are similar to the dark-skinned Somalis or the Zulu; on the other hand, they are not as dark, suggesting that Kôr's original "great" people were a light-skinned race, perhaps of a vaguely Oriental or Arabic origin, as nineteenth-century readers would have imagined it. Their deterioration, then, proceeds from the mixture of an "advanced" civilization with a "savage" one, such as Gobineau cautioned against.

Chrisman, in "The Imperial Unconscious? Representations of Imperial Discourse," describes the Amahagger's degeneration in a slightly different way, as the result of the once-great people of Kôr contaminating their line with *either* the "superior Oriental or . . . the savage black other" (503); thus, in her view, their adulteration comes from an indeterminate source. (Chrisman bases her opinion on Ayesha's description of Kôr's people as mixing with "[t]he barbarians from the south, or . . . the Arabs" [*She* 181]). This indeterminacy, Chrisman asserts, is the analog to the indeterminacy of imperial discourse. Although I would agree with Chrisman's larger point about *She*'s inconsistencies and ambiguities being a sign of imperialism's shifting rationale, in this specific instance I would argue that the Amahagger's degeneration comes from their mixing with black people such as the Somali or the Zulu. Thus, while Kôr's original inhabitants might be "Oriental," their eventual debasement comes from miscegenation with dark-skinned peoples—a significant point in light of nineteenth-century discourses of racial hybridity. In my view, rather than being indeterminate, the Amahagger are a conflation of several persistent myths. This conflation, as I argue, relates to Ayesha's multivalent signification.

The mixture of dark and light races that *She* delineates for the Amahagger is the prerequisite to their depiction as savage and cannibalistic. They are known, for example, for their especially cruel form of killing by placing burning-hot pots on their victims' heads (a reference perhaps to the human meal that the victim will soon become). Ayesha herself is disparaging of the people over whom she rules, calling them "[d]ogs and serpents" and "[e]aters of human flesh" (174) in contrast to the original "great people" (181) of Kôr. Moreover, the Amahagger's savagery correlates to their racial description. Unlike Ayesha, who has "a most beautiful white hand (white as snow)" [142]) and speaks a "pure" Arab dialect ("much purer and more classical Arabic than the Amahagger talk" [142]), the Amahagger are "yellowish in colour," as observed above (76–77). Holly continues with his detailed description of the Amahagger, connecting their physical characteristics with their moral:

> Their features were aquiline, and in many cases exceedingly handsome . . . [b]ut . . . on the whole, I had never seen a more evil-looking set of faces. There was an aspect of cold and sullen cruelty stamped upon them that revolted me, and which in some cases was almost uncanny in its intensity. (77)

The Amahagger's cruelty is etched in the very contours of the body, a body debased through centuries of racial intermixing with lesser people. The history of Kôr, then, is the history of a "great" people whose depraved sexual appetites for intermarriage with a less civilized race gave birth to an even more depraved "bastard brood" of man-eating savages (*She* 181).

The charge of cannibalism against the Amahagger is significant because it demonstrates the extent to which they have become debased.[18] In my reading, moreover, it needs to be seen both in relation to scientific claims about the dangers of interbreeding and as part of a long tradition of colonial myth-making. As Peter Hulme notes:

> Human beings who eat other human beings have always been placed on
> the very borders of humanity. They are not regarded as *in*human because
> if they were animals their behavior would be natural and could not cause
> the outrage and fear that "cannibalism" has always provoked. (14)

In contrast to its corollary, "anthropophagy," the word "cannibalism" conjures up a particularly frightening image of human degradation. Hulme observes that unlike "anthropophagy," which derives from the Greek, the term "cannibalism" evolved within a colonial context that was from the beginning layered with confusion and misunderstanding. As Hulme explains, we get the word "Cannibals" from Columbus's record, which is in itself dubious on several counts. Supposedly, "Cannibals" originally referred to a group of Caribs in the Antilles, but this information comes by way of their enemies and is then passed on to Columbus, who barely speaks the language. There are more uncertainties having to do with the validity of Columbus's journal, but Hulme's point is that the word comes to us through ambiguity, accusation, and a European distrust of racial others.

The term "cannibal" as used in the nineteenth century contained the ambiguity and suggested degradation of its early modern usage, but with an increased attention to racial specificity. Late Victorian accounts of cannibalism among Europeans existed, but as the century progressed and colonial incursions into Africa and other non-European countries became more widely reported, images of the cannibal became more firmly associated with nonwhite bodies. Malchow observes, for instance:

> [A]s the century progresses, such allusions [to domestic cannibals such as
> the Scottish Sawney and the Irish Sweeney] shift their reference in the
> mind of the reader, away from Defoe's tamable savage and toward a grow-
> ing colonial discourse, which ultimately objectified the idea of cannibalism

as an inherent racial characteristic rather than merely a barbaric practice. Cannibalism as a primitive practice in the eighteenth century
meant something quite different from cannibalism as a racial characteristic in the midnineteenth. (48)

Malchow charts the development of the cannibal image within nineteenth-
century British culture, observing that cannibalism in late-Victorian England
was specifically linked to inborn racial characteristics, a connection supported in part by "the pseudoscientific discourse of phrenologists and comparative anatomists" (Malchow 48–49). The changing view of cannibalism
was part of a general development of racist discourse in the latter half of the
century which owed much both to imperialist ideology and scientific beliefs,
such as I have outlined above. Brantlinger attributes "the success of the anti-
slavery movement, the impact of the great Victorian explorers, and the
merger in the social sciences of racist and evolutionary doctrines" to the
more brutal depictions of Africans by the British which became standard
after 1860 (*Rule of Darkness* 174). Before 1840 or 1860, Brantlinger
explains, descriptions of ritual human sacrifice or other instances of brutality
were seen as isolated incidents not indicative of Africans in general. Aboli-
tionist discourse, in particular, depicted Africans as "perhaps noble but also
innocent or simple savages" (*Rule of Darkness* 176). Although derogatory and
patronizing, these earlier writings did not focus unduly on cruelty.

My point about the portrayal of the Amahagger as man-eaters is that in
the context of late-Victorian imperial ideology and scientific beliefs, cannibalism is a sign of physical and moral pathology. The Amahagger are debased
both because they carry the stigma of the "savage" as defined by colonial discourse and because their race combines a "superior" people with an "inferior" black one. The result is that they are physically diseased, and that
disease is passed on from one generation to the next. In this narrative, then,
blackness is a disease, one that is manifested in the body.

The corollary to the pathologized African body here is the diseased
African landscape. The lost city of Kôr and the surrounding area are depicted
as stagnant and deadly. Holly, for instance, describes an endless terrain of
"foetid water" (73) and "death-breeding swamp[s]" (66) which give off an
"[awful] stench" (65); the protagonists' fears of malaria cause them to stop
repeatedly to "swallow precautionary doses of quinine" (65). Disease seems
to permeate every aspect of the landscape, as Holly details in his description
of the view: "Now that the sun was getting high it drew thin sickly looking
clouds of poisonous vapour from the surface of the marsh and from the
scummy pools of stagnant water" (63). Moreover, the "poisonous vapours"

and "foetid water" permeating the atmosphere suggest a specifically miasmatic theory of disease, an idea prevalent in the nineteenth century. This
medical concept held that rotting vegetation and other discarded remains led
to stagnant air which then caused various illnesses. There were numerous
challenges to this theory in the second half of the century, but the concept
persisted in many circles even in the face of new medical evidence.[19]

The miasmatic theory caught hold of the bourgeois imagination in
part because it suggested that the social habits of the poor were responsible
for outbreaks of diseases such as cholera. The theory was especially current
during the 1840s and 1850s, when Edwin Chadwick promoted sanitary
reform in England.[20] As Poovey demonstrates in a study analyzing the role
of sanitation reform in the support of bourgeois ideology, Chadwick connects ideas about inferior sanitation with what he describes as the habits of
the poor: idleness, drinking, overcrowding, prostitution, extramarital sexual relations, crime, and so on. His "crowded haunts of sin and filth"
repeatedly link concepts of non-bourgeois morals with poor sanitation
(235–36; quoted in Poovey, *Social Body* 120). As Poovey explains, Chadwick believed that the "effluvia exhaled by 'depraved' human beings [was]
more poisonous than the miasma created by decomposing organic matter"
(*Social Body* 123). Thus, although strictly speaking, miasmatic gases were
the product of poor sanitation, airborne diseases were imaginatively connected to the "immorality" of the poor. Chadwick's report was widely read,
constituting a hold over bourgeois thinking for years to come. Like the
urban slums of Victorian London, Africa's "unmapped" spaces are depicted
as supporting a corrupt existence which results in a diseased environment.
Holly's frequent references to "fever-inducing swamps" do more than neu-
trally describe deadly tropical diseases; they carry implications of unwhole-
someness which are similarly reflected in the unwholesome practices of
Ayesha and her cannibal followers.

Both the portrayal of the African landscape as diseased and the description of the Amahagger as pathological occur within the context of the narrative's "scientific" approach to its material. Our knowledge of Africa and its
inhabitants comes to us through Holly, whose authoritative tone approxi-
mates the "objective" style of scientific language and description. In Foucault's terms, Holly wields a kind of medical or scientific gaze, in this case
combining the language of the naturalist with the authority of the colonial
explorer. The scientific gaze brought to the study of the life sciences the relationship between subject and object which had already existed in the natural
sciences. The scientist of the human body, like the natural scientist, was a
detached observer. Both approaches are operative in *She,* signaling not only

the metaphorical connection between body and landscape in the text, but also the shared role among scientific discourses in the construction of nineteenth-century imperial ideology. The discourse of the naturalist, like that of the life scientist, is one which colonizes its others or objects; the rhetorical modes of the scientist—description, denotation, categorization, and so on—are instruments of possession and control.[21]

In her seminal study on travel writing and European expansion, Mary Louise Pratt analyzes the crucial role the naturalist played in European imperialism in the second half of the eighteenth century:

> From one angle, what is told is a story of urbanizing, industrializing Europeans fanning out in search of non-exploitive relations to nature, even as they were destroying such relations in their own centers of power. . . . [W]hat is also told is a narrative of 'anti-conquest,' in which the naturalist *naturalizes* the bourgeois European's own global presence and authority. This naturalist's narrative was to continue to hold enormous ideological force throughout the nineteenth century, and remains very much with us today. (28; emphasis added)

In effect, the naturalist duplicates the relations of power operative in the metropolis while at the same time asserting his or her innocence. Moreover, Pratt states, "natural history conceived of the world as a chaos out of which the scientist *produced* an order. It is not, then, simply a question of depicting the planet as it was" (30). The natural scientist "discovers" what was presumably always there, while securing his or her status as an authority and neutral observer. Like the natural scientist, the scientist of the human body relegates the subject of study to the role of object and lays claim to knowledge of a preordained order. Using the tools of the naturalist and the human scientist, *She*'s male protagonists, like the colonial explorer, are able to appear non-aggressive, on an altruistic quest to expand human knowledge.

By invoking the scientific gaze through his descriptions of the African landscape and African people, Holly establishes his superiority and fitness to rule while appearing to be merely seeking knowledge for its own sake. Through the varied discourses of the anthropologist, the ethnographer, the medical doctor, and the naturalist, Holly's descriptions confirm his intellectual command of all he surveys. Merely commenting on the local flora and fauna, as he does throughout the narrative, places him in the position of authority. (Holly states, for instance, "[we secured] the boat fast to a beautiful tree with broad shining leaves, and flowers of the magnolia species, only they were rose-coloured and not white . . ." [61].) Holly similarly comments on the social organization of the Amahagger, the ancient civilization of Kôr, and the African terrain, seemingly an expert on all he surveys. The scientific gaze has a double thrust, however, because it not only dominates its object simply through invoking a discourse of possession and control, but it also reserves for itself the right to decide what is healthy or pathological, natural or unnatural. Holly's observations have the double effect of both establishing his intellectual hegemony and defining the African land and its people as fundamentally unsound.

Such an effect occurs during a curious passage in which Billali discloses to Holly his fascination, as a boy, with the embalmed corpse of a beautiful woman: "I would creep up to her and kiss her cold face, and wonder how many men had lived and died since she was, and who had loved her and embraced her in the days that long had passed away" (111). Billali's mother, fearing that he was "bewitched" (111), sets the corpse on fire. Later Billali returns and cuts the unburnt feet from the corpse, wrapping them in a piece of linen and hiding them. Holly is amazed when Billali unwraps a "rotting rag" and produces "a beautifully shaped and almost white woman's foot, looking as fresh and as firm as though it had but now been placed there" (112). After a brief, impassioned ode to the foot ("Poor little foot! . . . Shapely little foot!" [112]), Holly takes the foot and "put[s] it away in [his] Gladstone bag, which [he] had bought at the Army and Navy Stores" (113). Clearly Holly shares Billali's erotic fascination with the foot; similar echoes appear later when Holly rhapsodizes over Ayesha's "little sandalled foot" (189). Yet at the same time distinct differences emerge between Billali's and Holly's perspectives. Billali's orientation towards the corpse is entirely erotic: he kisses it and imagines it in sexual contexts. Further, his mother's concern about his being "bewitched" locates African beliefs within the realm of superstition and witchcraft, a system of reasoning which is diametrically opposed to Holly's own scientific methods. Holly, in contrast, has already established himself as an authority on ancient civilizations and, although the foot has erotic resonances for him, he ultimately defines it in historical and scientific terms. For him, the foot is a "relic of the past" (113), a scholarly glimpse into the ancient world; by storing it in his Gladstone bag, he invokes a sweeping vision of British military rule and imperial order. Like other Victorian collectors before him, his find will become evidence of his scientific ability, something mounted on the wall or under glass. Here, Africa becomes a place of intellectual darkness and disturbing, unnatural desires, while the England of the Gladstone bag becomes a place of method, order, and scientific reasoning.

Holly's "scientific" descriptions of the "diseased" African environment, along with his "detached" observations of the land and its inhabitants, not only establish him as an authority but validate the European colonial presence, ignoring the ways that Europeans themselves contributed to the spread of disease. As Porter explains, "diseases were not features waiting to be discovered, like the source of the Nile; they had often been aggravated or even created by imperialism. Bringing war, the flight of peoples, clearings, settlements, encampments, roads and railways and other ecological disruptions, and the reduction of native populations to wage-labour or to marginal lands, colonization spread disease" (*Greatest Benefit* 465). Narratives of colonial exploration such as *She* reinforce patterns of domination: of the learned over the uneducated, of the metropolis over its peripheries, and of the healthy European subject over its diseased others.

AMAZONS, SAVAGES, AND THE MYSTERIOUS ORIENTAL

Just as Holly and Leo's journey into Africa is a journey into a diseased, abnormal landscape, so too is it a journey into the female body. The underground caves and tunnels of the lost city of Kôr, where Ayesha resides, for example, mirror female anatomy in unsubtle ways. From Kôr, Holly and Leo travel to a large "cavern" (287) where they enter the "very womb of the Earth" (286). This association of the African landscape with the female body relates to a number of cultural concepts linking women with colonial territories and racial others. While in the last section I examined the pathologization of the African body and landscape, in this section I will examine the way in which the female body was metaphorically associated with this same African body/landscape. Both in the text of *She* and in the cultural context of Victorian Britain, discourses of colonial possession, racial alterity, and medical pathology made these associations explicit.

When Freud stated (in 1926) that "the sexual life of adult women is a 'dark continent' for psychology," he drew upon a long cultural tradition connecting the female body and female sexuality to colonial exploration and racial otherness (Freud, "Question of Lay Analysis" 212). As the first European explorers travelled into unknown territories, metaphors connecting the female body to remote geography and savage customs multiplied. Anne McClintock remarks, for instance:

> Female figures were planted like fetishes at the ambiguous points of contact, at the borders and orifices of the contest zone. Sailors bound wooden female figures to their ships' prows and baptized their ships—as exemplary threshold objects—with female names. Cartographers filled the blank seas of their maps with mermaids and sirens. Explorers called unknown lands "virgin" territory. (24)

Not only were women associated with exploration and mysterious land-scapes, but also more particularly with a sexualized female body controlled by male authority. Loomba observes, for instance, that colonial space in the early modern period was associated with a specifically sexual view of women's bodies. As she explains, "The two 'Indies' were repeatedly identified with female sexual parts, both in literary accounts, as in John Donne's 'Love's Progress,' where the lover sails towards his mistress's 'India,' and in travel narratives, as in Columbus's statement that the earth was a breast with the Indies as its nipple" (30). Thus, the colonial landscape was itself sexualized through erotic images of female availability and male control.

Yet the connection between women's bodies and colonial travel was not always benign or playfully suggestive. To the European explorer, women also figured as threatening, mysterious, and savage. This is apparent, for instance, in stories about Amazons who inhabited unknown territories thought to be wild and dangerous. The legend of the Amazons, originally a Greek myth, adapted itself easily to the colonial context. According to the myth, the Amazons were female warriors who forced their men to take care of domestic tasks and killed or maimed their male children. Their monstrosity lay in their complete reversal of gender conventions: refusing household duties, fighting and killing instead of nurturing others or making themselves sexually compliant. Moreover, as Loomba notes, within the context of colonial exploration the Amazon came to be identified not only with war and fighting, but more particularly with cannibalism and barbarity. The European explorers, she observes, located Amazons in Africa and the Americas, countries thought to engage in unspeakable horrors. As she states, "The association of the Amazon with America, seen as a land of savagery and cannibalism, transformed the former from a figure who mutilated men into one who literally ate them" (Loomba 28). In reversing gender expectations, the Amazon signified deviance and complete degradation.

The correlation of Amazons with deviance and degradation received a more specifically biological treatment in the nineteenth century by the historian J.J. Bachofen, as Gilman has observed. In *Mother Law*, an 1870 publication, Bachofen identifies Amazons as examples of sexual degeneracy. Gilman comments, in particular: "While *Mother Law* does not overtly discuss the medical aspects of human sexuality, it does analyze the question of sexual degeneracy" (*Difference* 194). In Bachofen's estimation, matriarchy is an early stage in human history; as society matures, patriarchy becomes the preferred mode of social organization (*Difference* 194). "[T]he violence of the Amazon," Gilman explains, "was labeled by Bachofen as 'savage degeneration.' The cruel and unnatural domination of the male by the woman warrior in

Amazon society was a vestige of an aberrant but necessary stage in human development" (*Difference* 194). Thus, Bachofen's view of Amazon social organization claimed that all primitive society was deviant; only modern, "civilized" society approached anything like normality or health.

This association between a female-ruled society and sexual deviance is enacted in *She* through the construction of the Amahagger as not only pathological in the biological sense, as discussed above, but also in a social sense, in reversing gender relationships. As a matriarchal society, they transpose Victorian gender conventions and express their deviant sexual appetites (for a less "civilized" race) within that inverted framework. Holly reports, for instance, that "women among the Amahagger are not only upon terms of perfect equality with the men, but are not held to them by any binding ties. Descent is traced only through the line of the mother" (81). Moreover, sexual alliances are initiated by the women, who "signif[y] [their] preference by advancing and embracing [the chosen man] publicly" (81). The man can choose not to return the embrace, but if he accepts it, they are considered united until "one of them wearie[s] of it" (81). Ustane approaches Leo in this way and is his companion until she dies trying to save him from attack. The narrative treats this all rather humorously, and Ustane is clearly in the "noble savage" category of primitive characterization, yet all other descriptions in *She* contradict this benign view of Africans. The Amahagger are, in fact, ruthless cannibals and sexual degenerates; at the highest level, moreover, their matriarchy is governed by Ayesha, whose brutality is legend.

Nineteenth-century views associating women with savages gained a firm scientific footing through the doctrine of recapitulation. According to recapitulation theory, individual human development follows the same evolutionary trajectory as the development of the human species. Thus, each single organism "recapitulates" the history of evolution in its own life history, moving from primitive stages of biological organization to more advanced stages as the individual matures. This theory served multiple purposes among scientists, most particularly in that women, children, and nonwhite people ("savages," according to Russett) were located at the bottom of an evolutionary scale which placed white men at the top.[22] In one sense, women were compared to savages and children because all three were considered childlike. Men were at a later evolutionary stage and thus more mature in thought and intellect. In another sense, however, deviant women were connected to children and savages because all three were thought to have little control over their passions.

Lombroso makes some of these analogies when he identifies criminals with a primitive form of humanity. Thus, he classifies the criminal not only with the savage, but also with the child who cannot control his instincts:

[T]he most horrible crimes have their origin in those animal instincts of which childhood gives us a pale reflection. Repressed in civilized man by education, environment, and the fear of punishment, they suddenly break out in the born criminal without apparent cause, or under the influence of certain circumstances. . . . (*Crime* 368)

In this logic, children begin life with "animal instincts" which are subdued through the processes of civilization in the case of the normal individual, but in the case of the "born criminal," these (savage) instincts cannot be controlled. Although Lombroso's comments in this volume are, for the most part, aimed at the male criminal, his brief words on the female criminal connect her too with the savage. In his discussion of female crime he declares, for instance, that "abortion is a widespread practice among savages" (*Crime* 188). According to Lombroso, offenses such as abortion and infanticide occur more frequently in lesser civilizations, especially among adult offenders. He explains that while the "more civilized" regions (such as northern Italy) often see very young women commit these crimes because of public censure against unmarried pregnancies, the "less civilized" areas (such as southern Italy) experience a greater degree of adult women committing the same crimes because standards are lower (*Crime* 188). In other words, adult females (between the ages of "21 and 40") engage in abortion and infanticide more often in less civilized areas because the primitive inhabitants see these acts as viable solutions (*Crime* 188). The female criminal, like the male, then, is lower on the evolutionary scale than the more civilized members of society. Thus, the specifically feminine "crime" of abortion is a sign, in Lombroso's view, of innate female savagery.

In many cases, doctors and scientists identified female sexual abnormality with savagery and blackness in a specifically physical manner. Gilman has demonstrated, for instance, that nineteenth-century doctors looked for biological ways to link deviant female sexuality with the "savage" black woman. As I have outlined in Chapter One, Gilman examines medical reports which identified similarities between the genitalia and buttocks of white female prostitutes and black African women. In this study, Gilman first explores the cultural context of such associations, noting that painting and literature often linked the sexualized white woman with the image of the black servant. As he remarks, "[t]he black, both male and female, becomes by the eighteenth century an icon for deviant sexuality in general, almost always, however, paired with a white figure of the opposite sex" (81). Manet's acclaimed 1863 *Olympia,* for example, depicts a black female servant in the company of a nude white female. The cultural associations between black women and sexualized white women entered into medical and scientific discourse in the nineteenth century when experts made authoritative claims about the strong sexual appetite of the African woman and her "primitive" genitalia and then, in turn, compared the white prostitute's body to the African's. Much attention was placed on the physical appearance of the Hottentot's labia, which by the late nineteenth century were determined to be biologically abnormal.[23] At the same time, doctors scrutinized the prostitute's body for similar signs of abnormality: the skull, the ear, the labia, or buttocks were all possible indications of physical difference. Her bodily aberration was thought to be a sign of her difference from the sexually "normal" woman. Gilman notes, for instance, that according to Lombroso, "the prostitute's labia are throwbacks to the Hottentot, if not the chimpanzee; the prostitute, in short, is an atavistic subclass of woman" (*Difference* 98). What is interesting here in the comparison between the prostitute and the black woman is that overt sexuality in the white woman is specifically marked as deviant and not merely erotic. Scientists thus looked for ways to align European stereotypes about libidinous black sexuality with biological models of abnormality.

I have been arguing that concepts of female deviance in the nineteenth century were intimately connected with images of savagery and racial otherness. However, *She*'s racial topography includes not only the impression of the "black savage," as I have been discussing, but also that of the "mysterious Oriental." In *She*, the female body is associated with racial otherness both through analogies between women and the African landscape, and through Ayesha's complex racial profile: as a white woman of Arabic descent ruling over a hybrid race of black and vaguely Oriental people. Thus, Ayesha embodies three different races at once—white, black, and yellow—as these categories were defined in the nineteenth century. Her proximity to the Amahagger alone connects her to the concept of blackness, savagery, and sexual deviance, while colonial and biomedical discourses give an added emphasis to these associations. Although some of the racial stereotypes I have discussed apply both to Western constructions of black Africans and to constructions of Middle Eastern and north African peoples (all of whom were seen as savage and mysterious), the "Oriental" has its own lexicon, combining brutality and sexuality, nobility and base desires.[24]

A number of contradictory views coalesce in the characterization of Ayesha which can be attributed, in part, to her identification as an Oriental.[25] She is beautiful but despotic, pure in some ways but impure in others. Holly states, for instance, that "[Ayesha's] beauty, with all its awful loveliness and purity, was *evil*" (155). The "evil" aspect of her character can be attributed to her murderous inclinations and to a sensuality that contradicts the chaste sensibilities of the domestic angel. Yet this evilness exists alongside a "purity" that is based, to a large extent, on racial purity: Ayesha speaks the "pure" Arab language (142) and is of "true Arab blood" (146), for instance. There is a sense, on the one hand, that the Arabic civilization was a great one, worthy of admiration, although its time has passed. On the other hand, the contrast between Ayesha and her English companions suggests that it is and was also a corrupt civilization, capable of a brutality unimaginable in European society. Said, in his seminal work on Orientalism, comments on this contradictory assessment of the East, observing that Western culture imagines the East as simultaneously distinguished but counter to European ideals:

> The Orient is not only adjacent to Europe; it is also the place of Europe's greatest and richest and oldest colonies, the source of its civilizations and languages, its cultural contestant, and one of its deepest and most recurring images of the Other. In addition, the Orient has helped to define Europe (or the West) as its contrasting image, idea, personality, experience. (*Orientalism* 1–2)

Ayesha embodies all of these inconsistencies: a sense of past grandeur but also of absolute incompatibility with Western standards. Moreover, such inconsistencies are suggested by her simultaneous portrayal as "white" and "Arab." The extreme whiteness of her hand would seem to be the corollary to her ostensible purity (her hand is "a most beautiful white hand (white as snow)" [142], for example). This insistent whiteness demonstrates the extent to which she is both a figure of desire and of fear: a European construction of Oriental sensuality and despotism in one person. She is thus foreign, yet desirable; her whiteness is a function of the Western imagination, something that makes her an erotic object, masking for a moment her crucial difference and allowing the combination of purity and evil to inhere in her body.

Ayesha's multivalence is significant to my analysis because it enables her to embody all the associations of brutality, savagery, and sexual debasement that the Amahagger exhibit while allowing them to recede into the background. Ayesha is, after all, the eponymous heroine of the narrative, taking center stage even before she appears as an actual character. The reader's attention, then, is displaced from the diseased African landscape onto the debased African body, and finally onto Ayesha, who contains all of these associations. David Bunn makes a similar observation about *She:*

> [C]ontradictions are evident in the way the narrative constructs its subjects, for, once the Amahagger are described . . . as degeneration from an

original, romantic age, this does not mean that they are simply susceptible to conquest. Rather, it is as though they are emptied of imaginative
interest. The narrative overcomes this disappointment by leading us
away from the Amahaggar periphery to the centre of imperial control,
located in Ayesha. . . . The marker of exoticism has shifted from the
Amahaggar to the figure of Woman. (Bunn, "Embodying Africa" 19)

While in my analysis I do not view Ayesha as "Woman," since that term has
connotations of universalism which run counter to my historicization of the
female body, Bunn's comments nevertheless capture my point about narrative displacement. Moreover, as I am arguing, this displacement does not
merely leave other plot lines unresolved, but draws together contradictory
associations of these other accounts and locates them in one figure.

REPRODUCTION, DEVOLUTION, AND DEGENERATION

Ayesha's body, I am asserting, is emblematic of the multiple pathologies portrayed in this text: the diseased African landscape, the degenerate Amahagger, and gender abnormality. By depicting an aggressive and sexualized
femininity which does not accord with domestic ideology, Ayesha represents
a sexual monstrosity which metaphorically reflects the diseased land and history of the Amahagger. Ayesha's gender behavior and sexual appetites are
highly aberrant, moreover, within the context of late-Victorian medicine.
British and American doctors, for instance, believed that normal women did
not experience sexual passion, subscribing to the theory of female passionlessness. Rather than sexual passion, the respectable Victorian woman chan-
neled her emotional energy into maternal love and familial devotion. Ayesha
violates all the tenets of domestic ideology: she is a ruler of cannibals, a killer,
a temptress. She is aggressive in her sexual predilections, murdering
Kallikrates when he does not return her affections and making her desire for
Leo (who she believes is the reincarnated Kallikrates) apparent. She is, then,
in all ways a monstrous version of the Victorian angel, scorning all other
authority but her own.[26] When she tells Holly and Leo of her plans to domi-
nate the world along with Leo/Kallikrates, for example, overthrowing Queen
Victoria and destroying whomever is in her way, Holly cautions her against
violating the law and Ayesha responds: "'The law,' she laughed with scorn—
'the law! Canst thou not understand, oh Holly, that I am above the law, and
so shall my Kallikrates be also? All human law will be to us as the north wind
to a mountain'" (255). Not content merely to be reunited with Kallikrates,
she revels in her complete disregard of all laws, obeying no one, killing at
will, and indulging her passions. Holly shudders to think of what would

happen if Ayesha did go to England; her mental and physical powers are so extensive, it is conceivable that she could rule England by force. What makes Ayesha especially threatening, however, is that she considers herself to be not only above judicial law, but also above patriarchal law: the law of the father. Ayesha is monstrous in this sense because she violates cultural prohibitions against improper desires. Her desire for the married Kallikrates and her limitless desire for power violate deep social taboos about gender in the nineteenth century.

Ayesha transgresses patriarchal law and Victorian gender ideology, moreover, through a rejection of reproductive sexuality and the maternal ideal. The image of the sexually aggressive woman directly opposes that of the nurturing mother and chaste wife. Stott notes, for instance, that the late-Victorian New Woman, whom she identifies with Ayesha, was censured because she was an "unnatural woman, unnatural because of her supposed rejection of motherhood and marriage" ("Cannibal Mothers" 158). This rejection of the maternal ideal is significant in *She* because the image of nonreproductive and diseased wombs is a recurring motif in the text, reflecting in the landscape what is represented in Ayesha's body. Thus, the African terrain is not only rendered as diseased, but more specifically as a diseased female body. Along with the conventional associations of women's bodies with colonial exploration, *She* displays a more specific reference to numerous caverns and caves suggestive of poisonous wombs. Kôr itself, with its masses of underground tombs and piles of dead bodies, resembles a vast "womb/tomb," as Gilbert has termed it (45). The image of deadly wombs is made more complete when Holly reports that the Amahagger kill their human prey by placing red-hot pots on their victims' heads. As Gilbert notes, "[t]his astonishing mode of execution, a cross between cooking and decapitation, which seems to have no real anthropological precedent, is such a vivid enactment of both castration fears and birth anxieties that it is hardly necessary to rehearse all its psychosymbolic overtones" (41). With its emphasis on killer wombs, *She*'s African topography and people evoke an atmosphere of nonreproductivity and sterility.

The conjunction of wombs and death, then, draws attention to the generally sterile atmosphere of Kôr and the savage civilization that now lives there; Kôr is not a place of life, but a place of death, as is demonstrated in the description of Kôr's underground caves. As Holly soon discovers, these caves are actually "vast catacombs" connecting tombs, embalming rooms, preserved bodies and elaborate pictures of the dead and dying (135). At one point the Englishmen are served dinner in an embalming room and at another time sleep on stone slabs meant for the dead. In addition to formal tombs, there is also a "great pit" which contains the bodies of Kôr's original population, destroyed by plague:

> We were standing in an enormous pit . . . and when the lamps were held
> up I saw that it was nothing but one vast charnel-house, being literally
> full of thousands of human skeletons, which lay piled up in an enor-
> mous gleaming pyramid, formed by the slipping down of the bodies at
> the apex as fresh ones were dropped in from above. . . . [W]hat made it
> even more dreadful was that in this dry air a considerable number of the
> bodies had simply become desiccated with the skin still on them, and
> now, fixed in every conceivable position, stared at us out of the moun-
> tain of white bones, grotesquely horrible caricatures of humanity.
> (181–82)

The scene Holly describes seals an already overdetermined connection between Africa, disease, and the female body. Kôr's massive womb/tomb underscores Ayesha's own sterility and her murderous rather than maternal practices. The recurring images of monstrous wombs are not only misogynis-tic, but they join discourses about women, reproduction, and unlawful desires with discourses of colonialism and racism.

She's sterile wombs and unmotherly women, moreover, suggest a dis-avowal of female reproduction in favor of what Showalter has termed "the fantasy of male reproductive autonomy" (*Sexual Anarchy* 84). As Showalter argues, *She* offers its own account of male self-reproduction, both in terms of Leo's personal genealogy and the genealogy of the narrative. Leo's ancestry, for instance, is traced through the male name, in contrast to the Amahagger, who trace their lineage through maternal descent. Showalter notes further that the narrative's layered stories are passed on through a succession of male custodians: Holly's guardianship of Leo occurs as a sort of "virgin father-hood" (*Sexual Anarchy* 84) granted to him through Leo's father, then under-taken by Holly and his male servant, Job, within an all-male academic community. Moreover, the main text of *She* is introduced and glossed by a fictional male editor to whom Holly entrusts his manuscript, so that the double meaning of biological and creative reproduction applies.

I would like to extend Showalter's analysis here and note that these contrasting modes of male and female reproduction can be seen as a further comment on the pathology of abnormal femininity rendered both as nonre-productive and racially inflected. Thus, *She* posits a healthy male homosocial community against the diseased and sterile community of Ayesha and her followers. The male community made up of Holly, Leo, and Job is mutually supportive, loyal, and nurturing, while the female-led community is marked by cruelty, insensitivity, and treachery. Both Holly and Job raise Leo lovingly from the time he is five years old, establishing an alternative family organization which becomes normative within the structure of the novel. In contrast, the African community headed by Ayesha does not show the signs of mutual support and healthy familial bonds necessary to thrive. When Billali nearly drowns, for example, his own men ignore his struggle and it is Holly who finally saves him. When, during the same incident, one of the men drowns, Holly tells us that "nobody seemed to grieve much over his sudden and final disappearance, unless, perhaps, it was the men who had to do his share of the work" (123). Sterility, I am arguing, is figured not so much in literal terms as in imaginative and emotional ones. We must assume that the Amahagger reproduce, for instance; yet rather than signs of life we see signs of death. Thus, Billali explains that every "second generation" when the men get tired of being governed by the women, they "rise, and kill the old [women] as an example to the young ones" (114). Holly even tells us that the population count is kept low by continual warring and fever: "Often the 'Households' made war on each other until *She* sent word that it was to stop, and then they instantly ceased. That and the fever which they caught in crossing the swamps prevented their numbers from increasing too much" (91). Disease and internal war, then, keep the numbers of the Amahagger in check. Rather than being an example of a healthy, self-nurturing, fertile society, the Amahagger manifest death and a decreasing population. Not surprisingly, the only reference to a child is to a dead one, when Holly views the embalmed corpse of a woman with "a little babe" (183) in her arms.

The suggestion of sterility and the text's preoccupation with deadly wombs brings us once again to the issue of the Amahagger's racial hybridity. The emotional, physical, and imaginative sterility of the Amahagger corresponds to nineteenth-century ideas about hybridity and racial classification. Questions about hybridity depended on making a clear distinction between a species (or race) and a variety, whether referring to plants or animals. The standard rule for distinguishing between a species and a variety was the existence of infertility in crossed species;[27] thus, hybrid races or species were not expected to be fertile. This rule did not satisfy everyone, however, in determining the distinction between species and varieties. Robert Young notes, for instance, in *Colonial Desire: Hybridity in Theory, Culture and Race,* that it was clear even before Darwin's *Origin* that white and black people mixed and had children who in turn went on to have children of their own, thus putting the fertility rule into doubt.[28] Moreover, as Young notes, Darwin did not clarify the distinction between the two terms, but instead attested to the mutability of both. One of the features of natural selection, for instance, was that species were constantly evolving. Darwin complicated this situation further by discussing the many different results that occurred with regard to fertility when both species and varieties were crossed. He states, for example:

> First crosses between forms sufficiently distinct to be ranked as species, and their hybrids, are very generally, but not universally sterile. . . . The sterility is innately variable in individuals of the same species, and is eminently susceptible of favourable and unfavourable conditions. The degree of sterility does not strictly follow systematic affinity, but is governed by several curious and complex laws. (*Origin* 288)

In Darwin's formulation, crossed species may exhibit sterility, but only under certain circumstances. Thus, the lack of any definitive conclusion on the subject of species and varieties led to much controversy about the relation of fertility to hybridity. As Young explains, there were discussions about hybridity between "remote species" and closely affiliated species, for example. Many felt that fertility was an issue, but that rather than total infertility, hybrids experienced a decline of fertility over generations or impeded fertility at some point.[29] Young outlines several of the competing theories that existed at the time, but observes that "the argument that hybridity varies between 'proximate' and 'distant' species [because] unions between allied races are fertile, [and] those between distant either are infertile or tend to degeneration . . . became the dominant view from the 1850s to the 1930s" (18). The association of the Amahagger with diseased wombs and low reproductive rates, then, follows logically from their racial hybridity.

The Amahagger's sterility further evidences their degeneration from a "mighty" people to a lesser one; it underscores the barrenness of the land and the poverty of the tribe's cultural existence. Sterility too brings together some of the main themes and motifs of the narrative, from the nonreproductive sexuality and gender deviance of Ayesha to the diseased African terrain represented as the female body. *She* tells us that this is a society that cannot bring anything fruitful or rich or enduring to the world. Thus, it is a story of desolation: of body, mind, and culture. Moreover, Ayesha's devolution from powerful seductress to withered monkey renders this multivalent desolation in literal terms. Ayesha's body, like the body of Africa(ns), regresses rather than evolves, enacting a biological narrative of failed species development.

Fittingly, then, the story of Kôr's decline—its degeneration from greatness to plague, miscegenation, and cannibalism—is almost literally imprinted on Ayesha's body in the story's denouement. Like the once-great civilization of Kôr, Ayesha's power and loveliness were unparalleled; her beauty was so dazzling that she wore a veil to protect others from her radiance. Yet all this is destroyed in the climactic scene when Ayesha undergoes a more than 2,000-year evolutionary regression. Holly describes the disaster (an unexplained accident) that occurs when she steps into the life-extending "Pillar of Life" (31):

> [S]maller and smaller she grew; her skin changed colour, and in place of the perfect whiteness of its lustre it turned dirty brown and yellow, like an old piece of withered parchment. She felt at her head: the delicate hand was nothing but a claw now, a human talon like that of a badly-preserved Egyptian mummy. . . . Smaller she grew, and smaller yet, till she was no larger than a baboon. Now the skin was puckered into a million wrinkles, and on the shapeless face was the stamp of unutterable age. . . . She, who but two minutes before had gazed upon us the loveliest, noblest, most splendid woman the world has ever seen, she lay still before us, near the masses of her own dark hair, no larger than a big monkey, and hideous—ah, too hideous for words. (293–94)

Thus, in this scene we see the truth beneath the veil: it is Ayesha, not Holly, who is the "baboon." Holly's earlier humiliation is vindicated, and the demarcation between savage and civilized is conclusive. Ayesha's decaying form parallels Kôr's own evolutionary decay, literally and figuratively embodying 2,000 years of degenerate practices and taboo sexuality. Her personal history of upstart pretensions to eternal beauty and world rule cannot be separated from the history of Kôr and its debased appetites. Ayesha, her people, and the Amahagger's "bastard brood" together comprise a species in decline against which the healthy bodies of the bourgeois male protagonists—and, by extension, the larger imperial body—prevail. It is a Darwinian moment, enacting an evolutionary decline of one species and the ascendance of another. Ayesha is transformed into a mummified monkey, the relic of a dead civilization; in contrast, Holly's simian masculinity is vital and powerful. The marks of Ayesha's ruined beauty—the yellowed skin, the innumerable wrinkles, the lifeless hair—draw attention to a sexuality rendered grotesque in relation to a bourgeois ideology of maternal grace and passive compliance. Ayesha's "hideous" body incorporates all othernesses within it, at once conflating imperial and bourgeois discourses about racial and sexual others.

Her regression, moreover, dramatizes the scientific logic at work in the text; it returns Ayesha to her "natural" state and "true" origin, demonstrating her absolute unfitness to rule. Ayesha's power was, after all, always a transgression and a fraud, something stolen from the male keeper of the Fire,

Noot, as the narrative explains (*She* 280). Holly states, moreover, that Ayesha violated the "eternal Law":

> Ayesha strong and happy in her love, clothed in immortal youth and godlike beauty, and the wisdom of the centuries, would have revolutionised society, and even perchance have changed the destiny of Mankind. Thus *she opposed herself against the eternal Law,* and, strong though she was, by it was swept back to nothingness. . . . (295; emphasis added)

Ayesha's transgression is, then, a transgression against a law rooted in culture but rendered in nature. Unlike her English visitors, she lacks the innate characteristics that justify the assumption of authority. The abnormal female body, with its unnatural desires, is necessary here to construct the white male body as normative.

CONCLUSION

She's motif of killer wombs and mummified monkeys underscores the text's central preoccupation with the body. At the center of a text overfull with bodies, Ayesha's body is ostensibly the primary one; it is the point towards which events converge and the basis of Ayesha's ultimate weakness. Moreover, this focus on Ayesha's physical allure and frailty demonstrates that in this text, as in Victorian culture, the female body provided a nexus for competing ideologies about masculine authority, imperial power, and racial stereotypes. And, as I have been arguing, scientific discourses about gender and race in the late nineteenth century offered a way to justify the existing social hierarchy and gender ideology. Accordingly, Holly's ruminations on Ayesha's failed bid to power capture the close analogy between racial otherness and female deviance that *She* depicts: "[I]f . . . *She* were practically immortal . . . how was it that, with [unlimited wealth, power, and wisdom], she preferred to remain in a cave amongst a society of cannibals? The whole story was monstrous . . ." (120). Ayesha's desires are indeed "monstrous" because they are "against nature." By superimposing images of a monstrous, sterile female body onto the body of a debased, diseased Africa, Haggard brings together Victorian ideas about "unnatural" female desire and "natural" imperial hegemony. In this way, anxieties about reproductive decline and a degenerating African body are contained and displaced onto a site that promises to yield up its "truth." Ayesha's pathology, then, reveals the truth of the "dark continent."

Chapter Four

"Shapes like our own selves hideously multiplied": Sue Bridehead, Reproduction, and the Disease of "Modern Civilization"

Since the earliest responses to Thomas Hardy's *Jude the Obscure,* critics have read Sue Bridehead, the novel's female protagonist, as a "study in pathology" (Gosse 388). Her extreme nervous sensitivity, combined with an ambivalence about marriage in general and compulsory heterosexuality in particular, place her at the center of a number of nineteenth-century scientific discourses about female sexual pathology and nervous disorders. The text describes Sue as a woman on the brink of nervous exhaustion: "quivering [and] sensitive" (90), with a "nervous little face" (83) and a "tremulous" voice (81). Moreover, in the final chapters she experiences what has been termed a breakdown, characterized by religious obsession and sexual self-subjugation. Hardy himself suggested that Sue's nervous disposition was due to "modern conditions," citing both the effects of urbanization and changes in women's circumstances as possible influences. Paraphrasing a German critic, Hardy writes in the Postscript to the 1912 edition of *Jude the Obscure,* "Sue Bridehead [is] the intellectualized, emancipated bundle of nerves that modern conditions [are] producing, mainly in cities as yet; who does not recognize the necessity for most of her sex to follow marriage as a profession . . ." (8). Coinciding with Sue's nervousness is a sexual aloofness that develops into dread when Phillotson, her husband, desires sexual relations with her. Even with Jude, whom she loves, Sue is ambivalent in this aspect, prompting generations of commentators to see her variously as "neurotic and sexually maladjusted,"[1] "hysterical,"[2] a combination of "New Woman . . . [and] Frigid Woman,"[3] or exhibiting "'epicene' frigidity."[4] Yet while there is ample evidence to support such readings, my purpose here is not merely to locate her as such but to trace the way in which her assorted pathologies are symptomatic of a larger cultural malaise affecting the reproductive future of the entire social body. *Jude the Obscure* posits not one pathological figure, but many: an entire culture threatened with the hereditarian transmission of nervous disease. Not only Sue, but also Jude and his son, Little Time, exhibit the effects of what then was labeled neurasthenia—an umbrella term for a range of problems related to nervousness. Nevertheless, although Jude and Little Time bear the clear marks of neurasthenia, and in fact are portrayed as templates for the "coming universal wish not to live" (*Jude* 264), it is Sue Bridehead who carries the weight of reproductive failure that *Jude* augurs. Through a series of displacements made possible through biomedical discourse and the trope of urban modernity, Sue's body stands in for and contains the problems of a pathologized social domain.

NEURASTHENIA, SOCIAL UNREST, AND "MODERN CIVILIZATION"

Neurasthenia was considered by many to be a problem of increasing concern, affecting, in particular, the inhabitants of cities and all those feeling pressured by the fast pace of modern life. George Beard (1839–1883), an American doctor specializing in nervous disorders, brought neurasthenia to widespread attention with the 1881 publication of his first book on the subject, *American Nervousness,* which asserted that "The chief and primary cause of this . . . very rapid increase of nervousness is *modern civilization*" (vi). The concept of neurasthenia had been around for several decades before Beard published *American Nervousness,* but his work popularized the condition and consolidated many prior theories. The list of possible symptoms included here were many; anxiety, depression, indigestion, increased susceptibility to stimulants and narcotics, nearsightedness, tooth decay, sensitivity to heat and cold, headaches, insomnia, hay fever, and "in the extreme cases," epilepsy and insanity, all were possible indications of neurasthenia (*American Nervousness* 56). The problem, as Beard and many of his contemporaries saw it, was that the conditions of modern life had simply overtaxed the nervous system. Inventions such as steam power, the periodical press, and the telegraph contributed to a sense of hurry in everyday life and an over-stimulation of the senses. Adding to this, Beard thought, the American climate acted on a weakened nervous system, resulting in more stress upon the body. Even more seriously, increased intellectual activity threatened to overwhelm the modern inhabitant of the city. The "mental activity of women" was an especial problem, yet men were also affected by excessive intellectual work (vi). According to Beard, "[n]ew [i]deas" (113) contributed to an excess of mental excitation for both men and women, while the "extending complexity of modern education" was driving more and more people to their breaking point (100). The educated person of the late nineteenth century was bombarded on all sides with a constant influx of ideas and stimulation.

Beard's second book, *Sexual Neurasthenia* (originally published in 1884 and followed by several reprints), duplicated the logic of its predecessor, identifying "modern civilization" as the root cause of a host of nervous ailments. This volume focused explicitly on impotence and other sexually-related complaints among men, correcting what Beard perceived as a lack of adequate medical attention to male sexual disorders. One of the many effects of neurasthenia, as Beard saw it, was an increase in male sexual complaints, including "sexual exhaustion" and various physical problems (26). As Beard explains:

> The causation of sexual neurasthenia, as of all the other clinical varieties, and of modern nerve sensitiveness in general, is not single or simple, but complex; evil habits, excesses, tobacco, alcohol, worry and special excitements, even climate itself—all the familiar excitants being secondary to the one great predisposing cause—civilization. (15)

All forms of neurasthenia, sexual or otherwise, were thought by Beard to be caused by the stimulation of modern living, particularly evident in the rapidly expanding cities.

Although some doctors argued, in contrast to Beard, that neurasthenia was a rural problem, relating to isolation and the difficulties of farming life, the emphasis on urban conditions prevailed.[5] Even Freud, writing from the vantage point of 1908, observed that most doctors believed that urban conditions were leading to an increase in nervous disorders. In "'Civilized' Sexual Morality and Modern Nervousness," Freud states:

> The physician is . . . frequently given matter for thought by observing that neurosis attacks precisely those whose forefathers, after living in simple, healthy, country conditions, offshoots of rude but vigorous stocks, came to the great cities where they were successful and were able in a short space of time to raise their children to a high level of cultural attainment. But, most cogent of all, neurologists themselves have loudly proclaimed the connection between the "increasing nervousness" of the present day and modern civilized life. (77–78)

Freud's ultimate goal here is to redefine the meaning of "modern civilized life" as it had been understood in the medical profession, dispelling the assumption that the sole cause of nervous disease was the frantic pace of work, play, and mental effort. Instead, he envisions "modern civilized life" as including an overly-restrictive conventional sexual morality which, he argues, was leading to nervous problems. Yet while Freud aims to break with tradition, he nonetheless assumes, like others before him, that the origin of nervous disorders lay in modern patterns of behavior, particularly those of the city dweller. Even in 1908, more than 25 years after the publication of *American Nervousness,* standard medical thought considered nervousness a product of modern life.

Beard's emphasis on the role of modern advances in the spreading of neurasthenia made the diagnosis a fairly attractive one. Because neurasthenia was connected with energy, dynamism, and a certain level of education, there was nothing shameful about the disease and, in fact, it bestowed a kind of compliment upon the patient. Beard had displayed more than a trace of national hubris by designating neurasthenia a particularly American disorder, relating to the country's rapid progress and expansion. In his preface to *American Nervousness,* he declares:

> A class of functional diseases of the nervous system, now beginning to be known everywhere in civilization, seem to have first taken root under an American sky, whence their seed is being distributed.
>
> All this is modern, and originally American; and no age, no country, and no form of civilization, not Greece, nor Rome, nor Spain, nor the Netherlands, in the days of their glory, possessed such maladies. Of all the facts of modern sociology, this rise and growth of functional nervous disease in the northern part of America is one of the most stupendous, complex, and suggestive. . . . (vii–viii)

Notwithstanding Beard's extravagant claims for American superiority, British and European doctors adopted the diagnosis of neurasthenia as their own. Medical professionals and patients across Europe soon became familiar with Beard's ideas and adapted them to their own uses. The new classification was not only an appealing label to many, but it enabled doctors to put a name on a confusing assortment of symptoms. As Oppenheim remarks, "Late Victorian and Edwardian medical men found neurasthenia a convenient term not only because it imposed an artificial coherence on a broad array of disparate symptoms, but also because it bestowed an air of precision on an indeterminate affliction whose amorphous contours had puzzled and embarrassed them for decades" (96). For the patient, neurasthenia was a fashionable ailment, and for the doctor, a convenient diagnosis.

Alongside neurasthenia, hysteria occupied a central place among discourses of nervous afflictions.[6] Often confused with neurasthenia, hysteria had a slightly less genteel connotation. Both maladies had similar symptoms, including headaches, insomnia, depression, and a host of other vague complaints. But while neurasthenia was identified as a problem affecting both men and women, hysteria was envisioned more specifically as a female condition. During the 1870s and 1880s, Jean-Martin Charcot, a French physician famous for his work with hysterical patients, had demonstrated that hysteria could also affect men, yet it continued to be identified with women throughout the century. It was not until World War I, when traumatized soldiers returned from the trenches in droves, that male hysteria became a common diagnosis. In general, the hysteric was viewed as a more troublesome patient than the neurasthenic, with symptoms becoming sometimes very marked. Partial paralysis, loss of voice, and even fits were not uncommon, along with habits of masturbation and other sexual behavior deemed unacceptable for women. On the whole, as Showalter comments, neurasthenia was "a more prestigious and attractive form of female nervousness than hysteria," and its diagnosis often depended on the perceived docility of the patient (*Female Malady* 134).

Nineteenth-century discourses of nervous disorders—especially neurasthenia—are central to my argument about *Jude the Obscure*. My purpose is to demonstrate that the pathologized female body represents the larger social body of modern urban culture and to explore the implications of such an analogy. Modern culture in *Jude* is depicted as causing the educated and aspiring classes to become so nervous and depressed that the general population is at risk of decline through a combination of premature deaths and falling reproductive rates. The text seems to make this point clear in certain passages, yet at the same time evades the issue by portraying Jude and Sue as unique individual types, unconnected to larger social trends. Jude and Sue's problems, on the one hand, seem hereditary in nature; they come from a family plagued with tragedy and failed marriages and are doomed to repeat those failures. Sue's sexual and emotional problems, on the other hand, are so magnified that they threaten to eclipse Jude's completely. Significantly, Sue's problems are specifically gendered, relating to her characterization as a "modern woman" and seemingly not applicable to men. Hardy himself supports this interpretation in his Postscript to the 1912 edition of *Jude* when he attributes Sue's problems to "modern conditions." In comparison to Sue, Jude seems almost normal. His neuroses and the neuroses of the social domain fade next to Sue's more obvious problems which, because of their exaggerated nature, seem more connected to female hysteria than to the less showy condition of neurasthenia. Thus, I am arguing that the pathological condition of modern urban culture is displaced onto the female body. By so doing, larger cultural anxieties are circumvented, seemingly solved by an implied diagnosis of female sexual pathology.

Despite clear indications of neurotic behavior on Jude's part and numerous critical references to such, few critics have analyzed the pathological aspect of Jude's problems to any great extent. Jude's neuroses are relevant to my study because I am asserting that Sue's problems are symptomatic of a larger cultural malaise which afflicts others: Jude, his son, and modern urban society. Thus Jude's pathology is the link to this larger social sphere. Moreover, in making this link I am asserting that neurasthenia has specific connotations in *Jude* that other commentators have not explored. Those that do make reference to Jude's neuroses usually attribute them to degeneration, a related field of medical inquiry which I discuss below but which is not the main focus of my argument. An early review of *Jude,* for example, written by Edmund Gosse in 1896, terms Jude "a neurotic subject in whom hereditary degeneracy takes an idealist turn" (386), yet Gosse does not examine this charge in any detail. Gosse makes a similarly cursory observation about Sue, whom he finds more seriously afflicted; she is, according to Gosse, "a poor, maimed 'degenerate,' ignorant of herself and of the perversion of her instincts" (388). A few months after this review, Havelock Ellis comments in direct contrast to Gosse, "it is clear that Mr. Hardy was not proposing to himself a study of gross pathological degenerescence, a study of the hereditary evolution of criminality" (*Concerning Jude* 19). Yet Ellis, like Gosse, does not take up the question of degeneracy in depth.

One of the few critics to pursue this line of inquiry is William Greenslade, whose *Degeneration, Culture and the Novel: 1880–1940* includes a comprehensive analysis of degeneration in *Jude.* Greenslade comments on neurasthenia in passing, but only in relation to Sue and in a cursory manner;[7] he identifies Jude as a degenerate type,[8] but not neurasthenic. Moreover, Greenslade grants both Sue and Jude a fair amount of agency, asserting that both attempt to resist the straightjacket of degeneration imposed upon them by their family history.[9] My analysis takes a different approach, in that my interest is not with Jude and Sue as individual agents, but as symptoms of a larger social and biological decline informed only in part by degeneracy theory. Although I agree with Greenslade that degeneration plays a role in *Jude,* by centering my argument more on neurasthenia and less on degeneration, I wish to illuminate a different set of assumptions. There is a certain amount of overlap between the two theories to the extent that degeneration was often considered to encompass or cause nervous disorders; yet neurasthenia was not necessarily assumed to relate to degeneration. Moreover, degeneration had connotations of moral debasement which were not usually applicable to neurasthenia, a far more respectable disorder. In some instances, certain prohibited sexual practices, such as masturbation, were believed to cause or relate to nervous disorders, but these issues were peripheral and not central to neurasthenia. Moreover, the male sexual problems that Beard addresses are not related to moral decline. Finally, there were differences in presumed causes for each malady. Degeneracy theory focused on the dangers of hereditarian transmission and placed much emphasis on individual moral and physical liability, whereas neurasthenia, in contrast, was assumed to have been caused by widespread cultural factors: a fast pace of life, increased intellectual effort, and hard-driving social ambition. Both afflictions are pertinent to my analysis, yet by shifting the emphasis to neurasthenia, issues having to do with widespread cultural pathology become visible. As such, I am interested in degeneration only as it relates to late nineteenth-century nervous disorders—especially neurasthenia but also, to a lesser extent, hysteria—and concepts of reproductive decline.

The second issue that differentiates my analysis from Greenslade's is my focus on the female body and its relation to modern urban culture. Greenslade's study does not concentrate on gender, although he does make passing reference to Sue's "neurasthenia" and its relation to "modern civilization."[10] However, whereas Greenslade sees disease and modernity in relation to Sue's characterization as a "strictly contemporary 'new woman'" (Greenslade 175), I see both neurasthenia and "modern civilization" in broader terms: as encompassing both women's issues and larger social issues unrelated to gender. My argument, then, is twofold: first, that the pathologized female body represents the diseased social domain because the problems in the social domain are related to reproduction; and second, that those larger social issues are concealed because of the more conspicuous problems with the female body. Thus, widespread social problems are seemingly eliminated or contained, displaced onto a single instance of female vulnerability.

Although there seems to be general critical agreement that Sue Bridehead's neuroses are prominently displayed, studies which actually address the biomedical issues involved are almost as limited as those relating to Jude. Thus, while feminist critics such as Boumelha and Ledger, discussed below, refer to Sue's pathologization, they focus the main part of their arguments on social and cultural issues. Two exceptions, however, are relevant to my study. Richard Dellamora has a brief but cogent appraisal of Sue's pathologization in *Masculine Desire: The Sexual Politics of Victorian Aestheticism* (214–217). Dellamora sees Sue as constrained by the dictates of compulsory heterosexuality. My discussion of compulsory heterosexuality in *Jude* expands Dellamora's central insight and relates it to reproduction and Sue's presumed frigidity. The other exception is Kristin Brady's "Textual Hysteria: Hardy's Narrator on Women," which offers an enlightening account of Sue Bridehead's construction as hysterical woman through Victorian medical discourses. My comments on hysteria, compulsory heterosexuality, and Sue's "frigidity" are elaborated on below. While I concur entirely with Brady's account of Sue's hysteria, my study differs from hers in that I relate Sue's pathology to that of the social domain. I am asserting, then, that Sue's disease covers up and contains the pathology of modern urban society.

In my view, the neurasthenic symptoms suffered by Jude and his son play a central role in the novel, connecting Sue's individual and gendered malady to the larger social body. Although Jude's neurotic symptoms relate on the one hand to his individual characteristics, on the other hand, they are more clearly aligned with the problems of the larger social sphere than are Sue's. A comprehensive analysis of Jude's nervous maladies are thus central to my analysis.

With his anxious, morose disposition, Jude Fawley follows the typical neurasthenic course outlined by Beard and others. Like Sue, Jude is "supersensitive" and given to feelings of deep despondency (*Jude* 240). He engages in strenuous intellectual activity, moves restlessly from town to town, holds "advanced" social and religious views, and is driven to move beyond the limits of the sphere to which he was born. Moreover, Jude's neuroses, although less spectacular than Sue's, establish a metonymic link to the anxieties of the larger cultural sphere, one that is fragmented by a changing political, economic, and social climate. As he strives throughout the story to attain a university education and later, when that becomes infeasible, a lay position in the Church, Jude sees himself not merely as an individual in conflict with the social customs of "modern civilization," but as an individual representative of that same civilization. It is, according to Jude, a civilization afflicted by a sense of restlessness and rootlessness leading ultimately to a shared cultural malaise. In one instance in the early part of the narrative, as Jude compares the importance of his current occupation as stonemason to that of his scholarly ambitions, he muses,

> here in the stone yard was a centre of effort as worthy as that dignified by the name of scholarly study within the noblest of the colleges. But he lost [this thought] under stress of his old idea. He would accept any employment which might be offered him on the strength of his late employer's recommendation; but he would accept it as a provisional thing only. This was his form of the *modern vice of unrest*. (69; emphasis added)

Although Jude acknowledges the importance of his job as church stonemason, he nevertheless is driven to pursue an education that is barred to him, the idea of which will keep him in a perpetual state of discontent. Later, when the university education has eluded him and he considers a career as a Church licentiate, he returns to the concept of a generalized social unrest:

> He feared that his whole scheme had degenerated to, even though it might have originated in, a *social unrest* which had no foundation in the nobler instincts; which was purely an artificial product of civilisation. There were *thousands of young men* on the same self-seeking track at the present moment. (103; emphasis added)

Jude worries that he is no longer driven by a worthy ambition but instead is caught up in a widespread desire for social advancement that is part of modern existence. Even more disturbing for him, his restlessness is no longer attached to a particular goal, but has become restlessness for its own sake. Social unrest and discontent have become a way of life for Jude and others like him.

Behind the mere drive to achieve is a rootlessness and turmoil produced by a shift from rural to urban patterns of living, apparent even in the countryside where Jude begins his life. Jude follows in the track of "thousands of young men" because he, like them, comes from an environment in which traditional patterns of living are changing rapidly. As Terry Eagleton notes, Jude's background is not one of rural stability, but of continual movement:

> The fact that he doesn't belong to Marygreen in the first place, but was dumped there one dark night (as his own son is later unloaded in Aldbrickham), is significant: Jude's own lack of roots is symptomatic of the generally deracinated condition of the place. Marygreen is not timeless but stagnant, not settled but inert; it is a depressed and ugly enclave bypassed by history, stripped of its thatched and dormered dwelling-houses as the tradesmen, craftsmen and lifeholders move from the land. (63)

The social ambition that inspires Jude is only one consequence of a general economic and social upheaval in the English countryside. Like thousands of other rural areas, Marygreen offers few economic opportunities and encourages a migration toward the urban centers. Such movements only contribute to a lessening of familial ties and a disruption of communities. For Jude, Marygreen holds no entree to higher education and only a tenuous family connection. His Aunt Drusilla, although tied to Jude by blood, is burdened by the "poor worthless boy" who only adds to her economic woes (12). After such an upbringing, Jude's rootlessness becomes a force of its own, interwoven with faint hopes but perpetuated long after those hopes have been destroyed.

From the time Jude is a small child, it is the image of Christminster, "[t]he heavenly Jerusalem," which fuels his hopes and aspirations (18). The city represents everything that is missing from his limited existence: intellectual scope, spiritual greatness, and social distinction. Like many others before him seeking escape from drudgery and poverty, Jude travels to the city in search of something unattainable. Yet while the country holds no prospects for Jude, the city brings its own disappointments, only exacerbating an existing agitation that results in continual movement. The chapter headings trace his urban migrations: "Part First, At Marygreen"; "Part Second, At Christminster"; "Part Third, At Melchester"; "Part Fourth, At Shaston"; "Part Fifth, At Aldbrickham and Elsewhere"; and "Part Sixth, At Christminster Again." Jude's urban wanderings underscore the logic of restlessness that drives the narrative. Each move is motivated by a hope for something better and a desire to escape memories of failure and trauma, up through his final decision to return to Christminster.

Jude's return to Christminster effects a sort of Freudian return of the repressed. Christminster, the scene of Jude's childhood fantasies of academic glory, is also the scene of his ultimate failure, where he realizes that a university education is barred to him forever. During this final return to the town in which he will later die, Jude addresses a crowd who has gathered for the university's annual Commemoration, setting forth his history of thwarted ambition and asserting his affiliation with others of his kind:

> It is a difficult question, . . . that question I had to grapple with, and which thousands are weighing at the present moment in these uprising times—whether to follow uncritically the track he finds himself in . . . or to . . . re-shape his course accordingly. (255)

Jude sees himself as part of a larger social phenomenon, in which the desire for social advancement is shared by "thousands" and shaped by "these uprising times." Jude goes on to assert:

> It takes two or three generations to do what I tried to do in one. . . . I was, perhaps, after all, a paltry victim to *the spirit of mental and social restlessness,* that makes so many unhappy in these days! (256; emphasis added)

Jude's personal restlessness is indicative of a generalized social restlessness that the text characterizes as mental trauma. Just as neurasthenia discourses pathologize social phenomena, so too does *Jude* pathologize similar phenomena. In both cases, social and economic obstacles are presumed to create anxieties which then take center stage rather than the original social causes. Thus, in a series of slippages and displacements, widespread social problems become individual neuroses. Although Jude acknowledges that "thousands" are wrestling with the same problems he has, rather than attributing his problems to the class system or the rigid hierarchy of the Church, he ultimately blames himself: he tried to do too much in one generation; he caught the virus of social ambition. In this manner, very real political, economic, and social problems are contained, displaced onto a model of pathology that oscillates between the individual and the social domain.

It is perhaps at this point that Jude's fragile state of mind is connected most closely to the concept of "modern civilization," demonstrating the novel's dual concerns with individual mental pathology and the larger social body. Jude's observation that "It takes two or three generations to do what [he] tried to do in one" (256) goes directly to the heart of neurasthenia, and is echoed more than a decade later by Freud:

> Occasionally a nervous patient will himself draw the physician's attention to the part played in the causation of his sufferings by the opposition between his constitution and the demands of civilization, and will remark: "We in our family have all become nervous because we wanted to be something better than what with our origin we were capable of being." ("'Civilized' Sexual Morality" 77)

Mirroring Jude's thoughts, these words illustrate the pervasive belief that social and intellectual ambition can cause nervous disease, and that something within civilization itself "demands" a push beyond what the body and mind can tolerate. Jude believes that his aspirations—not just the failure of those aspirations, but the simple desire to achieve—have caused him to become mentally agitated. The scenes which follow in the last chapter, after Jude's return to Christminster, are scenes of mental and physical decline not only for Sue, but also for Jude. Jude is still debilitated from a physical illness when he arrives in town and describes his defeated state to the crowd, who responds, "He do look ill and worn-out, it is true!" (256). Worse than physical weakness, however, Jude experiences a mental deterioration that has begun to affect his reasoning capacity. Still addressing the crowd, he states, "And what I appear, a sick and poor man, is not the worst of me. I am in a chaos of principles—groping in the dark—acting by instinct and not after example" (256). Jude, whose intellectual strengths have sustained him throughout his urban wanderings, arrives at the brink of a mental fatigue that renders his life senseless.

Jude's mental fatigue is so extensive that he is already at the breaking point before the chapter's final tragic events. His children's subsequent deaths and his abandonment by Sue only exacerbate a deep mental despair that pre-existed his return to Christminster. As Jude's mental state spirals downward, he ignores his physical health and in effect wills himself to death, enacting a suicide that duplicates his young son's earlier suicide. The general inability of both father and son to withstand life's traumas illustrates the tenuous hold that they and others like them have on life. Jude's words about Little Time's suicide and murder of his step-siblings could apply equally to his own situation:

> It was in his nature to do it. The doctor says there are such boys spring-ing up amongst us—boys of a sort unknown in the last generation—the outcome of new views of life. They seem to see all its terrors before they are old enough to have staying power to resist them. He says it is the beginning of the coming universal wish not to live. (264)

For Jude, the despair and suicidal thoughts experienced by his son extend beyond the individual sphere of personal circumstances to the larger sphere of civilization. "[T]he coming universal wish not to live" threatens all soci-ety; it is the collective wish of a frail species (264).

HEREDITY, DEGENERATION, AND RACIAL DECLINE

The similarity of father and son is no accident, but an indication of the extent to which heredity is central to the narrative's themes.[11] Heredity is the means through which neurasthenic symptoms are passed from father to son, and from the Fawley ancestors to Jude and Sue. It gives Jude his melancholic nature, Sue her hysterical edge, and Little Time his morose disposition. When Jude's Aunt Drusilla states "The Fawleys were not made for wedlock. . . . There's sommat in our blood that won't take kindly to the notion of being bound to do what we do readily enough if not bound," she refers to the seemingly inescapable force of biological inheritance and the threat of congenital affliction (58). Heredity in *Jude* works in several ways. Most obviously, it affects the Fawley family line and contributes to the physical and mental weakening of Jude, Sue, and Little Time; in this sense the novel participates in contemporary discourses of degen-eration, especially as they relate to nervous symptoms. At the same time, Jude's affinity with the "thousands" distressed by "these uprising times" and his belief in "the coming universal wish not to live" suggest a vast social landscape and a teleology of decline extending far beyond the Fawley family. In this larger sense hereditarian decline threatens an entire species, suggesting connections not only to degeneration, but also to discourses of racial deterioration, which are closely linked. Together, racial deterioration and degeneration provide a rationale which enables the transmission of neurasthenic symptoms to future generations.

Degeneration theory is more of an interlinking network of related approaches than a single concept; theories of racial decline and neurasthenia are just two of its many possible permutations. Despite its ambiguity, however, certain writings function as important points of departure for any discussion of degeneracy.[12] Two works by Bénédict Augustin Morel, a French psychiatrist, had a decided influence upon later research into the field of degeneracy. His *Traité des dégénérescences physiques, intellectuelles, et morales de l'espèce humaine,* and *Traité des maladies mentales,* published in 1857 and 1860, respectively, addressed national concerns about the rise of mental disorders and reports of large numbers of unhealthy military recruits.[13] According to Morel's line of reasoning, defects acquired during one's lifetime could be passed on to the next generation. On the one hand, these defects could be physical, relating to environmental poisons such as poor food, narcotics, or poisonous vapors in the air which weakened individuals and could be passed on to their children.[14] On the other hand, defects could be moral, such as the tendency to drink to excess or engage in criminal activities.[15] Morel's ideas opened up a wave of possibilities. If acquired defects could be passed on to one's children, then an entire race or species could degenerate physically, mentally, and morally as the result of hereditarian transmission.

Although theories of racial deterioration and degenerative decline had been circulating for some years after Morel's publications, the book that brought these theories to wide public attention was *Degeneration* by Max Nordau. First published in German in 1892 and appearing in English in 1895, *Degeneration* was crucial in making degeneracy theory known throughout Europe in the 1890s. Nordau's book derives much from Morel, whom he praises extensively, but to Morel's approach Nordau added his own apprehensions about urban living and the excessive stimulation which was part of modern existence. He comments:

> To [Morel's concern about environmental poisons], however, one more may be added, which Morel has not known, or has not taken into consideration—residence in large towns. *The inhabitant of a large town,* even the richest, . . . breathes an atmosphere charged with organic detritus; he eats stale, contaminated, adulterated food; he feels himself in a state of *constant nervous excitement,* and one can compare him without exaggeration to the inhabitant of a marshy district. The effect of a large town [is that] its population falls victim to the same fatality of degeneracy and destruction as the victims of malaria. (35; emphasis added)

Nordau places particular emphasis on the connection between urban living and nervousness, recalling earlier theories of neurasthenia but grafting those theories onto a model of hereditarian transmission. His work goes beyond others' in that he offers a fully developed theory, drawing upon many sources and applying his ideas with a wide brush. Allusions to neurasthenia and urban problems, moreover, tapped into pre-existing anxieties about the increasingly burdensome pace of modern life. Like Beard, Nordau believed that the current generation was suffering from physical and mental exhaustion brought on by excessive work, increased travel, intense mental stimulation, and a general sense of hurry and worry with which earlier generations did not have to contend. Numerous references in *Degeneration* to the problems of modern "civilization" echo Beard's language: the "victims of civilization" (41) and "civilized humanity" (40) all suffer from nervousness caused by modern patterns of living. The result, according to Nordau, was not only an increase, in the extreme cases, in "crime, madness and suicide" (40), but also, more commonly, in cases of hysteria and neurasthenia. In contrast to Beard, however, Nordau believed that these ailments could be passed on from generation to generation, with the outcome being that each generation would become progressively weaker. As he explains:

> The enormous increase of hysteria in our days is partly due to the same causes as degeneracy, besides which there is one cause much more general still than the growth of large towns—a cause which perhaps of itself would not be sufficient to bring about degeneracy, but which is unquestionably quite enough to produce *hysteria and neurasthenia*. This cause is the fatigue of the present generation. (36; emphasis added)

> . . .

> To speak without metaphor, statistics indicate in what measure the sum of work of civilized humanity has increased during the half-century. . . . It grew fatigued and exhausted, and this fatigue and exhaustion showed themselves in the first generation, under the form of *acquired hysteria;* in the second, as *hereditary hysteria.* (40; emphasis added)

In Nordau's view, hysteria and neurasthenia were not themselves degeneracy, but had the same root cause and were thus markers for society's threatened state of being.[16] The modern city-dweller was exhausted by the stimulations afforded by industrial advances and poisoned by environmental toxins, all of which resulted in a physical and mental decline that would be reproduced in the next generation.

Fears about the decline of the British race sometimes intermingled with degeneracy theory and at other times veered away in a different direction. Many medical authorities expressed the concern that "society"—meaning especially the more privileged classes—was becoming weak and prone to illness, and that this weakness was being passed on, through hereditarian transmission, to future generations. Weir Mitchell voices the misgivings of many of his contemporaries when he states:

> If any reader doubts my statement as to the physical failure of our city-bred women to fulfill all the natural functions of mothers, let him contrast the power of the recently imported Irish or Germans to nurse their babies a full term or longer, with that of the native women even of our mechanic classes. . . . There is indeed little doubt that the mass of our women possess that peculiar nervous organization which is associated with great excitability, and, unfortunately, with less physical vigor than is to be found, for example, in the sturdy English dames at whom Hawthorne sneered so bitterly. . . . I am . . . inclined to believe that climatic peculiarities have formed the groundwork of the evil, and enabled every injurious agency to produce an effect which would not in some other countries be so severe. I am quite persuaded, indeed, that *the development of a nervous temperament, with lessened power of endurance, is one of the many race-changes which are also giving us facial, vocal, and other peculiarities derived from none of our ancestral stocks.* (30–32; emphasis added)[17]

Mitchell does not specifically address degeneration or the question of moral decay, but he does speak to concerns about the deterioration of the British "race" through hereditarian transmission. He attributes what he sees as an increase in nervous problems among women to climatic changes and to tensions which are particular to modern, urban ("city-bred") women. The ideas he expresses here draw heavily upon theories of neurasthenia but evidence concerns about heredity that were absent in Beard's formulations. Like many of his contemporaries, Mitchell believed that the physical and mental debilities of the current generation did not exist in the first half of the nineteenth century. The "sturdy English dames" of the earlier generation have died out and the new generation of British women have become fragile and weak. In the pages following this passage, Mitchell elaborates on his ideas, citing excessive intellectual work and lack of physical exercise allotted to girls in public schools as the cause of ill health among so many American women. Mitchell's main concern was that the "race" of British women was becoming too feeble to raise healthy children, unlike the supposedly hardy Irish and

German immigrants. As he remarks, "If the mothers of a people are sickly and weak, the sad inheritance falls upon their offspring . . ." (30–31). For Mitchell, "race deterioration" was a physical rather than a moral problem, and in this sense he does not employ the language of moral degeneration used by Morel; rather, Mitchell's references to "ancestral stocks" and "race-changes" emulate the language of hereditarian thought and racial degeneration that became prevalent in Britain and Europe in the latter decades of the century.[18]

One of the many apprehensions evidenced by discourses of racial deterioration was a fear that Britain would not be able to sustain its strength as an imperial and military power. Oppenheim notes that concerns about "race suicide," as it was called, were fueled, in part, by a declining national birthrate in the last 25 years of the nineteenth century (266). As she states, "To make matters worse, studies revealed that the birthrate was not slowing down uniformly across the social spectrum: the decline was considerably more marked at the higher levels of society than at the lower," thus causing the more affluent classes to worry about their ability to sustain their numbers (266). Similar apprehensions about the vitality of the "race" existed in the United States, where some observers were less concerned with the national birthrate than they were about moral degeneration. Kellogg, for example, offers some pertinent remarks on the subject of "Race Deterioration": "Defects of body and mind, as well as of morals, are growing yearly more abundant. Two persons possessing these defects unite in marriage, and their defects are many times increased in their children" (385). For Kellogg, degeneration is a severe risk that all prospective parents should be aware of. While the discourses of racial deterioration took many forms, however, most British and American medical authorities agreed that large segments of society were becoming physically and mentally more fragile, and that hereditarian transmission was speeding the decline. As Oppenheim remarks, "In the confrontation between an optimistic emphasis on environmental reforms and an essentially pessimistic preoccupation with patterns of heredity, doctors who stressed defective inheritance believed that the key to the problem lay with the nerves" (267).

Jude, Sue, and Little Time are heirs to a degenerative decline, which is on the one hand, a family decline and on the other, a "universal" decline of the British as a race or species (the "coming universal wish not to live" [264]). The family history to which Jude's Aunt Drusilla repeatedly and ominously refers resembles the typical scenarios of crime, madness, and suicide outlined by Morel, Nordau, and other commentators on degenerative decline. As first cousins, connected by blood through Jude's father and Sue's mother, Jude and Sue are doubly cursed; each brings to the relationship a legacy reflected in the other's background. According to Drusilla's account, Jude's parents were unhappy together and eventually separated; sometime after the separation, Jude's mother drowned herself. Sue's parents were similarly miserable and, like Jude's parents, went their separate ways. Added to these stories of suicide and marital discord is an even gloomier tale of execution and madness. On the night before Jude and Sue's expected marriage, Mrs. Edlin, a family friend, recounts the story of Jude's ancestor who, following his wife's desertion and the death of their child, was caught and arrested for attempting to steal the dead child's coffin. As Mrs. Edlin explains, "[the father] was hanged and gibbeted on Brown House Hill. His wife went mad after he was dead" (222). The Fawley family history, with its allusions to madness and suicide, provides a biological rationale for the mental and physical deterioration experienced by Jude, Sue, and Little Time in the latter stages of the narrative.

The hereditary degeneration of the Fawley family line can be traced through Jude and Sue, ending finally in Little Time's suicide and the murder of his step-siblings. While commentators often see Little Time as Arabella's son, rather than Jude's[19]—since Jude himself is not entirely sure the boy is his own—there is nonetheless a clear resemblance between Jude's and Little Time's dispositions that recalls hereditarian theories of degeneration and racial deterioration. Morose and sober beyond his years, the boy is withdrawn, displays little curiosity in the world around him, and is never shown to enjoy himself in any way. Although he has never seen his father until the moment he arrives, at age seven, on Jude's doorstep, Little Time exhibits an inclination to melancholy that duplicates and even exceeds Jude's own. Kellogg's comments are particularly relevant to the portrayal of the father-son relationship in *Jude:*

> "Like father like son," is a homely adage, the correctness of which is rarely questioned; and "like mother like daughter" would be equally true. A careful study of the subject of heredity has established as a scientific fact the principle that sons as a rule most resemble the father, and daughters the mother, although there are often observed marked exceptions to the rule. (383)

Taking into account the emotional resemblance between Jude and Little Time, Kellogg's remarks support the logic of degenerative decline evident in *Jude,* suggesting that the boy is far more his father's son than his mother's. In this light, Little Time's suicide and the murder of his step-siblings emphasize a family decay that culminates in Sue's religious mania and Jude's self-willed death. The death of both father and son, combined with Sue's emotional decline and sexual reserve, severely limit, if not categorically end, the Fawley family line.

Just as the Fawley family line is threatened with decay, so too is the "race" threatened by "modern civilization." The universal decline of the species suggested in *Jude* takes some of its rationale from discourses of racial deterioration, insofar as it describes a nervous deterioration affecting large segments of the population. That it is a decline which heralds something new and unusual in modern society is clear. The "mental and social restlessness, that makes so many unhappy in these days" is part of the newly urbanized modern culture that Jude and Sue inhabit (256). *Jude* makes clear distinctions between an older, more emotionally pragmatic society, comfortable with the traditions of marriage and sexual relations, and a newer, more emotionally fragile society, for whom work, sexual relations, and marriage are fraught with complications. Mrs. Edlin, in several passages, captures this sense of a deep divide between two very different eras. Speaking to Jude and Sue, she exclaims:

> [S]akes if tidden—if this is what the new notions be leading us to! Nobody thought o' being afeard 'o matrimony in my time, nor of much else but a cannon-ball or empty cupboard! Why when I and my poor man were married we thought no more o't than of a game o' dibs! (226)

Similarly, speaking to Phillotson, Mrs. Edlin declares:

> I don't know what the times be coming to! Matrimony have growed to be that serious in these days that one really do feel afeard to move in it at all. In my time we took it more careless; and I don't know that we was any the worse for it! When I and my poor man were jined in it we kept up the junketing all the week, and drunk the parish dry, and had to borrow half-a-crown to begin housekeeping! (289)

Mrs. Edlin's final comment on the subject of marriage is:

> "*Weddings be funerals 'a b'lieve nowadays.* Fifty-five years ago, come Fall, since my man and I married! Times have changed since then!" (314; emphasis added)

Mrs. Edlin's remarks at various points in the narrative—to Jude and Sue, when they cannot bring themselves to go through with the legal act of marriage; to Phillotson, before he and Sue have remarried; and to herself, after

Sue has remarried Phillotson and is vacillating about joining him in his bed—function like those of a Greek chorus in that they comment on the main events of the story, offering sympathy but no remedy for the couple's problems. More importantly, they emphasize a sense of the modern period as being a unique point in history, a time when people are far more sensitive about human relations than they were only a half a century earlier. Like Beard, who deemed "Rapid Development and Acceptance of New Ideas" a significant component of neurasthenia (*American Nervousness* 113), Mrs. Edlin believes that "new notions" are leading to an unnecessary fastidious-ness about marriage and sexuality. In both cases, new ideas—presumably not only about gender, but also about politics, economics, and religion—are responsible, at least partly, for creating an unusually touchy and anxious modern individual. The emotional upheaval of the new era is so extensive that, as Mrs. Edlin says, "Weddings be funerals," or, put another way, mar-riage is a sign of death rather than life. The future of the new generation is a non-reproductive one.

REPRODUCTION, COMPULSORY HETEROSEXUALITY, AND THE FEMALE BODY

Reproduction is one of the central problems of the new era portrayed in *Jude the Obscure* and the issue around which many others crystallize; nervous dis-orders, the problems of hereditary transmission, sexual and marital misgiv-ings, all reach disastrous proportions through the disruption of the reproductive process. It is through reproduction that the species or "race" is threatened with extinction and the means through which Jude and Sue become templates for an imminent, widespread social decline. The mutual imbrication of reproduction, marriage, and neurasthenia is apparent in a dia-logue between Jude and Sue after witnessing a church wedding of an unknown couple. The wedding immediately follows Jude and Sue's last-minute decision not to marry after they have gone to the Registrar's office to do so and prompts Sue to comment on their own reluctance towards wed-lock. She says: "We are a weak, tremulous pair, Jude, and what others may feel confident in I feel doubts of"; Jude responds, "We are horribly sensitive; that's really what's the matter with us, Sue!" (225). But Sue goes on to point out that they are not at all unusual, stating:

> Everybody is getting to feel as we do. We are a little beforehand, that's all. In fifty, a hundred, years the descendants of these two [people get-ting married] will act and feel worse than we. They will see weltering humanity still more vividly than we do now, as

Shapes like our own selves hideously multiplied,[20]
and will be afraid to reproduce them. (225)

Sue's dire prediction and the lines she quotes—"Shapes like our own selves hideously multiplied"—strike at a central anxiety in the novel about reproduction and the future of the species. In themselves, Jude and Sue are, by their own admission, "weak, tremulous" and "horribly sensitive" (225); they possess neither the pragmatism nor the lightheartedness of the earlier, ostensibly simpler era of Mrs. Edlin's youth. Moreover, as forerunners of "weltering humanity," they usher in an age of pathology marked by an uncertain reproductive future. Marriage is no longer an appropriate institution for people who have become too nervous and too laden with doubts and fears to wear its yoke lightly. It is this nervous impairment, and not the institution of marriage in itself, that augurs reproductive decline.

In a very literal sense, Sue Bridehead is the embodiment of this age of pathology and reproductive decline; her body—and the female body in general—represents the larger social problems that the novel introduces but cannot resolve. Yet the broader social issues I have outlined, which are themselves figured as pathology, become obscured by Sue's individual neuroses, which the text construes as sexual dysfunction: a reluctance to engage in sexual relations with Jude and a sheer horror at doing so with Phillotson. I am arguing, then, that the text's preoccupation with Sue's supposed sexual pathology conceals and contains the fear of widespread social collapse. Thus, in a series of displacements, other important issues which cannot be resolved in the social sphere are sidestepped; Sue's individual pathology becomes the narrative problem, the result being that the other social problems diminish in comparison. In a two-step process, broad social issues having to do with class limitations are displaced, first, onto Jude, who blames himself and a generalized "social restlessness" instead of the social system for his inability to get into the university. Problems which are cultural in nature—political, economic, and social—are transformed into Jude's personal medical pathology: an over-eager wish for social advancement that causes him to become depressed and anxious. A second displacement occurs when Jude's neuroses are overshadowed by Sue's, which then become the focus of the narrative. Sue's pathology, although multivalent in its causes, ultimately centers on her presumed sexual dysfunction, which in turn points to the less visible issue of reproductive decline in the species. In this manner, Sue's anxiety about heterosexual relations becomes the disease that conceals larger issues which haunt the text and which cannot be resolved: gender restrictions on female education and autonomy; social and class limitations; and the threat that social problems have become so serious that the educated and aspiring classes are fated to self-destruct. As such, the issue of nonreproductivity is one that is concealed by Sue's presumed sexual pathology, yet it is this issue that links the female body to the social body and so brings the larger cultural issues to light.

Thus, although the Fawley family history is littered with degenerative outcasts, although both Jude and his son are classic neurasthenics, and although the problems of neurasthenia threaten potentially all of modern civilization, it is, nonetheless, Sue's female body that bears the burden of nervous disease and reproductive crisis because both biomedical and literary narratives equate the female body with reproductive problems and disease. As the novel's central female character, she represents the biological function of reproduction. Her nervous problems manifest themselves in response to reproductive issues such as sexuality, pregnancy, childbirth and motherhood. Yet even before any sexual or reproductive pressures come to bear on her, Sue is portrayed as the narrative's most emotionally fragile character, destined for a collapse that is in itself gendered. Personality traits such as "timidity, irresolution, and inconsistency" define her in conventionally female terms.[21] And despite her keen intelligence, she is seemingly irrational—at least to Jude, who exclaims in a moment of exasperation: "Is a woman a thinking unit at all, or a fraction always wanting its integer?" (276); and later, "I never knew such a woman for doing impulsive penances as you, Sue! No sooner does one expect you to go straight on, as the only rational proceeding, than you double round the corner!" (284). Add to these conventionally feminine characteristics a "nervous little face" (83), "tremulous" voice (81), and "quivering" and "sensitive" temperament (90), and the stage is set for a collapse that seems preordained by what Brady terms her "weak female body" (99).

It is Sue's "weak female body" that sets her up for a mental deterioration that occurs after her children die. Convinced that God has punished her for sexual wrongdoing, she descends into religious mania (Jude finds her, sobbing, "a heap of black clothes" on the church floor [274]) and, as a form of self-punishment, leaves Jude and remarries Phillotson. She makes herself utterly miserable, yet seems to revel in her own debasement. By remarrying Phillotson, Sue says, she is "doing a penance—the ultimate thing" (310); she forces herself to engage in sexual relations with him only because, as she explains, "It is my duty. I will drink my cup to the dregs!" (311). The specifically sexual nature of her self-punishment, combined with the appalling consequences that pregnancy, childbirth, and motherhood exert upon her body and mind, suggest that Sue's femaleness is a major factor in her nervous disposition. Brady succinctly summarizes the gendered aspects of Sue's breakdown:

> The loss of reproductive and nurturing activity destroys Sue's intellect, causing a hysterical reversal that exceeds all her earlier inconsistencies. The idea that motherhood is necessary for female mental stability is thus reinforced by the pathetic decline of Sue Bridehead—caused not by external forces but by an irresolvable conflict between her own perverse nature and her weak female body. The deterioration of Jude Fawley is blamed on his victimization by the institutions of class and bourgeois marriage—as well as, in his view, by women themselves. (99)

Brady's comments succinctly illustrate the way that conventional ideas about female biology and mental stability inform the novel.[22] Sue's "weak female body" and her "perverse nature" point to that most gendered of all Victorian ailments, hysteria.[23] In addition to displaying all the conventional signs of hysteria ("fits, fainting, . . . sobbing" [Showalter, *Female Malady* 129] and "sexual frustration" [Showalter, *Female Malady* 132]), the connection between the loss of her role as mother and her mental collapse suggests a specifically female pathology. As the hysterical woman, Sue seems to unfairly shoulder the responsibility for a pathology that exists in Jude and the culture at large.[24]

My argument extends Brady's analysis and looks at how Sue's pathologized body functions in the novel in relation to the larger cultural sphere. In contrast to Brady, I am arguing that Sue's gendered pathologies conceal and appear to resolve, through their disclosure, other important cultural pathologies that are irresoluble. My point is that in constructing Sue's nervous disorder as specifically gendered and as more severe than Jude's, the narrative covers over larger social problems which are conveniently forgotten. Thus, the reciprocal character of Jude and Sue's nervous problems, their shared neuroses, and the link between their individual neuroses and the social order become invisible, eclipsed by a revelation of gendered disease. By illuminating the medical aspects of Jude's problems and the way in which both Jude and Sue are shown to be part of a cataclysmic social decline, I wish to demonstrate the way that female sexual pathology functions in literary narratives.

Thus, it is important that Sue's claim to the pathological, or the pathologically feminine, does not rest on the charge of hysteria alone, but on an ambivalence about sexuality—specifically compulsory heterosexuality, as Dellamora has pointed out—that has led many to assume she is "frigid."[25] This charge is important to my argument because it distinguishes Jude's neurosis from Sue's and places her firmly in the category of sexual deviant. As such, when sexual dysfunction is added to hysteria, the result is magnified; Sue is not merely a hysteric, but a sexual hysteric. By the same token, she is not merely frigid, but a hysterical frigid woman. Her antipathy to heterosexual relations causes her hysteria, which then causes her to break down. Sue's problems, in other words, are of such a magnitude that other problems pale in comparison.

The charge of Sue's sexual "frigidity" rests on her connections with three male figures who are mentioned. There is first an unnamed "undergraduate" with whom Sue lived for 15 months in a sexless relationship; as Sue explains to Jude, "He wanted me to be his mistress, in fact, but I wasn't in love with him" (118). Next, in both of her marriages to Phillotson it is clear that she is repulsed by all of his sexual advances, in fact jumping out of the window at one point to get away from him. And finally, although her physical relationship with Jude is ambiguous, it is clear that she does not consummate their union (despite his wish to do so) until quite some time after they begin living together—not until she fears that Arabella is going to make a claim on him. These occurrences have caused several decades of critics to interpret Sue's behavior as sexual "frigidity," or something very close to it.[26] Later feminist scholars rejected the label of "frigid," citing an unjust depiction by Hardy or a reductive reading by critics. Boumelha, for instance, states, "It has become a critical reflex to refer to Sue Bridehead as sexless or frigid" ("Sexual Ideology" 60) and argues that her "reserve or coolness . . . should be seen, rather, as her response to the complexities and difficulties of her sexuality and its role in her relationships than as a straightforward denial of it" ("Sexual Ideology" 60–61). In contrast to some of these commentators, Ledger does not take issue with the designation of "frigidity," but uses it to mean simply the avoidance of heterosexual relations rather than the existence of sexual neurosis. She observes, "With [the suicide of her stepson and murder of her children] as the endpoint of Sue's acceptance of a sexual relationship with Jude, her initial 'frigidity' suddenly makes much more sense" (185). Ledger, like Boumelha, sees in Sue Bridehead's actions a response to specific personal and social pressures rather than sexual pathology.[27] While I agree with feminist critics that the charge of "frigidity" is a misleading and overly simplistic one, I would like nevertheless to examine what such a charge means in the context of social and medical discourses of the time.

Strictly speaking, it is somewhat anachronistic to talk of Sue's "frigidity" because the word didn't come into general usage until about the 1920s, when sexologists first began using it to describe a number of sexual scenarios.[28] Although medical discourses on frigidity did not develop until after World War I, Sue represents an early prototype of the frigid woman of later medical discourses. Such later discourses, of course, did not materialize out of thin air, but were themselves comprised of earlier cultural discourses, including literary ones. Sexology had brought the topic of "normal" and "abnormal" sexual desire to public attention; and while male homosexuals were the focus of the sexologists' first studies, the question of normal female desire was the next logical consideration. *Jude* demonstrates that by the time of its original publication in 1894[29] there was already a public discourse connecting medical pathology with female aversion to heterosexual relations. Although not yet labeled "frigidity," the logic of later medical interpretations is apparent in Sue Bridehead's characterization. Sheila Jeffreys' observations on the construction of the "frigid" woman are thus valuable here:

> It was assumed [by the sexologists] that the "normal" woman would enthusiastically embrace sexual intercourse. The deviant woman who failed to respond with enthusiasm was classified as "frigid." . . . The fear of being labelled "frigid" was to be used as a weapon, by the sexologists and their popularisers, to force women to adapt themselves to the demands made by the new role for sexual intercourse. The attack on the resisting women within marriage was combined with a massive renewed onslaught of propaganda against spinsters, feminists, "manhaters," lesbians; all those categories of women who were seen as rejecting not only sexual intercourse but marriage itself. (169)

Jeffreys also notes:

> It should be clear at this point that frigidity was not understood to mean lack of sexual response. Lesbianism and masturbation were likely to include some sexual response and were cited as cause and result of frigidity. Frigidity was quite simply woman's failure to respond with enthusiasm to one particular sexual practice, sexual intercourse. (171–72)

Jeffreys' comments elucidate a number of points, and illustrate why the move from late-Victorian discourses of female sexuality—of which neurasthenia and hysteria were a significant part—to a post-Victorian discourse of female sexual "frigidity" was an easy one. Sue functions as a prototype for this version of female sexual pathology in several important ways.

In the late nineteenth century, hysteria was sometimes attributed to either an excess of sexual feeling or a denial of that feeling. As Elaine Showalter notes, "The idea that sexual frustration was a significant cause of hysteria was a traditional one, which had been strongly revived in the mid-nineteenth century" (*Female Malady* 132).[30] And in 1905, long before the official entrance of the "frigid woman" upon the sexology scene, Freud attributed "Dora's" (Ida Bauer's) hysteria to a repression of sexual feeling for her father's friend, Herr K.[31] Moreover, both "frigidity" and hysteria referred to women who renounced traditional roles of feminine behavior. Just as the female hysteric rejected her role as housewife and mother, so too the "frigid" woman rejected compulsory heterosexuality as it came to be envisioned by sexologists and others in the post-Victorian era. Most importantly, the "frigid" woman was grouped with a number of others—"spinsters, feminists, 'manhaters,' [and] lesbians"—who, like Sue Bridehead, did not carry out the function of reproduction that compulsory heterosexuality demanded. As Richard Dellamora observes, "for Sue, Hardy sketches only two alternatives: a disabling normalcy or degrees of deviance. His position foreshadows the formulation of the lesbian type two years later by Havelock Ellis" (215). Like the label of "lesbian type," the label of "frigidity" carried with it a covert mandate to propagate the species. The charge of Sue's "frigidity," besides placing her in the category of sexual deviant, points to her uncertain reproductive future and the future of those like her.

For Sue Bridehead, reproduction and the circumstances surrounding it—conception, pregnancy, childbirth, and motherhood—present an endless series of hazards and obstacles that must be negotiated at every turn. Somewhat paradoxically, *Jude* demonstrates both that "motherhood is necessary for female mental stability"[32] and that motherhood poses incalculable dangers. Although some pregnancies and births occur during a two and a half-year gap in the story—characterized by the narrator as "not without its pleasantness"—the pregnancies that occur within the narrated portion are fraught with problems (243). While painting an Aldbrickham church, for example, Jude and Sue are expelled from their job when locals realize Sue is pregnant and the couple is not married. One observer asks, "'She's his wife, I suppose?'"; and when the answer is negative, declares, "'Then she ought to be, or somebody's—that's very clear!'" (237). Sue herself comments that it is "droll" that she and Jude are painting the Ten Commandments, laughingly saying "'You a reprobate, and I—in my condition. . . . O dear!'" (239; ellipses in original). Despite the humor with which they take their expulsion from the church, the results are pitiful. When the two are ostracized from the community and business falls away, they are forced to move, auctioning off most of their possessions and slipping into a "shifting, almost nomadic, life" (243). Sue's next recounted pregnancy leads to even more misfortune. When Jude and Sue arrive in Christminster with their three children and one more visibly on the way, they are turned away from potential lodgings. One person "scrutinize[s] Sue's figure a moment" before turning them away and another simply says "we don't let where there are children" (259). Sue wraps her cloak around her to hide her body and they finally find a place that will accept her and the children, if Jude will agree to go elsewhere. It is at this point that the novel's most tragic events occur. Little Time murders his step-siblings and takes his own life after realizing that the family is having difficulty finding lodgings because there are too many children. Sue's announcement of another child to come puts the boy into a spin: "O God, mother, you've never a-sent for another; and such trouble with what you've got!" (262) and the next morning she awakes to find the children dead and a terse note: "Done because we are too menny" (264). But Sue's reproductive woes do not end here; in a final blow to her mental stability, soon after the deaths she gives birth to a premature, stillborn child, sounding a final note of doom to her reproductive life. Ledger's statements neatly summarize the terrible effects of such events:

> The sexual consummation of [Jude and Sue's] relationship involves Sue in the processes of pregnancy and childbirth which, far from being the "natural" goal of womanhood (as the dominant ideology would have it), are shown to be horribly encumbered with social proprieties and rigid social expectations. The freedom and happiness of their partnership comes to an abrupt end when they have children, with Sue forced into a dependency on Jude and both of them forced into a feigned "respectability." . . . (185)

Ledger's comments demonstrate not only that the reproductive process makes Sue's life an ordeal, but also that it is circumscribed by circumstances beyond her control. Sue's misfortunes illustrate the specific social and economic pressures that sexuality and reproduction exerted upon women of the 1890s while also imbuing *Jude* with a larger sense of reproductive disaster.

MODERNITY AND THE PATHOLOGICAL CITY

Despite the very real social and economic dimension of Sue's reproductive traumas, those traumas evaporate under the narrative's vision of the modern city. *Jude*'s vision of the city is also a biomedical one; it is a city tainted with the concept of modernity-as-illness. "Modernity" as I am using it here is a literary trope and a medical rationale, both of which find expression in narrative form. Within such literary and medical narratives, the city functions as modernity's sign—the visible evidence of an indistinct concept. Under the medical model, "modernity"—as represented in the city—causes disease, and this disease is visited upon individuals such as Jude and Sue. *Jude*'s narrative, like biomedical narratives, constructs modernity as the problem, but this problem conceals real, insoluble social, economic, and political problems.

Thus, the narrative of urban pathology points to individuals such as Jude and Sue who then become the focus of the story's problems. And finally Sue, who, as a "modern woman," is seen as even more afflicted than Jude, becomes the ultimate signifier of disease in the social domain. As such, *Jude* begins with a problem—or numerous ones—of social constraints and gender injunctions which are then contained or seemingly solved at a narrative level by pointing to Sue's sexual dysfunction. By identifying the central dilemma as Sue's sexual neurosis, the novel renders the political, economic, and social issues of the "modern" city irrelevant.

The trope of modernity in *Jude* is significant, moreover, because it points in two directions: towards the individual and towards the social whole. My purpose here is to illuminate the logic of modernity, thereby demonstrating the systemic nature of pathology in this text. The effects of neurasthenia and degeneration, for example, devolve onto the bodies of Jude and Sue, but both characters are products of the urban environment. Before Sue is ever called upon to confront the specific social and economic circumstances that burden her, she is portrayed as a fragile being deeply etched by her urban experience. One of the first things Jude learns about Sue (after noticing a photograph of her on his aunt's mantelpiece) is that she lives in Christminster, the city which has been the focus of his childhood fantasies. Jude's Aunt Drusilla explains early on that Sue was brought up in London by her mother after her parents separated. Like Nordau, who feared that "The inhabitant of a large town . . . feels himself in a state of constant nervous excitement" (35), Jude's aunt attributes Sue's "tight-strained nerves" to her being a "townish girl" (90). Consequently, Jude casts Sue in a similar light later when he first meets her, thinking:

> [T]hough she was a country-girl at bottom, a latter girlhood of some years in London, and a womanhood here, had taken all rawness out of her. . . . There was nothing statuesque in her; all was nervous motion. . . . She was quite a long way removed from the rusticity that was his. How could one of his cross-grained, unfortunate, almost accursed stock, have contrived to reach this pitch of niceness? London had done it, he supposed. (73)

Here, rural and urban domains are contrasted, with the coarser characteristics of the "rustic" and "cross-grained" Fawley "stock" pitted against the more refined but overwrought "nervous motion" and "niceness" of the London specimen. This contrast is accentuated further in a conversation between Jude and Sue about the effects of "civilization" upon her disposition. The two are in the country, spending the night at a shepherd's home, when Sue says:

> "I rather like this. . . . Outside all laws except gravitation and germination."
>
> "You only think you like it; you don't: you are quite a product of civilization," said Jude. . . .
>
> "Indeed I am not, Jude. I like reading and all that, but I crave to get back to the life of my infancy and its freedom."
>
> "Do you remember it so well? You seem to me to have nothing unconventional at all about you."
>
> "O, haven't I! You don't know what's inside me."
>
> "What?"
>
> "The Ishmaelite."
>
> "An urban miss is what you are." (111)

Jude and Sue's description of urban and rural spheres depicts a division between the stress of the city and the comparative freedom of the country. Whereas the country is "Outside all laws"—a place of "freedom" and "unconventional[ity]"—the city, in contrast, is a place of restraint, of conventionality, and of enforced law, and thus also a place of tension and disease. Moreover, the city is associated with reading, and thus with intellectual work, suggesting the adverse effects of "[n]ew [i]deas" and "modern education."[33] Sue's keen intellect—Jude describes her as "a woman whose intellect was to mine like a star to a benzoline lamp"—is accordingly the result of modern influences affecting women's education (315). As "a product of civilization," as Jude terms her, Sue is enmeshed firmly in the urban sphere, caught up in the same kind of social and intellectual restlessness that affects Jude himself.

Against this unhealthy environment of modern pressures and changing expectations, *Jude* depicts the rural sphere as backward but robust: a fecund contrast to the neurasthenic city. Along with Mrs. Edlin, Arabella is the main emblem of the rural tradition, a remnant of a dying way of life. Pragmatic and coarse, uninterested in learning for its own sake, Arabella is more in tune with the past of Mrs. Edlin's imagination than the "modern" age of Jude and Sue. Arabella looks upon Jude's intellectual and social ambitions as worthless, and so distances herself from some of the main components of neurasthenia as seen by Beard and his contemporaries. "How like Jude," she remarks, "always thinking of Colleges and Christminster, instead of attending to his business!" (232). Instead of "Colleges and Christminster," Arabella is concerned with practical matters, such as killing the family pig by slow bleeding so that she and Jude can get the best price for its meat. Untroubled by the pig's suffering, as Jude is, Arabella sums up the matter by stating that "Pigs must be killed" and "Poor folks must live" (54). She shares none of Jude's and Sue's sensitivities towards animals and is, in fact, not a woman to burden herself with too much inward reflection. Accordingly, Arabella's unreflecting disposition renders her unperturbed in matters of sexuality. From her first meeting with Jude, punctuated by her hurling of a pig's penis against his ear, to her three marriages (one is bigamous) and numerous sexual encounters, Arabella displays a straightforward but always canny attitude towards sexuality. Marriage, sexual relations, and reproduction alike are entered into with chilling rationality, totted up like so many pounds or shillings. Unlike Sue, Arabella's attitude toward reproduction and mothering is matter-of-fact; she abandons Little Time as thoughtlessly as she conceived him. Yet despite her insensitivity towards living creatures, she is, nonetheless, associated with unproblematic fertility. As Boumelha has observed, "Arabella is always connected with both sexuality and fecundity" ("Sexual Ideology" 69), not the least as when she is shown carrying a "cochin's egg" between her breasts in an approximation of a live incubator (*Jude* 47). In response to Jude's curiosity about the egg, Arabella says, "I suppose it is natural for a woman to want to bring live things into the world" (47). The healthy, fertile, rural world which Arabella inhabits is thus the direct counterpoint to the more infirm urban sphere of Jude and Sue that equates reproduction with death. The greater vigor of this rural sphere is demonstrated further when Arabella outlives Jude at the story's conclusion; the suggestion is that she will also outlive the frail Sue Bridehead. In this context, it is not surprising that Arabella's words are the last in the novel. Both Arabella and Mrs. Edlin—those hardy remnants of the rural past—conclude the narrative with much clucking and sighing over the "[t]ired and miserable" (322) Sue Bridehead and the corpse of the "poor boy" (321) who lacked the strength to endure life's hardships.

The rural sphere of Arabella's blunted emotions serves to highlight the strained and feeble milieu of the city. Both city and country are imagined not so much as separate geographical places, but as conflicting strands of a single, fragmented body. Raymond Williams describes "Hardy country" as a "border country": "between custom and education, between work and ideas, between love of place and an experience of change" (*Country* 197). I would add that this border country is also, in *Jude,* a physical body that is so conflicted within itself that no geographical space can contain it adequately, so that movement—from town to town, from city to country and back again— is the corollary to a physical being that experiences constant turmoil. In this border country, physical and psychological cohesion is not possible; the country is not an antidote to the city, but merely the remains of a social entity that survives in body but succumbs in spirit. In this domain, pathology is the outward expression of an inner conflict.

CONCLUSION

The trope of modernity, then, in *Jude* allows a narrative slippage from social body to individual female body through the use of scientific logic. Biomedical discourses of degeneration and neurasthenia utilize the idea of modernity to re-envision widespread cultural problems as individual pathologies. Thus, the narrative of urban pathology becomes a narrative of female sexual dysfunction. By tracing the biological and social associations between the female body and the larger social body, I have attempted to make visible the supplanted narrative of widespread social unrest and reproductive decline. *Jude the Obscure* portrays a "modern civilization" plagued by urban ills and fostering an unhealthy reproductive future for the educated and aspiring classes. Jude and Sue's fate is conceivably the fate of all those affected by the pressures of a changing world. Yet these problems cannot be solved in the terms in which they are rendered; they are insoluble, and the text conveniently circumvents these problems and substitutes medical diagnosis for social resolution. In one substitution, the social sphere is itself pathologized, but that larger pathology is eclipsed by the individual pathologies exhibited by the two central characters. In another substitution, Sue's nervous problems eclipse Jude's. In this way, Jude's personal neuroses, Little Jude's suicidal despondency, and the social restlessness of "thousands" are displaced, relegated to a secondary position beside Sue's more prominent mental turmoil. Her sexual neurosis and eventual breakdown, then, become the narrative's answer to social discord; social dysfunction becomes female sexual dysfunction.

My procedure has been to trace this movement from social pathology to female pathology and back again. Through the logic of gendered science, Sue's aversion to heteronormative sexual relations is a rejection of "normal" female sexual desire and also of her reproductive destiny. Thus, while modernity provides the transition from the social body to the individual female body, reproduction provides the transition from the female body back to the larger social sphere. In this larger context, then, Sue's female body stands in for a less-than-robust species facing reproductive decline. The implied diagnosis of her "perversion" enables the resolution of a cultural crisis.

Female Deviance in the Twenty-First Century: From Martha Stewart to Lynndie England

A few months ago I sat with some friends discussing the impending verdict of Martha Stewart, on trial for allegedly engaging in stock fraud and dumping her 4,000 shares of ImClone on the market before the price plummeted. We examined the various accusations: Did she engage in insider trading? Did she lie to federal investigators? Did she scream on the phone when her stockbroker tried to put her on hold? The biggest question for us, though, was whether the severity of her offense in any way matched that of other recent corporate scandals. Ken Lay, for example, chairman of Enron, was accused of putting 5,000 employees out of work and destroying the retirement investments of millions.[1] Some months earlier, Bernie Ebbers, CEO of the now bankrupt WorldCom, had been indicted for allegedly engaging in an $11 billion securities fraud that resulted in the largest corporate bankruptcy in U.S. history,[2] eventually devastating innumerable investors. Stewart's crime seemed to pale in comparison; millions of retirees were not going to have to work at the local copy center to make ends meet as a result of her dealings.

We were not alone in our musings. Nationwide, women—and men—crowded online chat rooms and ranted in blogs. Elaine Lafferty, Editor in Chief of *Ms.* magazine, posted online "An Open Letter from Ms. in Support of Martha Stewart," calling Stewart's high-profile prosecution a "bitch hunt." "The fact is," Lafferty writes, "that there is a reserve of cultural hostility toward powerful women—particularly if their personalities border on arrogance, as many would say Martha's does." Certainly many, like Lafferty, felt that Stewart was receiving an unfair amount of flak for her crime. After all, Stewart's offense came down to lying to federal agents—not scamming investors out of millions or billions.[3] Others, in contrast, felt that she received exactly what she deserved. One indignant pollster declared, for example: "If every greedy whitecollar criminal was sent up the river, you better believe that kind of behavior would stop" ("Two Cents"). The media were saturated with parodies, news updates, sly references, and at least one television biopic, starring Cybill Shepherd. However, although Stewart's story received an enormous amount of public notice, Americans remained skeptical of the idea that her prosecution had anything to do with gender. In a poll taken in March, 2005, for example, respondents were divided equally as to whether they felt Stewart's actions were "illegal and 'seriously wrong' or illegal but 'not seriously wrong,'" yet a full two-thirds said that "they didn't think Stewart was being singled out because she [was] a successful woman" ("Indepth: Martha Stewart"). Nevertheless, although many were not convinced that gender was a factor, Stewart's case received much more media attention and public response than other corporate misdeeds. If this was not about gender, then why did it resonate so deeply with the nation?

Despite the fact that women today take on roles in traditionally masculine fields and command greater financial parity with men than in earlier years, they are still, at some level, expected to act like "women." We may like to think that we have left quaint Victorian attitudes toward gender and sexuality far behind, but our culture is full of examples that indicate this is not so. As in the novels examined here, the deviant woman still has tremendous ideological significance today. The context may have changed; concepts of species decline and biological relatedness do not have the same urgency as they did in the nineteenth century. Yet the "unnatural" woman still has the capacity to embody larger, systemic problems in the social sphere and deflect attention away from them.[4]

Stewart's "deviance," though, however much in the news, was nothing in comparison to the gender scandal that broke in the wake of the Abu Ghraib prison disclosures in the spring of 2004. As photograph after photograph emerged showing ever more disturbing scenes of prisoner abuse, some in particular riveted the attention of the public. In several pictures of degraded Iraqi men, Lynndie England, a 21-year-old woman from a small town in West Virginia, appeared smiling and upbeat. In one, she stands holding a leash attached to the neck of a nude prisoner who lies on the floor in obvious discomfort. In another, a cigarette dangles from the corner of her mouth while she beams and points to the genitals of a naked Iraqi man who masturbates, a bag covering his head. Soon, these scenes of prisoner humiliation were followed by stories about England's background, with photos of a fresh-faced Lynndie smiling up at us at every turn.[5] We read, for example, about her "loving" family and "innocent" childhood,[6] and about her family's "hardscrabble" life in a trailer park.[7] We read, too, about her boyfriend, Charles Graner, "a former prison guard stateside who was accused of beating and stalking his ex-wife,"[8] and about England defying military orders, being caught time and time again in Graner's bed, and getting pregnant in spite of strict injunctions to the contrary.[9] There was so much information—there never seemed to be an end to it.[10]

The images of England and brutalized prisoners were just some of the many that surfaced, all of them shocking, both for the extent of dehumanization depicted and for the level of elaborate staging involved. It looked as if quite a bit of thought had gone into the scenes, which required specific props and a knowledge of the most effective means to humiliate Muslim men. As the story unfolded, people debated whether the illegal methods at Abu Ghraib were the work of a few delinquent individuals or a more widespread problem coming from further up the chain of command. Most of the accused soldiers said that they had been urged by their superiors, either through implication or outright request, to "loosen . . . up" the detainees for interrogation.[11] Gary Myers, a military defense attorney, asked Seymour Hersh of *The New Yorker,* "Do you really think a group of kids from rural Virginia decided to do this on their own? Decided that the best way to embarrass Arabs and make them talk was to have them walk around nude?" (Hersh, "Abu Ghraib" 44). Many thought as did Myers, surmising that others more knowledgeable about Islamic beliefs and interrogation methods had planned the abuse of the Iraqi inmates. In a series of articles investigating the scandal, Hersh asserted that the decision to employ harsh methods at the prison came from the very highest levels—from Secretary of Defense Donald Rumsfeld, on down through the ranks.[12] In addition to Hersh, other journalists questioned the roles not only of Rumsfeld, but also of Attorney General John Ashcroft. *Washington Post* reporter Susan Schmidt, for example, claimed that Ashcroft authored a memo stating, in effect, that "inflicting physical or psychological pain might be justified in the war on terror" (Schmidt, "Ashcroft"). Even after Ashcroft stepped down as Attorney General in early 2005, his replacement, Alberto Gonzales, came under similar scrutiny for advocating the use of ruthless interrogation techniques.[13] And while Rumsfeld and Ashcroft have vigorously denied sanctioning the use of torture at Abu Ghraib or elsewhere, questions remain.

The events surrounding the Iraqi prison revelations are far more complicated than I have outlined here, but my point is that there has been much public concern over whether the atrocities were authorized at very high levels of government. If such an authorization did occur at the top, then the effects would be felt far beyond Abu Ghraib. Rather than a circumscribed scandal involving a few depraved hate-mongers, the problem would be system-wide, with repercussions echoing throughout the military and political landscape.[14] Decisions about the treatment of military prisoners, coming from the Pentagon and the Executive Office, affect our standing within the international community and the handling of prisoners elsewhere, such as Guantanamo Bay. Yet although questions about responsibility have not been fully resolved, for many Americans those questions are far less intriguing than ones about the intimate doings of a young woman from West Virginia. Given this state of affairs, how was it that Lynndie England became, in the words of *Newsweek* writer Evan Thomas, "the poster girl for sexual humiliation and degradation at Abu Ghraib"?

To assert, as I am, that public outrage over England's involvement in the scandal diverted attention away from a more systemic problem in the upper reaches of government and the military is not to diminish the heinousness of England's actions or the actions of other Army personnel. It is, rather, to ask how that diversion took place and what cultural beliefs about gender enabled it. A brief survey of media sources, to begin with, tells us that domestic ideology is alive and well in the U.S. today. Ads about household cleansers and kitchen aids regularly feature more women than men, demonstrating that the domestic sphere is still a feminized one. In a similar manner, the theory of separate spheres is enacted nightly on network television in such popular shows as *Dr. Phil,* in which the host, Phil McGraw (a clinical psychologist), often urges his male guests to take on the role of "leader" within the family, while his wife, Robin, appears in occasional spots about beauty secrets and home decorating.[15] In this context, it is not surprising that contemporary religious, political, and cultural discourses still consider women, in some fundamental way, "different" from men: less aggressive, more sensitive, and perhaps more ethical. Barbara Ehrenreich—feminist historian and cultural critic—admits to encountering some of these biases in herself when faced with the knowledge of female involvement in the Abu Ghraib abuse. She states:

> A certain kind of feminism, or perhaps I should say a certain kind of feminist naiveté, died in Abu Ghraib. It was a feminism that saw men as the perpetual perpetrators, women as the perpetual victims and male sexual violence against women as the root of all injustice. . . . That was before we had seen female sexual sadism in action.
>
> But it's not just the theory of this naïve feminism that was wrong. So was its strategy and vision for change. That strategy and vision rested on the assumption, implicit or stated outright, that women were

morally superior to men. We had a lot of debates over whether it was biology or conditioning that gave women the moral edge—or simply the experience of being a woman in a sexist culture. But the assumption of superiority, or at least a lesser inclination toward cruelty and violence, was more or less beyond debate. (Ehrenreich, "Abu Ghraib")

Ehrenreich's candid observations indicate that gender assumptions are not just the purview of misogynists and political conservatives. They are, rather, witness to our own cultural construction within a discourse of embodiment. Yet we know that in extreme cases, gender assumptions can kill, as they do in certain hate crimes. In Lynndie England's case, gender assumptions in the cultural imagination allow that while men—especially groups of men—can be violent and unfeeling, women are not so, "by nature." Hazing rituals in male fraternities, for example, every so often result in death;[16] these occurrences are not presumed to be instances of deviance, but of male hormones gone wrong. Cruel, yes; illegal, maybe; "unnatural"—no.

Although Ehrenreich suggests that the supposition of women's moral superiority can be based upon cultural conditioning as well as biology, it is biology that gives the edge to such suppositions. The biological foundation of female moral superiority is not something that is argued by modern science—although some gestures in this direction could surely be found—but it is deeply embedded in a cultural logic that casts England as the sexual deviant and her male counterparts as merely vile. Without some degree of a biological assumption of innate feminine characteristics, England cannot take on the significance that she does in contemporary culture. Under a premise of inherent sexual difference, her participation in the mistreatment—and the jaunty poses that she strikes in the photographs—is transformed from brutal to abnormal. As an interrogation technique, the sexual degradation of prisoners is cold and calculating; her involvement, however, was read as something quite different. In cultural terms, England's deviation from gender norms was the result of an inherent pathology. The "unnatural" woman was a deviant; only the exposure of this deviance could reveal the "truth" behind the scandal at Abu Ghraib. And this leads us back to the body, for the biological presumption behind cultural constructions of feminine deviance requires a female body for its reference point.

Throughout this study, I have made a connection between female social transgression, at one time identified solely as a moral issue, and female sexual deviance, something inscribed upon the body by nineteenth-century scientific discourse. In this last chapter, my goal is to demonstrate how the same kind of gender ideology that provided a foundation for scientific paradigms in the Victorian era informs twenty-first-century cultural discourse and media. The intense public reaction to the stories of Martha Stewart and Lynndie England is a prime example of the way in which today's gender assumptions are the legacy of nineteenth-century thought; it illustrates how female social transgression, figured as gender transgression, morphs into an issue of "deviance" closely related to biological presuppositions. Female gender deviance in the twenty-first century, in other words, carries the taint of nineteenth-century pathology because it refers to a stable feminine "nature"—necessarily attached to a female body—for its logic. Today, then, as in the nineteenth century, figures of female deviance are able to displace widespread problems in the social sphere. In this way, Stewart and England embody troubling cultural issues: Stewart stands in for all corporate crime ("greedy whitecollar" crime, as one person put it), while England stands in for an entire torture scandal. Both substitutions effectively deflect scrutiny away from these larger political, economic, and social quandaries, enacting a kind of public exposure that appears, in some way, to reveal an inner truth.

So at this point we have come full circle, back to Dr. Bedford's pursuit of the female body and its "sealed mysteries," back to the full "light" of modern inquiry. In Bedford's case, this inquiry was specifically scientific; in ours, it is media-driven. Both have their conventions and their vanities. But, more importantly for my purposes, both aspire to tell us the "truth" about systemic disorders through the probing of the female body. Deviant women, it seems, still make good copy.

Notes

NOTES TO THE INTRODUCTION

1. Gunning S. Bedford, *Clinical Lectures on the Diseases of Women and Children*
   4. Bedford's text was widely circulated, going through several editions and
   being translated into French and German. This quotation is taken from the
   eighth edition, wherein Bedford, in the style of a grand master, expresses his
   gratitude "[f]or the flattering commendations of the medical press—at
   home and abroad" (Preface).

2. Throughout this study, the words "deviant," "deviance," and similar
   terms—"perverse," "abnormal," "unnatural," and "unhealthy," for example—are understood to be constructed by culture. The same is true of terms
   that denote normalcy, such as "healthy," "normal," and "natural." Moreover,
   I am using "deviance" in the broad sense, meaning a deviation from cultural, physical, or mental norms, including unconventional social behavior,
   sexual transgression, or supposed physical or mental aberrations.

3. Bedford's comments on the importance of the uterus are typical of the
   period. Across the Atlantic, for example, London physician Charles West
   warned his readers:

   > Women may apply to you, who seem out of health, and in
   > whom you may, perhaps, at first, suspect the existence of
   > uterine disease; but they appear annoyed at inquiries with
   > reference to their sexual functions, or perhaps deny, and
   > with perfect truth, the existence of any pain in the uterus or
   > its immediate neighborhood. . . . [Yet] it is highly probable
   > that . . . anomalous symptoms will resolve themselves into
   > the effects of uterine disease. (*Lectures on the Diseases of
   > Women* 22)

   Like Bedford, West urges his readers to suspect the uterus as the cause of
   any and all complaints from his female patients, even if the patients themselves see no possible connection.

4. My use of the term "race" assumes that this is a constructed, rather than a biological, category. In this I follow Henry Louis Gates, who observes that "[r]ace, as a meaningful criterion within the biological sciences, has long been recognized to be a fiction" ("Writing 'Race'" 4). See also Lyndsay Andrew Farrall's *The Origins and Growth of the English Eugenics Movement 1865–1925* and Nancy Stephan's *The Idea of Race in Science* for a discussion of "race" in the scientific context. Farrall summarizes the issue succinctly:

    > [J]ust as "species" could be defined but still be the centre of a long scientific controversy because biologists could not agree on the significance of the definition and its implications, so "race" was defined without such definition meaning that all biologists agreed about the significance and the implication of the term. That there was some confusion about the term is illustrated by the full title of Darwin's famous work, *On the Origins of Species by Means of Natural Selection, or the Preservation of Favoured Races in the Struggle for Life.* Although "species" and "races" were not used as equivalents in the title it gave the distinct impression that they were very similar. "Race," however, was an inappropriate concept to use in relation to different groups of men. (298)

    As Farrall and others point out, there is no scientific basis for a biological understanding of "race."

5. See George Stocking, *Victorian Anthropology* 131–32.
6. Susan Walsh notes, for example, that "[t]he homologous relationship between the social body and the human body has a long history, from Plato's *Republic* to Hobbes' *Leviathan* to Herbert Spencer's writings on political economy" ("Bodies of Capital" 75).
7. See Adam Smith, *The Wealth of Nations.*
8. Thomas Malthus, *An Essay on the Principle of Population* 262 and *passim.* See also my discussion on Malthus in Chapter One.
9. I owe this formulation to Fredric Jameson, who states that texts appear to "solve" problems that are irresolvable in social and political terms. As Jameson explains, "the individual narrative, or the individual formal structure, is to be grasped as the imaginary resolution of a real contradiction" (*The Political Unconscious* 77). I have adapted Jameson's insight to include biomedical discourses, which function as do literary narratives. Through a series of analogies, elisions, and substitutions, then, the text attempts to explain and resolve, at the narrative level, problems which are otherwise insoluble.
10. One critic, for example, examines the social body in Blake and Mary Shelley not in a biological or Spencerian sense but in a broader cultural sense. Glen Brewster notes that "the cultural significance of the Creature's *monstrous*

body [in *Frankenstein*] has become a sort of free-floating signifier of the dominant anxieties of the changing times, from Gothic fears of sexuality to fears of new technologies to an exemplar of Lacanian otherness" ("Disintegration of the Social Body" 75). While Brewster does not consider the social body as a female body, much of what he says about the monstrous body taking on the anxieties of the larger social order are applicable to my analysis. In contrast to Brewster, however, I see the female body as being particularly redolent with biological associations.

11. Catherine Gallagher, "The Body Versus the Social Body in the Works of Thomas Malthus and Henry Mayhew."

12. An excellent example of the feminist treatment of Spencer can be found in Nancy Paxton's *George Eliot and Herbert Spencer: Feminism, Evolutionism, and the Reconstruction of Gender.* Paxton does not address the issue of the social body in any specific manner, but is very illuminating on Spencer's ideas about women's biological inferiority.

13. Other passing references to Spencer's theory of the social body in the context of women's studies can be found, for instance, in Penny Boumelha's *Thomas Hardy and Women: Sexual Ideology and Narrative Form.* Boumelha comments briefly on the parallels between social organization and biological thinking as a general trend in Darwinian and post-Darwinian thought, stating that "[t]he transfer from biological law and organisation to social, which seems so obviously metaphorical, is sometimes made with a directness so explicit as to make 'organicism' a barely adequate characterisation" (12); she does not pursue this thought at any length and does not discuss Spencer's concept of the social organism in particular. In a later reference to Spencer she refers to his reformulation of Darwin's thought as a "struggle for survival" and explains that the "metaphor" at work was between human society and evolutionary theory (103). While I certainly agree that there is a metaphorical link here—especially illustrated in the theory of recapitulation, which I discuss in Chapter One—I am pursuing a slightly different train of thought in which the biological parallel suggests not an evolutionary struggle but a vulnerability to pathology.

Sally Ledger makes a similar comment about Darwin's and Spencer's "evolutionist thought on [Olive] Schreiner's work," stating briefly that "Spencer's work persuaded Schreiner that the social order reflected a deeper biological order, and that progress was a law that underpinned the whole or organic creation" (73). Ledger's point here is that Spencer's work motivated Schreiner's belief in a unity in nature.

Similarly, in *The Female Malady: Women, Madness, and English Culture, 1830–1980,* Elaine Showalter observes that the "body metaphors of late Victorian social analysis" were pervasive, and goes on to state that "such exponents of an organic social view as Herbert Spencer described the body politic in terms of the governing male as the Head, the workers as Hands, and middle-class women as the Heart" (109). Thus, for Showalter, the "body metaphor" is used to maintain gender hierarchy, but not to suggest widespread pathology. Later in the text Showalter makes the more usual remarks about Spencer regarding his contribution to the theory of sexual difference, noting that he believed "women depleted, or sacrificed their energy in the reproductive process [and thus were] heavily handicapped, even developmentally arrested, in intellectual competition" (122).

Jill Conway makes similar observations about Spencer in "Stereotypes of Femininity in a Theory of Sexual Evolution." As Conway remarks, Spencer surmised that "[f]emale energy expended in reproduction was not available for psychic and intellectual growth" (141).

14. For general studies of health and medicine in the nineteenth century, see W.F. Bynum, *Science and the Practice of Medicine in the Nineteenth Century;* Bruce Haley, *The Healthy Body and Victorian Culture;* and Roy Porter, *The Greatest Benefit to Mankind: A Medical History of Humanity.* Works that specifically take up the question of sexuality during the nineteenth century but which do not focus exclusively on the female body include Jonathan Dollimore, *Sexual Dissidence: Augustine to Wilde, Freud to Foucault;* Michael Mason, *The Making of Victorian Sexuality;* and Frank Mort, *Dangerous Sexualities: Medico-Moral Politics in England since 1830.* Dollimore has a particularly illuminating chapter on Freud's theory of sexual perversion.

15. Other worthwhile studies that explore nineteenth-century medical and scientific attitudes towards female sexuality include George Chauncey, "From Sexual Inversion to Homosexuality: Medicine and the Changing Conceptualization of Female Deviance"; L.J. Jordanova, "Natural Facts: A Historical Perspective on Science and Sexuality"; and Jill Matus, *Unstable Bodies: Victorian Representations of Sexuality and Maternity.*

16. Also useful is Paula Bartley's more recent *Prostitution: Prevention and Reform in England, 1860–1914,* which concentrates on the reform movement.

17. Many feminists have objected to Foucault's formulation of sexuality, arguing that it undermines the struggle that women have undergone in fighting for political emancipation. Foucault's poststructural view of the body minimizes the significance of biological differences between men and women and instead focuses on the discursive constructs that enable gender classifications. My approach to Foucault follows Judith Butler and others who adopt a poststructuralist concept of the female body as constructed by discourse. See *Gender Trouble: Feminism and the Subversion of Identity* for Butler's critique of the "naturalness" of gender categories. Also, for a comprehensive account of the feminist debate on Foucault, see Margaret McLaren, *Feminism, Foucault, and Embodied Subjectivity.*

18. See Edwin Chadwick, *Report on the Sanitary Condition of the Labouring Population of Great Britain.*

19. See also Chapters One and Three below, in which I discuss Chadwick in reference to bourgeois ideas about contagion.

20. As noted earlier, Catherine Gallagher argues that Malthus's theory on population contradicts the popular assumption that vigorous reproduction in the individual signaled health in the larger social sphere. However, she also states that "[b]y insisting that healthy bodies eventually generate a feeble social organism, Malthus departed from nearly all his contemporaries" ("The Body" 83). Similarly, Russett observes that the concept of the social organism promoted by Spencer was also advanced by Auguste Comte and "a host of lesser social theorists" (*Sexual Science* 86). Thus, the pervasive thinking in the eighteenth and nineteenth centuries was that individual bodies bore a resemblance to the larger social body. Moreover, I emphasize that this concept became specifically related to biology in the nineteenth century.

NOTES TO CHAPTER ONE

1. See, for example, Brewster's observations on the "healthy 'social body'" according to Edmund Burke and others: "Burke's healthy individual body—a paradigm for nature divinely ordered—is a perfect microcosm of the 'social body.' As the body 'naturally' imposes hierarchy—head over heels, for example—it follows that the natural head of the family is the father and that the king is the natural head of the social body" ("Disintegration of the Social Body" 67).

2. For a comprehensive overview of evolutionary thought in the nineteenth century, see George Stocking's *Victorian Anthropology.* This volume is especially enlightening on the Victorian construction of savagery. Russett's *Sexual Science: The Victorian Construction of Womanhood* covers evolutionary and scientific thought from a feminist perspective. Also, the chapter on "Neurotic Women" in Janet Oppenheim's *"Shattered Nerves": Doctors, Patients, and Depression in Victorian England* offers some useful perspectives on Spencer and, to a lesser extent, Darwin, in relation to gender ideology.

3. Spencer has been more closely identified with supporting Lamarck than has Darwin, an identification which, according to some scholars, has led to a subsequent devaluation of Spencer's contributions to evolutionary thought. Robert M. Young, for example, summarizes the problem succinctly:

> The problem about Spencer is . . . to get historians to see how central his work and influence were to the nineteenth-century debate, both among scientists and the broader public. His reputation has suffered most among the leaders of thought in the period because subsequent scientists (followed dutifully by historians) have anachronistically dismissed him for holding a "Lamarckian" theory of the

mechanism of evolution. . . . [It should be noted, however,] that it was a theory which, although embattled, was taken seriously throughout the nineteenth century and indeed, was given increasing weight by Darwin (just as Spencer allowed the increasing role for natural selection). (Qtd. in Paxton 4)

4. See Russett 50.

5. I use the terms "race" and "species" with the understanding that there was much slippage between both in nineteenth-century writing. See Farrall's comments on this occurrence in footnote 4 to my Introduction.

6. Gallagher's essay on Thomas Malthus and the social body, discussed in my Introduction, argues that Malthus contradicts the traditional correspondence between the healthy individual and the healthy society when he suggests that "the healthy, and consequently *reproducing,* body" of the individual will undermine the health of the general population ("The Body" 85). Although Gallagher illuminates an important inconsistency in Malthus's thought, my analysis focuses on the traditional analogy between healthy body/healthy society illustrated through the depiction of the *morally* healthy (ironically, *non*reproducing) body. Malthus views the man who marries without being able to support a wife and children, for example, as committing an "immoral act" (*Essay* 262). See also footnote 20 to the Introduction.

7. In Chapter Two, on Dickens's *Hard Times,* I examine the text's satirization of such social theories. In *Hard Times* the "natural" social body imagined by social theorists such as Smith, Malthus, and others is more precisely an "unnatural" one, threatened with self-extinction.

8. See Foucault, *The Birth of the Clinic* 3–35; and Roy Porter, *The Greatest Benefit to Mankind* 306–314.

9. Qtd. in Rosario, "Homosexual Bio-Histories" 6. See also Georges Canguilhem, *The Normal and the Pathological,* which gives a fuller account of the development of these divisions in medicine.

10. Both Poovey, in *Making a Social Body: British Cultural Formation, 1830–1864* and Stallybrass and White, in *The Politics and Poetics of Transgression,* analyze the relationship between Chadwick's report and middle-class attitudes towards the poor and working classes. While Stallybrass and White, however, look at the polarization between the bourgeois body and the "body of the Other" in Chadwick's report and in bourgeois society, Poovey concentrates more on the way that Chadwick's study supports a view of the social aggregate as a unified entity.

11. For studies of Lombroso, see Mary Gibson, *Born to Crime: Cesare Lombroso and the Origins of Biological Criminology;* William Greenslade, *Degeneration,*

Culture and the Novel: 1880–1940; and Daniel Pick, *Faces of Degeneration: A European Disorder, c. 1848–c. 1918.*

12. For a closer examination of the concept of "race" in nineteenth-century science, see *The Mismeasure of Man,* by Stephen Jay Gould; *Outcasts from Evolution: Scientific Attitudes of Racial Inferiority, 1859–1900,* by John S. Haller, Jr.; and *The Idea of Race in Science: Great Britain 1800–1960,* by Nancy Stepan. See also Chapter Three, below, on Rider Haggard's *She.*

13. Jeffrey Weeks records the publication of Samuel Tissot's *On Onania* as 1758.

14. Primary sources for sexology texts include: Richard von Krafft-Ebing, *Psychopathia Sexualis, with Especial Reference to Contrary Sexual Instinct: A Medico-Legal Study;* Havelock Ellis, *Studies in the Psychology of Sex;* and Ellis and John Addington Symonds, *Sexual Inversion.* There are many good studies of early sexology in relation to culture, but see especially Lucy Bland and Laura Doan, *Sexology in Culture: Labelling Bodies and Desires;* Vernon Rosario, *Science and Homosexualities;* Carroll Smith-Rosenberg: "Discourses of Sexuality and Subjectivity: The New Woman, 1870–1936" and *Disorderly Conduct: Visions of Gender in Victorian America;* Jennifer Terry and Jacqueline Urla, *Deviant Bodies: Critical Perspectives on Difference in Science and Popular Culture;* and Weeks, *Sex, Politics and Society: The Regulation of Sexuality Since 1800* and *Sexuality and Its Discontents: Meanings, Myths & Modern Sexualities.* Also of interest is Lillian Faderman's section on sexology and lesbian sexuality in *Surpassing the Love of Men: Romantic Friendship and Love Between Women from the Renaissance to the Present.*

15. Ellis's and Symonds's *Sexual Inversion* later became the first volume to Ellis's seven-volume *Studies in the Psychology of Sex.*

16. Writers on sexology vary in their responses to the sexologists. Weeks's *Sexuality and Its Discontents,* for instance, focuses more on the pathologizing aspects of Krafft-Ebing, while Gayle Rubin emphasizes the useful value that some sexologists—including Krafft-Ebing—exerted. See especially Rubin's "The Traffic in Women: Notes on the 'Political Economy' of Sex" and her interview with Judith Butler, "Sexual Traffic. *Interview.*"

17. The theory of nineteenth-century domestic ideology, or separate spheres, is well known among feminist scholars. While there are many studies on the topic, Davidoff & Hall's *Family Fortunes: Men and Women of the English Middle Class, 1780–1850* offers a comprehensive historical appraisal of the period. Of interest also is Nancy Armstrong's *Desire and Domestic Fiction: A Political History of the Novel,* which examines domestic ideology especially as developed in conduct manuals and novels. Additionally, Lynda Nead's *Myths of Sexuality: Representations of Women in Victorian Britain* contains an excellent shorter analysis of domestic ideology and related topics.

18. Mary Wollstonecraft's *A Vindication of the Rights of Woman* turns on a similar incongruity, not within the prevailing eighteenth-century discourse

about "proper ladies," but between that discourse and the liberal one of the "Rights of Man." As she makes clear throughout *Rights of Woman,* the two doctrines are diametrically opposed.

19. Russett 78.
20. See Elizabeth Garrett Anderson's trenchant response to Maudsley's assertions in "Sex in Mind and Education: A Reply."
21. Conway 141.
22. Conway 141.
23. Conway 141.
24. My account of Geddes and Thomson is based on Russett's *Sexual Science* and Conway's "Stereotypes of Femininity in a Theory of Sexual Evolution."
25. Russett 90.
26. Russett 91.
27. Ornella Moscucci, *The Science of Woman: Gynaecology and Gender in England, 1800–1929* 2.
28. Moscucci, *Science of Woman* 10.
29. My comments on midwives and nineteenth-century medicine in this section are compiled from Moscucci, *The Science of Woman,* and Barbara Ehrenreich and Deirdre English, *For Her Own Good: 150 Years of the Experts' Advice to Women.* Bynum covers similar material in *Science and the Practice of Medicine* 202–08.
30. Ehrenreich & English, *For Her Own Good* 111.
31. See Oppenheim, *"Shattered Nerves"* 181–232; and Barbara Ehrenreich and Deirdre English, *For Her Own Good* 101–140.
32. Sally Shuttleworth 48.
33. Shuttleworth 48.
34. For a comprehensive appraisal of ovariotomies in the nineteenth-century, see Moscucci, *The Science of Woman.* Although Moscucci sees the increase of ovariotomies as related to "the social construction of femininity," she also specifically denies that they are "an expression of medical mysogyny" (135). Ehrenreich and English, on the other hand, emphasize the practice of unnecessary ovariotomies in the regulation of feminine mental and emotional disorders.
35. For primary materials on clitoridectomies in nineteenth-century England, see Isaac Baker Brown, "On Some Diseases of Woman Admitting Surgical Treatment." Secondary materials include Moscucci's "Clitoridectomy, Circumcision, and the Politics of Sexual Pleasure in Mid-Victorian Britain," which gives an extensive analysis of the subject; additionally, Showalter's *Female Malady* describes the use of clitoridectomies in treating female mental patients.
36. Ehrenreich and English state, for instance, that the last known clitoridectomy performed in the U.S. was in 1948, on a child of five, as a cure for masturbation (*For Her Own Good* 123).
37. Moscucci, "Clitoridectomy" 62.

38. For secondary sources on nineteenth-century neurasthenia, see Sander Gilman, *Difference and Pathology: Stereotypes of Sexuality, Race and Madness;* Oppenheim, *"Shattered Nerves";* and Showalter, *Female Malady.* Additionally, my discussion in Chapter Four, on *Jude,* examines the issue in more detail. For primary materials, George Beard, *American Nervousness: Its Causes and Consequences* and *Sexual Neurasthenia,* are the central medical texts on neurasthenia. Other primary texts of interest on the subject include Archibald Church and Frederick Peterson, *Nervous and Mental Diseases,* which has a section on neurasthenia; Thomas Stretch Dowse, *On Brain and Nerve Exhaustion. Neurasthenia, its nature and curative treatment;* and Thomas D. Savill, *Clinical Lectures on Neurasthenia.* See also C.H.F. Routh, *On Overwork and Premature Mental Decay: Its Treatment,* which addresses the conditions that came to be known as neurasthenia.

39. The literature on hysteria, both primary and secondary, is extensive. The names most prominently associated with the study of hysteria are those of Sigmund Freud and Jean-Martin Charcot. Freud and Josef Breuer, *Studies on Hysteria,* is a basic text. Charcot's studies of hysteria in the 1870s and 1880s are also fundamental; see especially *L'hystérie.* Other nineteenth-century studies of interest are: Church and Peterson, *Nervous and Mental Diseases;* Thomas Laycock, *A Treatise on the Nervous Diseases of Women; Comprising an Inquiry into the Nature, Causes, and Treatment of Spinal and Hysterical Disorders;* George J. Preston, *Hysteria and Certain Allied Conditions;* and F.C. Skey, *Hysteria.* For secondary sources, see: Gilman, *Hysteria Beyond Freud;* Oppenheim, *"Shattered Nerves";* and Showalter, *Female Malady.*

40. Both Roy Porter's *Madness: A Brief History* and Showalter's *Female Malady* contain useful summaries of moral management; Showalter's analysis here is especially extensive.

41. Porter, *Madness* 167–172.

42. Porter, *Madness* 106. See also Philippe Pinel, *A Treatise on Insanity.*

43. Porter, *Madness* 104.

44. Showalter, *Female Malady* 52.

45. Nancy Cott's "Passionlessness: An Interpretation of Victorian Sexual Ideology, 1790–1850" offers one of the first feminist accounts of this theory.

46. Poovey, "Speaking of the Body" 31.

47. Walkowitz 33.

48. Walkowitz 33.

49. Poovey, "Speaking of the Body" 31.

50. Poovey, "Speaking of the Body" 31.

51. Walkowitz 1.

52. Walkowitz 1.

53. Walkowitz 90–112.

54. Heteronormativity, of course, did not suddenly come into being in the late nineteenth century. Henry Abelove argues, for instance, that towards the end of the eighteenth century "sexual intercourse" was redefined to exclude acts such as "mutual masturbation, oral sex, anal sex, [and] display and watching" (340), formerly practiced on a cross-sex and same-sex basis, and to refer mainly to cross-sex genital intercourse ("penis in vagina, vagina around penis" [337]). Abelove's point is that there is an interesting parallel between a reported increase in sexual intercourse, so defined, at the end of the eighteenth century and beyond and a rise in industrial production, during which time "work" was redefined to exclude frequent and extended periods of rest. Just as the reformulation of "sexual intercourse" meant that some sexual acts became defined as incidental "foreplay," Abelove asserts, so too was rest consigned a secondary role. Abelove's theory of the construction of sexual intercourse corresponds to Rich's formulation of compulsory heterosexuality in that both constructs designate reproductive sexuality as the norm. Compulsory heterosexuality as I am using the term, however—in relation to a change in medical attitudes towards female sexual desire—came into being much later than the period Abelove cites; in my formulation, it is a product of late nineteenth-century sexological discourse.

55. This redefinition of female sexual deviance is especially relevant to my analysis of *Jude the Obscure* in Chapter Four.

56. There are many publications on the New Woman, but see especially Sally Ledger's *The New Woman: Fiction and Feminism at the* Fin de Siècle for an extensive overview; and *The New Woman in Fiction and in Fact:* Fin de Siècle *Feminisms,* edited by Angelique Richardson and Chris Willis, for a collection of recent appraisals. Also see Carroll Smith-Rosenberg's "Discourses of Sexuality and Subjectivity: The New Woman, 1870–1936," which I discuss in this section.

NOTES TO CHAPTER TWO

1. There has been much discussion about whether or not Dickens's understanding of utilitarianism was accurate. See Robin Gilmour's article, "The Gradgrind School: Political Economy in the Classroom," for instance, for a full discussion of the debate about Dickens's understanding of utilitarianism and Victorian materialism. Gilmour argues that Dickens's Gradgrind school had a historical referent. Raymond Williams also supports the view that *Hard Times* has an accurate historical foundation. In "Dickens and Social Ideas" Williams notes that utilitarianism and *laissez-faire* economics did overlap for a time, despite their apparent differences:

> At a certain point in the real history of England . . . the teachings of utilitarianism and of philosophical radicalism

became inextricably entwined with the teachings of classical economics and of restraint of the poor. When Dickens was writing, the utilitarian emphasis was a compound of rationalism and *laissez-faire* economics, in spite of the substantial contradiction between an appeal to general utility and a recommendation of noninterference. (90)

More recently, Nicholas Coles has argued, in "The Politics of *Hard Times:* Dickens the Novelist versus Dickens the Reformer," that Dickens's goals as a social reformer were different from his goals as a novelist. As reformer, he edited and wrote articles on social conditions, and as novelist he provided amusement and diversion for readers. Coles also discusses the debate about Dickens's attack on statistical data gathering (146–147).

2. See also my discussion of Smith in Chapter One.
3. See also my discussion of Malthus in Chapter One.
4. See my Introduction for more on Spencer and this line of thought.
5. For an in-depth discussion of divorce in *Hard Times,* see Anne Humpherys's "Louisa Gradgrind's Secret: Marriage and Divorce in *Hard Times*" and John Baird's "'Divorce and Matrimonial Causes': An Aspect of *Hard Times.*"
6. Amy King examines the development of a language of nature and plant life in the eighteenth- and nineteenth-century British novel in *Bloom: The Botanical Vernacular in the English Novel.* Her detailed study of the rise of botanical science and the use of botanical language in literature lends support to my broader claims about the importance of the natural world in scientific and literary discourses.
7. For an interesting discussion of *Hard Times'* attitude towards environmental influences, see Williams, "The Reader in *Hard Times.*" Williams observes that the novel both promotes a "Godwinian version of a shaping environment" and a contradictory assumption of inborn characteristics (170).
8. Three articles are cited by Schacht, all written by the medical journalist E. A. Hart (1835–98): "Birth of Plants" (*Household Words;* 18 Feb. 1854: 1–4); "Nature's Changes of Dress" (*Household Words;* 13 May 1854: 304–06); and "Plant Architecture" (*Household Words;* 25 Mar. 1854: 129–32).
9. Critical work on sibling incest in the British novel has focused to a great extent on Romantic literature. In this respect, Alan Richardson's, "The Dangers of Sympathy: Sibling Incest in English Romantic Poetry" and "Rethinking Romantic Incest: Human Universals, Literary Representation, and the Biology of Mind" are especially insightful. Glenda A. Hudson's *Sibling Love and Incest in Jane Austen's Fiction* and Julie Shaffer's "Familial Love, Incest, and Female Desire in Late Eighteenth- and Early Nineteenth-Century British Women's Novels" are also excellent resources that address trends throughout the eighteenth and early nineteenth centuries rather than only

the Romantic period. For broader studies that do not focus exclusively on sibling incest, see Ellen Pollak, *Incest and the English Novel, 1684–1814* and Jane M. Ford, *Patriarchy and Incest from Shakespeare to Joyce*. Pollak asserts, in particular, that studies of eighteenth-century incest narratives unfairly privilege "Romantic models of culture and human desire" (2).

10. Shaffer 71.

11. Shaffer 71. Critical examinations of the public controversy over marriage to a deceased wife's sister are of interest here in that they address Victorian attitudes towards sibling relationships. Elisabeth Rose Gruner, for example, notes that "debates over the Deceased Wife's Sister Bill (1835–1907) exemplify the broader cultural anxieties over the positions of women and the family in the period and demonstrate the Victorian elevation of the brother-sister bond" ("Born and Made" 424). Also of interest on the subject are Karen Chase and Michael Levenson, *The Spectacle of Intimacy: A Public Life for the Victorian Family*, Chapter Five; and Margaret Morganroth Gullette, "The Puzzling Case of the Deceased Wife's Sister: Nineteenth-Century England Deals with a Second-Chance Plot."

12. Shaffer borrows this word from Tony Tanner's *Adultery in the Novel: Contract and Transgression*.

13. Richardson, "Dangers of Sympathy" 739.

14. Catherine Waters discusses these same passages from Spilka and Slater in "Ambiguous Intimacy: Brother and Sister Relationships in *Dombey and Son*."

15. See Catherine Waters, "Ambiguous Intimacy," for a full and insightful analysis of the way in which Florence's relationship with Walter mirrors and is conflated with her earlier relationship to Paul.

16. Waters argues against Schelly's conclusions, stating that "the relationship between Paul and Florence is shown, I think, to be neither blatantly incestuous nor nostalgically pre-lapsarian" (17). In my view, the adult world in *Dombey and Son* and *David Copperfield* is seen as seriously compromised and sibling-like alliances modeled on childhood offer a way to avoid the mistakes of adult behavior. Russell Goldfarb's chapter on incest and orphans in Dickens's writing also brings together the themes of childhood and incest, yet Goldfarb sees these themes as being opposed to each other, each one representing different poles of what he describes as Dickens's sexual repression.

17. In *Dickens and the Politics of the Family*, Catherine Waters makes a slightly different argument about *Dombey and Son*, a novel with striking parallels to *Hard Times*. Where Waters sees the merging of public and private spheres to be the central issue in *Dombey*, I see the problem in *Hard Times* to be the application of public-sphere thinking to the private sphere, with the ideal being the other way around; thus, the public sphere in *Hard Times*, even as a separate entity, is deeply flawed. Nonetheless, many of Waters's comments on *Dombey* can be applied to *Hard Times*. In particular, the relationship

between Mr. Dombey and Florence, his daughter, has many similarities to the relationship between Gradgrind and Louisa. As Waters observes, "Above all, in the relationship between Mr. Dombey and his daughter, the novel documents the consequences of a failure to understand the crucial role of the domestic woman in symbolically resolving some of the anxieties associated with the rapid growth of industrial capitalism" (39–40). In both novels, female sexuality provides the link between the bourgeois family and industrial society. The many resemblances between the two novels make Waters's section on *Dombey* especially valuable reading.

18. Fabrizio 78.
19. Under the law of coverture, a married woman's identity was subsumed under that of her husband's. For more information on the legal status of women at this time, see Mary Lyndon Shanley's *Feminism, Marriage, and the Law in Victorian England.*
20. The image of the fallen woman was also made familiar in many mid-century paintings. See Augustus Egg's *Past and Present,* no. 1, 1858; E.H. Corbould's *Go and Sin No More,* 1842; and D.G. Rossetti's *Found,* 1854, for example.
21. Baird 408.
22. I am making the argument that *Hard Times* depicts the environment as a shaping influence upon children; thus, children begin life as healthy specimens but, through outside influences, become unhealthy. There is also the suggestion (in the depiction of a systemic, ongoing problem in all of Coketown) that, once damaged, heredity passes on the weakness to successive generations. This kind of reasoning can be seen in biomedical discourses (especially in the latter decades of the century) of heredity and acquired afflictions such as hysteria, insanity, alcoholism, and nervous diseases. See Chapter Four for a more extended analysis of heredity and nervous disorders. Additionally, in connection with environmental conditioning, see Williams' views in "The Reader in *Hard Times.*"
23. Gallagher, "Hard Times" 82–83.

NOTES TO CHAPTER THREE

1. For studies that look at the connections between the female body and the African landscape in *She,* see especially Sandra Gilbert, "Rider Haggard's Heart of Darkness"; and Showalter, *Sexual Anarchy: Gender and Culture at the* Fin de Siècle. *She* has received far less attention than Haggard's other works, particularly *King Solomon's Mines,* which also posit a similar analogy between African landscape and female body. In this regard see, for example, David Bunn, "Embodying Africa: Woman and Romance in Colonial Fiction"; Anne McClintock, *Imperial Leather: Race, Gender and Sexuality in the Colonial Contest;* and Rebecca Stott, "'Scaping the Body: Of Cannibal

Mothers and Colonial Landscapes." McClintock's analysis of colonial power and gender is especially useful. Also of interest is Lindy Stiebel's "Imagining Empire's Margins." Stiebel focuses on Haggard's *King Solomon's Mines* and *Nada the Lily,* linking the "sexualizing of the African landscape" with Northrop Frye's comments about the "the mistress' body [and] the paradisal garden" (Stiebel, "Imagining Empire's Margins" 134).

2. Several terms have been used to denote the genre of late-Victorian male adventure writing: "imperial gothic," "imperial romance," and late-Victorian "male romance" are some of the phrases used most often in this respect. For an examination of this genre and its relation to British culture, see Stephen Arata, *Fictions of Loss in the Victorian* Fin de Siècle; Patrick Brantlinger, *Rule of Darkness: British Literature and Imperialism, 1830–1914;* Showalter, *Sexual Anarchy;* and Stiebel, "Imagining Empire's Margins."

3. Patrick Brantlinger's article, "Victorians and Africans: The Genealogy of the Myth of the Dark Continent," offers an excellent short overview of Britain's explorations into Africa in the nineteenth century, with particular attention paid to their cultural implications. See also Chapter 6 of *Rule of Darkness: British Literature and Imperialism, 1830–1914,* also by Brantlinger, which presents the same material in a slightly revised form. For a detailed historical analysis of Britain's involvement with Africa, see *Britain and the Conquest of Africa* by G.N. Uzoigwe. Also, Chapter 6 of V.G. Kiernan's *The Lords of Human Kind: Black Man, Yellow Man, and White Man in an Age of Empire* contains an absorbing discussion of Africa in relation to the U.S. and Europe, focusing in particular on the cultural attitudes of colonizing countries.

4. See, for example, David Livingstone, *The Last Journals of David Livingstone in Central Africa, from 1865 to His Death,* published just three years before *She.*

5. In this connection, see Haley's chapter on "The Healthy Man" in *The Healthy Body and Victorian Culture.* Haley notes, for instance, that the second half of the nineteenth century saw a marked increase of interest in sports and gymnastics. As he comments, "[t]he time was soon to come when Englishmen would be converting their back lawns into tennis courts, making yearly assaults on the Alps, and packing the grandstands at rugby matches" (124).

6. Throughout this analysis, I am treating the "Oriental" as a discursive construction.

7. For a discussion of Haggard's attitudes towards "race" in the context of a more widespread European racism, see Wendy Katz, *Rider Haggard and the Fiction of Empire.* She states, in particular: "To accuse Haggard, who probably knew more about and had more sympathy for African society than most of his contemporaries, of having been a racist is to grant that he was very

much a man of his time and his class. . . . Seeing Haggard's racism in its entirety, then, means seeing it as a significant part of the British body politic" (148–49). I am not making any particular claims about Haggard himself, but am analyzing the text of *She* as part of a larger discourse of racial stereotyping.

8. Michael Biddiss's study, *Father of Racist Ideology: The Social and Political Thought of Count Gobineau,* contains a full discussion of Gobineau's life and work.

9. The same kind of "scientific" reasoning can be found in medical treatises such as Maudsley's *The Physiology of Mind.* Maudsley states, in particular:

> The brain of the Negro is superior to that of the Bushman, but still it does not reach the level of the white man's brain; the weight of the male Negro's brain is less than that of the average European female. . . . Among Europeans it is found that, other circumstances being alike, the size of the brain bears a general relation to the mental powers of the individual, although apparent exceptions to the rule sometimes occur. (103)

10. More detailed information on Lombroso can be found in *Born to Crime: Cesare Lombroso and the Origins of Biological Criminology,* by Mary Gibson; *Degeneration, Culture and the Novel: 1880–1940,* by William Greenslade; and *Faces of Degeneration: A European Disorder, c. 1848–c. 1918,* by Daniel Pick.

11. Lombroso's *The White Man and the Coloured Man* was first published in 1871 as *L'uomo bianco e l'uomo di colore: Letture sull'origine e le varietà delle razze umane.*

12. Lombroso's *Crime: Its Causes and Remedies* was first published in French in 1899.

13. See Robert Young's *Colonial Desire: Hybridity in Theory, Culture and Race* for an extended treatment of the subject of hybridity. Also, H.L. Malchow's *Gothic Images of Race in Nineteenth-Century Britain* contains an excellent chapter on the image of the half-breed in relation to the Victorian gothic genre.

14. Both Young's *Colonial Desire* and Stephen Jay Gould's *The Mismeasure of Man* discuss Agassiz in relation to hybridity.

15. This information comes from Young, who states, "[u]ntil the word 'miscegenation' was invented in 1864, the word that was conventionally used for the fertile fusion and merging of races was 'amalgamation'" (9).

16. Letter to S.G. Howe dated August 9, 1863 (Gould 48).

17. Daniel Karlin, Introduction to *She* 327; *Genesis* 21:9–21.

18. For analyses of the cannibal as a cultural image and literary trope, see Peter Hulme, *Colonial Encounters: Europe and the Native Caribbean, 1492–1797;* Maggie Kilgour, *From Communion to Cannibalism: An Anatomy of Metaphors of Incorporation;* and H.L. Malchow's *Gothic Images of Race in Nineteenth-Century Britain.*

19. See, for example, George Godwin, *Town Swamps and Social Bridges* (1859). Godwin states, in particular: "The connection between disease and defective structural and economic arrangements continues to demand the most serious attention. The relationship of cholera, and fever, and crime, to cesspools, imperfect drainage, impure water, overcharged graveyards, and want of ventilation, is a great sanitary question" (48). The idea here is that disease will be spread through breathing impure fumes, not through bacterial contamination.

20. There are numerous studies which examine Chadwick's report and the larger question of urban disease in relation to bourgeois attitudes. For a useful discussion of Chadwick and sanitary reform in England in the nineteenth century, see Chapter 6 in Poovey's *Making a Social Body*. Also, Chapter 3 of Stallybrass and White's *The Politics and Poetics of Transgression* contains a short discussion of Chadwick in connection with a longer analysis of bourgeois attitudes towards urban disease and the poor. Elizabeth Wilson's *The Sphinx in the City: Urban Life, the Control of Disorder, and Women* addresses some of the same issues that Stallybrass and White address and also contains a section on the miasmatic theory of disease. Both Chadwick and the miasma theory are discussed in Porter's history of medicine, *The Greatest Benefit to Mankind.*

21. For an examination of the naturalist's role in colonial discourses, see Mary Louise Pratt, *Imperial Eyes: Travel Writing and Transculturation,* discussed herein. Also of interest is Shawn Malley, "'Time Hath No Power Against Identity': Historical Continuity and Archaeological Adventure in H. Rider Haggard's *She.*" Malley analyzes *She* in relation to Victorian archaeological thought, noting that "through the authenticating aegis of archaeology, Holly and Leo materially consolidate their English heritage" (275).

22. See Russett's *Sexual Science* for a discussion of recapitulation theory and the female body. Gould's *The Mismeasure of Man* contains an excellent section on recapitulation theory, but with less attention focused on the issue of women.

23. Gilman, *Difference* 89.

24. Edward Said's *Orientalism* is the classic study of the Western construction of the East and its inhabitants.

25. See Hager Ben Driss, "Closed to Oriental Heroines: Ethos of the Colonial Text," for an analysis of the discursive construction of the Oriental woman in *She* and other Haggard texts. Driss focuses in particular on the colonial gaze. He states, for example: "The veiled Ayesha sustains the European stereotype of the latent sexuality waiting to be unveiled. Ayesha is represented as the

embodiment of the passionate, sensual, inviting Oriental female" ("Closed to Oriental Heroines" 167).

26. Some critics have seen in Ayesha's violation of Victorian gender ideology a reference to the New Woman. See, for instance, Gilbert's "Rider Haggard's Heart of Darkness"; Arata's *Fictions of Loss in the Victorian* Fin de Siècle; and Stott's "'Scaping the Body."

27. Young, *Colonial Desire* 7–8.

28. Young, *Colonial Desire* 8.

29. Young, *Colonial Desire* 8.

NOTES TO CHAPTER FOUR

1. Albert J. Guerard, *Thomas Hardy: The Novels and Stories* 109.

2. Kristin Brady, "Textual Hysteria: Hardy's Narrator on Women" 99.

3. Cedric Watts, *Thomas Hardy: Jude the Obscure* 101.

4. A. Alvarez, *Beyond All This Fiddle: Essays 1955–1967* 184.

5. Oppenheim observes that the differences between the two camps may be due to individual circumstances. As she states, "Beard, the New Yorker, interpreted neurasthenia as a disorder precipitated by the fast pace of urban life, while Van Deusen [a medical superintendent of the Michigan Asylum for the Insane], working in a community of farmers, attributed it to rural isolation, aptly illustrat[ing] neurasthenia's immense capacity to be all things to all medical men" (93).

6. See also my discussion of hysteria in Chapter One.

7. Greenslade 175.

8. Greenslade 174 and *passim.*

9. Greenslade 174–75.

10. Greenslade 175.

11. The theme of heredity in Hardy's work has been taken up by critics in numerous ways—especially in relation to *Tess of the D'Urbervilles*—yet only a few refer to *Jude.* Darwinian studies of Hardy often see heredity as part of a larger evolutionary schema which has reduced the significance of human beings in world history. Roger Robinson in "Hardy and Darwin," captures the gist of some of these approaches when he remarks that "Loss, instability, disorientation, incoherence and, above all, the reduction of man's significance in his own sight . . . are the experiences which Hardy . . . renders through poetry and fiction" (129). Robinson also makes some brief remarks specifically about *Jude,* noting that the story portrays an "over-evolution of sensitivity" in Jude's and Sue's characters (134). Other responses that address *Jude* in this light include, for example, Perry Meisel's *Thomas Hardy: The Return of the Repressed,* which examines interiority and exteriority in *Jude* as these concepts relate to Darwinian notions of organism and environment. More recently, Ross Shideler, in *Questioning the Father: From Darwin to*

Zola, Ibsen, Strindberg, and Hardy, examines the way in which Darwin's thought displaced notions of Christian patriarchal authority.

12. For general appraisals of degeneracy theory, see especially Pick, *Faces of Degeneration* and Oppenheim, *"Shattered Nerves."* Important primary sources include Bénédict Augustin Morel's *Traité des dégénérescences physiques, intellectuelles, et morales de l'espèce humaine* and *Traité des maladies mentales;* and Max Nordau's *Degeneration.*

13. Oppenheim 270.

14. Oppenheim 270.

15. Oppenheim 270.

16. Many medical professionals conflated hysteria and degeneracy. Preston, for example, in his 1897 text on hysteria, states: "It frequently happens that degeneracy is confounded with hysteria, and, as a matter of fact, it is often not an easy thing to draw the line between the two conditions, for the reason that after prolonged mental hysteria there may be seen some degeneration" (156).

17. Mitchell's volume on nervous problems (*Wear and Tear, or Hints for the Overworked*) was first published in 1871 and went through several editions, due to its immense popularity.

18. References to the hereditarian transmission of nerve-related problems can be found throughout medical literature of the period. Maudsley, for instance, states that "individuals do sometimes inherit a positive tendency to a particular nervous disease from which one or other of their parents or ancestors has suffered. The son of an insane person carries in his organization a distinctly greater liability to an outbreak of insanity under the ordinary conditions of life than the son of perfectly sane parents . . ." (*Mental Disease* 40–41). Similarly, Church and Peterson, writing about hysteria, comment: "*Heredity* plays an important part. Hysterics usually belong to neuropathic families. Hysteria in the mother is very frequently followed by hysteria in the daughter" (562). Savill expresses a similar belief that heredity plays a strong role both in hysteria and insanity; to these maladies he adds "a predisposition [to the development of nervous disease] even still greater appears in the children of *alcoholic parents*" (53).

19. Greenslade, for instance, calls Little Time "Arabella's son" (179).

20. From Shelley's *Revolt of Islam.*

21. Mary Jacobus, "Sue the Obscure" 313.

22. In contrast to Brady, Boumelha sees Sue's breakdown as relating to social and economic forces rather than defects which are specifically feminine. As Boumelha states, "Sue's 'breakdown' is not the sign of some gender-determined constitutional weakness of mind or will, but a result of the fact that certain social forces press harder on women in sexual and marital relationships, largely by virtue of the implication of their sexuality in child-bearing" ("Sexual Ideology" 70). While I would agree that social pressures play a

major role in Sue's breakdown, I would also argue that social and economic issues are completely imbricated with medical and biological ones. This is as true for Jude as it is for Sue; both are afflicted with neurasthenic symptoms as a result of the pressures of modern living, which are multifold: social, economic, political, religious. Sue's "weak female nature," however, makes her a candidate for a breakdown that is feminized while also being representative of larger social pressures.

23. See also my discussion of hysteria in Chapter One.

24. It is worth noting that Sue Bridehead's nervousness and breakdown can be seen not only as aspects of degeneration and neurasthenia, but also in relation to nineteenth-century medical views on female intellectual work. Medical texts of the period contain numerous references to the deleterious effects of mental exertion upon the feminine reproductive system. In an 1891 edition of a much-reprinted medical textbook, Gaillard Thomas claims, for example:

> Girls of tender age are required to apply their minds too constantly, to master studies which are too difficult, and to tax their intellects by efforts of thought and memory which are too prolonged and laborious. The results are—rapid development of brain and nervous system, precocious talent, refined and cultivated taste, and a fascinating vivacity on the one hand; a morbid impressibility, great feebleness of muscular system, and marked tendency to disease in the generative organs on the other. (37)

Sue Bridehead is a walking textbook example of Thomas's principles. Her keen intellect and brilliant conversation are matched by emotional instability and reproductive frailty. See also my discussion in Chapter One regarding Mitchell's and Kellogg's observations of female mental exertion.

25. As Dellamora explains, "[Hardy] enforces upon [Sue Bridehead] what [Adrienne] Rich sees as one prime element of compulsory heterosexuality, namely, 'the socialization of women to feel that male sexual "drive" amounts to a right'" (215). For Dellamora, "frigidity" is not so much the issue as "compulsory heterosexuality," a term used by Adrienne Rich to mean the cultural directive to engage in heteronormative sexual relations. See also my discussion in Chapter One about compulsory heterosexuality.

26. For instance, D.H. Lawrence in 1936 describes Sue as "physically impotent" (415); Guerard, in 1949, terms Sue "neurotic and sexually maladjusted" (109); in 1961 Alvarez more specifically refers to Sue's "'epicene' frigidity" (184); Rosemarie Morgan, in 1988, mentions Sue's "sexual repressions and inhibitions [and] her lack of . . . sensuality" (*Women and Sexuality* 137); and

as recently as 1992, Watts states that "Hardy makes Sue a compound of New Woman, lily with a brain, [and] Frigid Woman" (101).

27. Other feminist responses to Sue's "frigidity" include: Kate Millett, who believes that Sue has been portrayed unjustly by Hardy as "an iceberg" (*Sexual Politics* 133); and Jacobus, who sees in Sue, rather than frigidity, a "sexual awakening" that Sue herself betrays (315).

28. See especially Wilhelm Stekel's *Frigidity in Woman in Relation to Her Love Life;* and Walter Gallichan's *Sexual Antipathy and Coldness in Women.*

29. *Jude the Obscure* was first published in 1894–95 in serial form and in 1895 as a novel.

30. Laycock, for example, writes: "The action of the erotic feeling upon the nervous system and its capability of exiting hysteria is evident from many facts. Erotic grief is well known to the hysterical [patient] . . ." (176).

31. See Freud, "Fragment of an Analysis of a Case of Hysteria."

32. Brady 99.

33. Beard, *American Nervousness* 113; 100.

NOTES TO THE AFTERWORD

1. "Was Martha Stewart Targeted Because She Is a Major Democratic Contributor and a Woman? Where Is Ken Lay?"

2. Ken Belson, "Ebbers Mounts an I-Never-Knew Defense." Ebbers was indicted in March of 2004. On March 15, 2005, a federal jury found Ebbers guilty of "securities fraud, conspiracy and seven counts of filing false reports with regulators" (Belson, "Ex-Chief of WorldCom Is Found Guilty in $11 Billion Fraud" A1). Ebbers's conviction has come as good news to many, but his case has not generated the same kind of public response as Stewart's.

3. The government dropped its original allegation of insider trading and instead charged Stewart with "lying during an investigation . . . whether it was insider trading or not" (Harvey Silverglate; interview with Amy Goodman and Juan Gonzalez). Moreover, the charge of security fraud—the most serious accusation—was later dropped by the judge ("Was Martha Stewart Targeted . . . ?"). The remaining counts were relatively minor: "one charge of conspiracy, one charge of obstruction of justice and two charges of making false statements to investigators" ("Indepth: Martha Stewart"). As Elaine Lafferty points out, "John Ashcroft's Justice Department spent millions of dollars overzealously pursuing a case in which Martha Stewart saved herself $52,000 in stock losses by following an insider stock tip. And she wasn't even prosecuted for that—she was busted for *lying* about whether or not she'd sold her stock based on that tip" ("An Open Letter").

4. Gender deviance is not only a serious matter for women, of course, but also for men, transsexuals, and transgendered individuals. Presumed gender and sexual "deviance" of all kinds has the potential to command public scrutiny and divert attention away from larger political, social, and economic problems—

witness the recent national preoccupation with gay marriage, for example, which began as a single act of civil disobedience in my hometown of San Francisco and eventually emerged as a major political issue in the 2004 presidential campaign. Many voters perceived "moral" issues such as gay marriage to be more important than political and economic concerns, both domestic and international. Despite the immense relevance such matters have to contemporary politics and society, however, my analysis does not attempt to cover all such contingencies, but focuses instead on the very distinctive place "unnatural" women hold in the cultural imagination.

5. See the picture in the *Newsweek* article by Evan Thomas, for example, "Explaining Lynndie England."
6. Thomas, "Explaining Lynndie England."
7. Lynne Duke, "A Woman Apart."
8. Thomas, "Explaining Lynndie England."
9. Duke, "A Woman Apart." Duke notes, for example, that "[g]etting pregnant in combat theater is forbidden; soldiers are not deployed to such areas if they are pregnant."
10. I am not accusing the media of orchestrating public reaction to the Lynndie England or the Martha Stewart stories; I see the media as being in constant dialogue with readers and viewers, simultaneously reflecting and shaping attitudes.
11. Seymour Hersh, "Torture at Abu Ghraib" 45.
12. See Hersh, "Torture at Abu Ghraib" and "The Gray Zone."
13. In an interview with Amy Goodman and Juan Gonzalez of *Democracy Now!*, Michael Ratner, president of the Center for Constitutional Rights, said, for example: "[By appointing Gonzales as Attorney General] we're putting in someone who really has his hands deep in the blood of the conspiracy of torture in this country. He is the one who wrote the memo saying the Geneva Conventions shouldn't apply. He is the one who asked for the memo, redefining torture so narrowly that the worst abuses we've seen would not constitute torture under his definition."
14. See Jane Mayer, "Outsourcing Torture: The Secret History of America's 'Extraordinary Rendition' Program" for an examination of some of the broader issues regarding U.S. policies on torture.
15. There is a rich irony here in that such suggestions of separate spheres for men and women come from a twenty-first century medical "expert." To be fair, male leadership in McGraw's terms does not mean total control over family decision making, but he does expect men to take on the more dominant role in a marriage. It is a rather familiar separate-but-equal model.
16. The most recent such hazing incident resulted in the death of Matthew Carrington of Chico State University on February 2, 2005. Fraternity members forced Matthew and others to drink gallons of water, do push-ups, and endure extremes of cold (Meredith May, "Chico").

Works Cited

PRIMARY TEXTS

Acton, William. *The Functions and Disorders of the Reproductive Organs.* 1875. *The Sexuality Debates.* Ed. Sheila Jeffreys. New York and London: Routledge, 1987. 57–73.

———. *Prostitution.* 1857. Ed. Peter Fryer. New York: Praeger, 1968.

Anderson, Elizabeth Garrett. "Sex in Mind and Education: A Reply." *The Fortnightly Review* 15. 1874. *Gender and Science: Late Nineteenth-Century Debates on the Female Mind and Body.* Ed. Katharina Rowold. Bristol: Thoemmes Press, 1996. 54–68.

Beard, George. *American Nervousness: Its Causes and Consequences.* 1881. New York: Arno, 1972.

———. *Sexual Neurasthenia: Its Hygiene, Causes, Symptoms, and Treatment.* 1884. 5th ed. New York: Treat, 1898. New York: Arno, 1972.

Bedford, Gunning S. *Clinical Lectures on the Diseases of Women and Children.* 1855. 8th ed. New York: W. Wood and Co., 1863.

Brown, Isaac Baker. "On Some Diseases of Woman Admitting Surgical Treatment." 1866. *The Sexuality Debates.* Ed. Sheila Jeffreys. New York: Routledge & Kegan Paul, 1987. 27–41.

Chadwick, Edwin. *Report on the Sanitary Condition of the Labouring Population of Great Britain.* 1842. Edinburgh: Edinburgh UP, 1965.

Charcot, J[ean]-M[artin]. *L'hystérie.* Ed. É. Trillat. Toulouse: Privat, [1971].

Church, Archibald and Frederick Peterson. *Nervous and Mental Diseases.* 3rd ed. Philadelphia: W.B. Saunders, 1901.

Darwin, Charles. *The Descent of Man, and Selection in Relation to Sex.* 1871. 2 vols. Princeton: Princeton UP, 1981.

———. *The Origin of Species by Means of Natural Selection or the Preservation of Favoured Races in the Struggle for Life.* 1859. Ed. J.W. Burrow. Harmondsworth: Penguin, 1968.

Dickens, Charles. *Hard Times.* 1854. London: Penguin, 1995.

Dowse, Thomas Stretch. *On Brain and Nerve Exhaustion. Neurasthenia, Its Nature and Curative Treatment. A Paper Read Before the Medical Society of London.* London: Baillière, Tindall, and Cox, 1880.

Ellis, Havelock. *Concerning Jude the Obscure.* 1896. [London: The Ulysses Bookshop, 1931.]

———. *Studies in the Psychology of Sex.* 1896–1928. 7 vols. Philadelphia: F.A. Davis, 1928.

Ellis, Havelock, and John Addington Symonds. *Sexual Inversion.* London: Wilson and Macmillan, 1897.

Freud, Sigmund. "'Civilized' Sexual Morality and Modern Nervousness." 1908. *Collected Papers, Volume II.* London: Basic Books-Hogarth Press, 1959. 76–99.

———. "Fragment of an Analysis of a Case of Hysteria." 1905. *Dora: An Analysis of a Case of Hysteria.* Introd. Philip Rieff. New York: Simon & Schuster, 1963. 1–112.

———. "The Question of Lay Analysis: Conversations with an Impartial Person." 1926. *The Standard Edition of the Complete Psychological Works of Sigmund Freud.* Ed. James Strachey. Vol. 20. London: Hogarth, 1959. 183–250. 24 vols. 1953–74.

Freud, Sigmund, and Josef Breuer. *Studies on Hysteria.* 1895. Trans. and ed. James Strachey. New York: Basic Books, [1957].

Gallichan, Walter. *Sexual Antipathy and Coldness in Women.* London: T. Werner Laurie, 1927.

de Gobineau, Arthur. *The Inequality of Human Races.* 1853. Trans. Adrian Collins. New York: Howard Fertig, 1915.

Godwin, George. *Town Swamps and Social Bridges.* 1859. Introd. Anthony D. King. New York: Leicester UP, 1972.

Gosse, Edmund. Rev. of *Jude the Obscure,* by Thomas Hardy. *Cosmopolis* January 1896. Rpt. as "From *Cosmopolis.*" *Jude the Obscure.* Ed. Norman Page. New York: Norton, 1978. 383–388.

Haggard, H. Rider. *She.* 1887. Ed. Daniel Karlin. Oxford: Oxford UP, 1991.

Hardy, Thomas. *Jude the Obscure.* 1895; rev. 1912. Ed. Norman Page. 2nd ed. New York: Norton, 1999.

Kellogg, John Harvey. *Ladies' Guide in Health and Disease, Girlhood, Maidenhood, Wifehood, Motherhood.* 1882. Battle Creek, MI: Modern Medicine Publishing Co., 1905.

Krafft-Ebing, Richard von. *Psychopathia Sexualis, with Especial Reference to Contrary Sexual Instinct: A Medico-Legal Study.* Trans. Charles Gilbert Chaddock, M.D. Philadelphia: F.A. Davis, 1892.

Laycock, Thomas. *A Treatise on the Nervous Diseases of Women; Comprising an Inquiry into the Nature, Causes, and Treatment of Spinal and Hysterical Disorders.* London: Longman, 1840.

[Livingstone, David.] *The Last Journals of David Livingstone in Central Africa, from 1865 to His Death. Continued by a Narrative of His Last Moments and Sufferings,*

Obtained from His Faithful Servants Chuma and Susi. Introd. Horace Waller. 2 vols. London: J. Murray, 1874.

Lombroso, Cesare. *Crime: Its Causes and Remedies.* Trans. Henry P. Horton. Boston: Little, Brown, and Co., 1911. Trans. of *Le crime, causes et remèdes.* 1899.

Malthus, Thomas. *An Essay on the Principle of Population.* Introd. Donald Winch. Cambridge: Cambridge UP, 1992. Based on the 1803 text with subsequent revisions.

Maudsley, Henry. *The Physiology of Mind. Being the First Part of a Third Edition, Revised, Enlarged, and in Great Part Rewritten, of "The Physiology and Pathology of Mind."* New York: D. Appleton, 1877.

———. *Responsibility in Mental Disease.* London: H.S. King, 1874.

———. "Sex in Mind and Education." *The Fortnightly Review* 15 (1874). *Gender and Science: Late Nineteenth-Century Debates on the Female Mind and Body.* Ed. Katharina Rowold. Bristol: Thoemmes Press, 1996. 32–53.

Mitchell, S. Weir. *Wear and Tear, or Hints for the Overworked.* 1871. 5th ed. Philadelphia: Lippincott, 1887.

Morel, Bénédict Augustin. *Traité des dégénérescences physiques, intellectuelles, et morales de l'espèce humaine.* 1857. New York: Arno Press, 1976.

———. *Traité des maladies mentales.* Paris, 1860.

Nordau, Max. *Degeneration.* 1895. Intro. George L. Mosse. Lincoln: U of Nebraska P, 1968.

Pinel, Ph[ilippe]. *A Treatise on Insanity.* Facsimile of the London 1806 edition. Trans. D.D. Davis. Introd. Paul F. Cranefield. New York: Hafner, 1962.

Preston, George J. *Hysteria and Certain Allied Conditions: Their Nature and Treatment, with Special Reference to the Application of the Rest Cure, Massage, Electrotheraphy, Hypnotism, Etc.* Philadelphia: P. Blakiston, 1897.

Routh, C.H.F. *On Overwork and Premature Mental Decay: Its Treatment.* London: Baillière, Tindall, and Cox, 1876.

Ruskin, John. "Of Queens' Gardens." *Sesame and Lilies.* 1865. Ed. Harold Bloom. New York: Chelsea, 1983. 68–113.

Savill, Thomas D. *Clinical Lectures on Neurasthenia.* New York: W. Wood & Co., 1899.

Skey, F.C. *Hysteria.* New York: A. Simpson, 1867.

Smith, Adam. *The Wealth of Nations.* 1776. Introd. Andrew Skinner. Harmondsworth: Penguin, 1982.

Spencer, Herbert. "The Development Hypothesis." 1852. *Essays: Scientific, Political, and Speculative.* Vol. 1. New York: D. Appleton, 1904. 1–7.

———. *Principles of Sociology.* 2 vols. New York: D. Appleton, 1896.

———. "The Social Organism." 1860. *Essays: Scientific, Political, and Speculative.* Vol. 1. New York: D. Appleton, 1904. 265–307.

———. "The Study of Sociology: No. XV–Preparation in Psychology." 1873. *Gender and Science: Late Nineteenth-Century Debates on the Female Mind and Body.* Ed. Katharina Rowold. Bristol: Thoemmes Press, 1996. 23–31.

Stekel, Wilhelm. *Frigidity in Woman in Relation to Her Love Life.* Trans. James S. Van
　　Teslaar. 2 vols. New York: Liveright, 1926.

Thomas, T. Gaillard. *A Practical Treatise on the Diseases of Women.* 6th ed. Paul F.
　　Mundé. Philadelphia: Lea Brothers, 1891.

Tilt, Edward John. *The Change of Life in Health and Disease: A Clinical Treatise on
　　the Diseases of the Ganglionic Nervous System Incidental to Women at the Decline
　　of Life.* 4th ed. New York: Bermingham, 1882.

West, Charles. *Lectures on the Diseases of Women.* 2nd American ed. Philadelphia:
　　Blanchard and Lea, 1861.

Wollstonecraft, Mary. *A Vindication of the Rights of Woman.* 1792. Ed. Carol H. Pos-
　　ton. New York: Norton, 1988.

SECONDARY TEXTS

Abelove, Henry. "Some Speculations on the History of 'Sexual Intercourse' During
　　the 'Long Eighteenth Century' in England." *Nationalisms and Sexualities.* Ed.
　　Andrew Parker, Mary Russo, Doris Sommer, and Patricia Yaeger. 335–342.

Alvarez, A. *Beyond All This Fiddle: Essays 1955–1967.* London: Penguin, 1968.

Arata, Stephen. *Fictions of Loss in the Victorian* Fin de Siècle. Cambridge: Cambridge
　　UP, 1996.

Armstrong, Nancy. *Desire and Domestic Fiction: A Political History of the Novel.* New
　　York: Oxford UP, 1987.

Baird, John. "'Divorce and Matrimonial Causes': An Aspect of 'Hard Times.'" *Victo-
　　rian Studies* 20:4 (1977): 401–412.

Bartley, Paula. *Prostitution: Prevention and Reform in England, 1860–1914.* London:
　　Routledge-Taylor & Francis, 2000.

Bell, Shannon. *Reading, Writing, and Rewriting the Prostitute Body.* Bloomington:
　　Indiana UP, 1994.

Belson, Ken. "Ebbers Mounts an I-Never-Knew Defense." *New York Times.* 1 Mar.
　　2005, late ed.: C1+.

———. "Ex-Chief of WorldCom Is Found Guilty in $11 Billion Fraud." *New York
　　Times.* 16 Mar. 2005, natl. ed.: A1+.

Biddiss, Michael D. *Father of Racist Ideology: The Social and Political Thought of
　　Count Gobineau.* London: Weidenfeld and Nicolson, 1970.

Bland, Lucy, and Laura Doan, ed. *Sexology in Culture: Labelling Bodies and Desires.*
　　Chicago: U of Chicago P, 1998.

Boone, Joseph A., and Deborah E. Nord. "Brother and Sister: The Seductions of
　　Siblinghood in Dickens, Eliot, and Brontë." *Western Humanities Review* 46:2
　　(1992): 164–188.

Boumelha, Penny. *"Jude the Obscure:* Sexual Ideology and Narrative Form." *Jude the
　　Obscure.* Ed. Penny Boumelha. New York: St. Martin's Press, 2000. 53–74.

———. *Thomas Hardy and Women: Sexual Ideology and Narrative Form.* Madison: U
　　of Wisconsin P, 1982.

Brady, Kristin. "Textual Hysteria: Hardy's Narrator on Women." *The Sense of Sex: Feminist Perspectives on Hardy.* Ed. Margaret R. Higonnet. Chicago: U of Illinois P, 1993. 87–106.

Brantlinger, Patrick. *Rule of Darkness: British Literature and Imperialism, 1830–1914.* Ithaca: Cornell UP, 1988.

———. Brantlinger, Patrick. "Victorians and Africans: The Genealogy of the Myth of the Dark Continent." *Critical Inquiry* 12.3 (1985): 166–203.

Brewster, Glen. "From Albion to Frankenstein's Creature: The Disintegration of the Social Body in Blake and Mary Shelley." *Romantic Generations: Essays in Honor of Robert F. Gleckner.* Ed. Ghislaine McDayter, Guinn Batten, and Barry Milligan. Lewisburg: Bucknell UP, 2001. 64–82.

Bunn, David. "Embodying Africa: Woman and Romance in Colonial Fiction." *English in Africa* 15:1 (May 1988): 1–28.

Butler, Judith. *Gender Trouble: Feminism and the Subversion of Identity.* New York: Routledge, 1990.

Bynum, W. F. *Science and the Practice of Medicine in the Nineteenth Century.* Cambridge: Cambridge UP, 1994.

Canguilhem, Georges. *The Normal and the Pathological.* Introd. Michel Foucault. Trans. Carolyn R. Fawcett and Robert S. Cohen. New York: Zone Books, 1989.

Cannon, Susan Faye. *Science in Culture: The Early Victorian Period.* New York: Science History Publications, 1978.

Chase, Karen, and Michael Levenson. *The Spectacle of Intimacy: A Public Life for the Victorian Family.* Princeton: Princeton UP, 2000.

Chauncey, George. "From Sexual Inversion to Homosexuality: Medicine and the Changing Conceptualization of Female Deviance." *Salmagundi* 58 (1982–83): 114–146.

Chrisman, Laura. "The Imperial Unconscious? Representations of Imperial Discourse." *Colonial Discourse and Post-Colonial Theory: A Reader.* Ed. Patrick Williams and Laura Chrisman. New York: Columbia UP, 1994. 498–516.

Coles, Nicholas. "The Politics of *Hard Times:* Dickens the Novelist versus Dickens the Reformer." *Dickens Studies Annual* 15 (1986): 145–179.

Conway, Jill. "Stereotypes of Femininity in a Theory of Sexual Evolution." *Suffer and Be Still: Women in the Victorian Age.* Ed. Martha Vicinus. 140–154.

Cott, Nancy F. "Passionlessness: An Interpretation of Victorian Sexual Ideology, 1790–1850." *Signs: Journal of Women in Culture and Society* 4.2 (1978): 219–236.

Davidoff, Leonore, and Catherine Hall. *Family Fortunes: Men and Women of the English Middle Class, 1780–1850.* Chicago: Univ. of Chicago Press, 1987.

Dellamora, Richard. *Masculine Desire: The Sexual Politics of Victorian Aestheticism.* Chapel Hill: U of North Carolina P, 1990.

Deneau, Daniel P. "The Brother-Sister Relationship in *Hard Times.*" *The Dickensian* 344 (Sept. 1964): 173–177.

Dollimore, Jonathan. *Sexual Dissidence: Augustine to Wilde, Freud to Foucault.* Oxford: Oxford UP, 1991.

Driss, Hager Ben. "Closed to Oriental Heroines: Ethos of the Colonial Text." *Middle Eastern Studies Association Bulletin* 36 (Winter 2003): 164–89.

Duke, Lynne. "A Woman Apart: For Soldiers, Lynndie England's Role at Abu Ghraib Is Best Viewed from a Distance." *Washington Post.* 19 Sept. 2004. 2 Mar. 2005 <http://www.washingtonpost.com>.

Eagleton, Terry. "The Limits of Art." *Thomas Hardy's Jude the Obscure.* Ed. Harold Bloom. New York: Chelsea, 1987. 61–71.

Ehrenreich, Barbara and Deirdre English. *For Her Own Good: 150 Years of the Experts' Advice to Women.* New York: Anchor-Doubleday, 1978.

Ehrenreich, Barbara. "What Abu Ghraib Taught Me." *AlterNet.* 20 May 2004. 10 Mar. 2005 <http://www.alternet.org>.

Fabrizio, Richard. "Wonderful No-Meaning: Language and the Psychopathology of the Family in Dickens's *Hard Times.*" *Dickens Studies Annual* 16 (1987): 61–94.

Faderman, Lillian. *Surpassing the Love of Men: Romantic Friendship and Love Between Women from the Renaissance to the Present.* 1981. New York: Perennial-Harper, 2001.

Farrall, Lyndsay Andrew. *The Origins and Growth of the English Eugenics Movement 1865–1925.* New York: Garland, 1985.

Flint, Kate. Introduction. *Hard Times.* By Charles Dickens. London: Penguin, 1995. xi–xxxiii.

Ford, Jane M. *Patriarchy and Incest from Shakespeare to Joyce.* Gainesville: UP of Florida, 1998.

Foucault, Michel. *The Birth of the Clinic: An Archaeology of Medical Perception.* Trans. A. M. Sheridan Smith. New York: Vintage-Random, 1975.

———. *The History of Sexuality, Vol. 1: An Introduction.* Trans. Robert Hurley. New York: Vintage-Random, 1990.

Gallagher, Catherine. "The Body Versus the Social Body in the Works of Thomas Malthus and Henry Mayhew." *The Making of the Modern Body: Sexuality and Society in the Nineteenth Century.* Ed. Catherine Gallagher and Thomas Laqueur. Berkeley: U of California P, 1987. 83–106.

———. "*Hard Times* and *North and South:* The Family and Society in Two Industrial Novels." *The Arizona Quarterly* 36:1 (1980): 70–96.

Gates, Henry Louis. "Writing 'Race' and the Difference It Makes." *"Race," Writing, and Difference.* Ed. Henry Louis Gates, Jr. Chicago: U of Chicago P, 1985. 1–20.

Gibson, Mary. *Born to Crime: Cesare Lombroso and the Origins of Biological Criminology.* Westport, Connecticut: Praeger, 2002.

Gilbert, Sandra M. "Rider Haggard's Heart of Darkness." *Reading* Fin de Siècle *Fictions.* Ed. Lyn Pykett. London: Longman, 1996. 39–63.

Gilman, Sander L. *Difference and Pathology: Stereotypes of Sexuality, Race, and Madness.* Ithaca: Cornell UP, 1985.

Gilman, Sander L., et al. *Hysteria Beyond Freud.* Berkeley: U of California P., 1993.

Gilmour, Robin. "The Gradgrind School: Political Economy in the Classroom." *Victorian Studies* 11:2 (1967): 207–224.

Gleadle, Kathryn. *British Women in the Nineteenth Century.* Houndmills, Basingstoke, Hampshire: Palgrave, 2001.

Goldfarb, Russell. *Sexual Repression and Victorian Literature.* Lewisburg: Bucknell UP, 1970.

Gould, Stephen Jay. *The Mismeasure of Man.* New York: Norton, 1981.

Greenslade, William. *Degeneration, Culture and the Novel: 1880–1940.* Cambridge: Cambridge UP, 1994.

Gruner, Elisabeth Rose. "Born and Made: Sisters, Brothers, and the Deceased Wife's Sister Bill." *Signs* 24 (1999): 423–47.

Guerard, Albert J. *Thomas Hardy: The Novels and Stories.* Cambridge: Harvard UP, 1949.

Gullette, Margaret Morganroth. "The Puzzling Case of the Deceased Wife's Sister: Nineteenth-Century England Deals with a Second-Chance Plot." *Representations* 31 (1990): 142–66.

Haley, Bruce. *The Healthy Body and Victorian Culture.* Cambridge, Massachusetts: Harvard UP, 1978.

Haller, John S., Jr. *Outcasts from Evolution: Scientific Attitudes of Racial Inferiority, 1859–1900.* Rev. ed. Carbondale: Southern Illinois UP, 1995.

Hersh, Seymour. "The Gray Zone." *The New Yorker.* 24 May 2004: 38–44.

———. "Torture at Abu Ghraib." *The New Yorker.* 10 May 2004: 42–47.

Hudson, Glenda A. *Sibling Love and Incest in Jane Austen's Fiction.* Hampshire: Macmillan, 1992.

Hulme, Peter. *Colonial Encounters: Europe and the Native Caribbean, 1492–1797.* London: Methuen, 1986.

Humpherys, Anne. "Louisa Gradgrind's Secret: Marriage and Divorce in *Hard Times.*" *Dickens Studies Annual* 25 (1996): 177–195.

Iglesia, Maria Angeles Toda. "Deadly Marriages: Masculinity and the Pleasures of Violence in H.R. Haggard's Romances of Adventure." *Dressing up for War: Transformations of Gender and Genre in the Discourse and Literature of War.* Ed. Aránzazu Usandizaga and Andrew Monnickendam. Amsterdam: Rodopi, 2001. 39–54.

"Indepth: Martha Stewart. Timeline." *CBC News Online.* 4 Mar. 2005. 9 Mar. 2005 <http://www.cbc.ca>.

Jacobus, Mary. "Sue the Obscure." *Essays in Criticism* 25 (1975): 304–28.

Jameson, Fredric. *The Political Unconscious: Narrative as a Socially Symbolic Act.* Ithaca: Cornell, 1981.

Jefferson, D.W. "Mr. Gradgrind's Facts." *Essays in Criticism* 35 (1985): 197–212.

Jeffreys, Sheila. *The Spinster and Her Enemies: Feminism and Sexuality 1880–1930.* London: Pandora-Routledge, 1985.

Jordanova, L.J. "Natural Facts: A Historical Perspective on Science and Sexuality." *Nature, Culture and Gender.* Ed. Carol P. MacCormack and Marilyn Strathern. Cambridge: Cambridge UP, 1980. 42–69.

Karlin, Daniel, ed. Introduction. *She.* By H. Rider Haggard. Oxford: Oxford UP, 1991. vii–xxxi.

Katz, Wendy R. *Rider Haggard and the Fiction of Empire: A Critical Study of British Imperial Fiction.* Cambridge: Cambridge UP, 1987.

Kiernan, V.G. *The Lords of Human Kind: Black Man, Yellow Man, and White Man in an Age of Empire.* 1969. New York: Columbia UP, 1986.

Kilgour, Maggie. *From Communion to Cannibalism: An Anatomy of Metaphors of Incorporation.* Princeton: Princeton UP, 1990.

King, Amy M. *Bloom: The Botanical Vernacular in the English Novel.* Oxford: Oxford UP, 2003.

Lafferty, Elaine. "An Open Letter from Ms. in Support of Martha Stewart." *Ms. Magazine* 16 July 04. 9 Mar. 05 <http://www.msmagazine.com/radar/2004–07–16-marthastewart.asp>.

Lawrence, D.H. "Male and Female." 1936. *Jude the Obscure.* Ed. Norman Page. New York: Norton, 1978. 412–24.

Ledger, Sally. *The New Woman: Fiction and Feminism at the* Fin de Siècle. Manchester: Manchester UP, 1997.

Levine, George. *Darwin and the Novelists: Patterns of Science in Victorian Fiction.* Cambridge: Harvard UP, 1988.

Loomba, Ania. *Shakespeare, Race, and Colonialism.* Oxford: Oxford UP, 2002.

Malchow, H.L. *Gothic Images of Race in Nineteenth-Century Britain.* Stanford: Stanford UP, 1996.

Malley, Shawn. "'Time Hath No Power Against Identity': Historical Continuity and Archaeological Adventure in H. Rider Haggard's *She.*" *English Literature in Transition (1880–1920).* 40 (1997): 275–97.

Mason, Michael. *The Making of Victorian Sexuality.* Oxford: Oxford UP, 1994.

Matus, Jill L. *Unstable Bodies: Victorian Representations of Sexuality and Maternity.* Manchester: Manchester UP, 1995.

May, Meredith. "Chico: Pledge Dies in Hazing at Chico Fraternity. House Was Kicked Off CSU Campus in 2002 for Infraction." *San Francisco Chronicle.* 3 Feb. 2005: B1+.

Mayer, Jane. "Outsourcing Torture: The Secret History of America's 'Extraordinary Rendition' Program." *The New Yorker.* 14 & 21 Feb. 2005: 106–23.

McClintock, Anne. *Imperial Leather: Race, Gender and Sexuality in the Colonial Contest.* New York: Routledge, 1995.

McLaren, Margaret A. *Feminism, Foucault, and Embodied Subjectivity.* Albany: SUNY Press, 2002.

Meisel, Perry. *Thomas Hardy: The Return of the Repressed.* New Haven: Yale UP, 1972.

Millett, Kate. *Sexual Politics.* Garden City, N.Y.: Doubleday, 1970.

Morgan, Rosemarie. *Women and Sexuality in the Novels of Thomas Hardy.* London and New York: Routledge, 1988.

Mort, Frank. *Dangerous Sexualities: Medico-Moral Politics in England since 1850.* 2nd ed. London: Routledge, 2000.

Moscucci, Ornella. "Clitoridectomy, Circumcision, and the Politics of Sexual Pleasure in Mid-Victorian Britain." *Sexualities in Victorian Britain.* Ed. Andrew H. Miller and James Eli Adams. Bloomington: Indiana UP, 1996. 60–78.

———. *The Science of Woman: Gynaecology and Gender in England, 1800–1929.* Cambridge: Cambridge UP, 1990.

Nead, Lynda. *Myths of Sexuality: Representations of Women in Victorian Britain.* Oxford: Basil Blackwell, 1988.

Nussbaum, Martha C. "The Literary Imagination in Public Life." *New Literary History* 22 (1991): 877–910.

Oppenheim, Janet. *"Shattered Nerves": Doctors, Patients, and Depression in Victorian England.* New York: Oxford UP, 1991.

Orwell, George. *A Collection of Essays.* New York: Doubleday, 1954.

Paxton, Nancy L. *George Eliot and Herbert Spencer: Feminism, Evolutionism, and the Reconstruction of Gender.* Princeton: Princeton UP, 1991.

Pick, Daniel. *Faces of Degeneration: A European Disorder, c. 1848–c. 1918.* Cambridge: Cambridge UP, 1989.

Pollak, Ellen. *Incest and the English Novel, 1684–1814.* Baltimore, Johns Hopkins UP: 2003.

Poovey, Mary. *Making a Social Body: British Cultural Formation, 1830–1864.* Chicago: University of Chicago Press, 1995.

———. "Speaking of the Body: Mid-Victorian Constructions of Female Desire." *Body/Politics: Women and the Discourses of Science.* Ed. Mary Jacobus, Evelyn Fox Keller, Sally Shuttleworth. New York: Routledge, 1990. 29–46.

Porter, Roy. *The Greatest Benefit to Mankind: A Medical History of Humanity.* New York: Norton, 1997.

———. *Madness: A Brief History.* Oxford: Oxford UP, 2002.

Pratt, Mary Louise. *Imperial Eyes: Travel Writing and Transculturation.* London: Routledge, 1992.

Ratner, Michael. Interview with Amy Goodman and Juan Gonzalez. "Michael Ratner: Gonzales 'Has His Hand Deep in the Blood of the Conspiracy of Torture.'" *Democracy Now!* 28 Jan. 2005. 9 Mar. 2005 <http://www.democracynow.org>.

Rich, Adrienne. "Compulsory Heterosexuality and Lesbian Existence." *Signs: Journal of Women in Culture and Society* 5.4 (1980): 631–660.

Richardson, Angelique, and Chris Willis, eds. *The New Woman in Fiction and in Fact: Fin-de-Siècle Feminisms.* New York: St. Martin's-Palgrave, 2001.

Richardson, Alan. "The Dangers of Sympathy: Sibling Incest in English Romantic Poetry." *Studies in English Literature: 1500–1900* 25:4 (1985): 737–54.

————. "Rethinking Romantic Incest: Human Universals, Literary Representation, and the Biology of Mind." *New Literary History* 31 (2000): 553–72.

Robinson, Roger. "Hardy and Darwin." *Thomas Hardy: The Writer and His Background.* Ed. Norman Page. London: Bell & Hyman, 1980. 128–50.

Rosario, Vernon A. "Homosexual Bio-Histories: Genetic Nostalgias and the Quest for Paternity." *Science and Homosexualities.* Ed. Vernon A. Rosario. New York: Routledge, 1997. 1–25.

Rosario, Vernon A., ed. *Science and Homosexualities.* New York: Routledge, 1997.

Rubin, Gayle. "The Traffic in Women: Notes on the 'Political Economy' of Sex." *Literary Theory: An Anthology.* Ed. Julie Rivkin and Michael Ryan. Malden, Mass: Blackwell, 1998. 533–560.

Rubin, Gayle, with Judith Butler. "Sexual Traffic. *Interview."* *Feminism Meets Queer Theory.* Ed. Elizabeth Weed and Naomi Schor. Bloomington: Indiana UP, 1997. 68–108.

Russett, Cynthia Eagle. *Sexual Science: The Victorian Construction of Womanhood.* Cambridge, Mass.: Harvard UP, 1989.

Said, Edward W. *Culture and Imperialism.* 1993. New York: Vintage-Random, 1994.

————. *Orientalism.* New York: Pantheon-Random, 1978.

Schacht, Paul. "Dickens and the Uses of Nature." *Victorian Studies* 34:1 (1990): 77–102.

Schmidt, Susan. "Ashcroft Refuses to Release '02 Memo; Document Details Suffering Allowed In Interrogations." *Washington Post.* 9 June 2004. 10 Mar. 2005 <http://www.washingtonpost.com>.

Sedgwick, Eve Kosofsky. *Between Men: English Literature and Male Homosocial Desire.* New York: Columbia UP, 1985.

————. *Epistemology of the Closet.* Berkeley: U of California Press, 1990.

Shaffer, Julie. "Familial Love, Incest, and Female Desire in Late Eighteenth- and Early Nineteenth-Century British Women's Novels." *Criticism* 41:1 (1999): 67–99.

Shanley, Mary Lyndon. *Feminism, Marriage, and the Law in Victorian England.* Princeton: Princeton UP, 1989.

Shideler, Ross. *Questioning the Father: From Darwin to Zola, Ibsen, Strindberg, and Hardy.* Stanford: Stanford UP, 1999.

Showalter, Elaine. *The Female Malady: Women, Madness, and English Culture, 1830–1980.* New York: Penguin, 1985.

————. *Sexual Anarchy: Gender and Culture at the* Fin de Siècle. New York: Penguin, 1990.

Shuttleworth, Sally. "Female Circulation: Medical Discourse and Popular Advertising in the Mid-Victorian Era." *Body/Politics: Women and the Discourses of Science.* Ed. Mary Jacobus, Evelyn Fox Keller, Sally Shuttleworth. New York: Routledge, 1990. 47–68.

Silverglate, Harvey. Interview with Amy Goodman and Juan Gonzalez. "Was Martha Stewart Targeted Because She Is a Major Democratic Contributor and a Woman? Where Is Ken Lay?" *Democracy Now!* 11 Mar. 2004. 9 Mar. 2005 <http://www.democracynow.org>.

Slater, Michael. *Dickens and Women.* London: J.M. Dent & Sons, 1983.

Smith-Rosenberg, Carroll. "Discourses of Sexuality and Subjectivity: The New Woman, 1870–1936." *Hidden from History: Reclaiming the Gay and Lesbian Past.* Ed. Martin Duberman, Martha Vicinus and George Chauncey, Jr. New York: Meridian-Penguin, 1990. 264–280.

———. *Disorderly Conduct: Visions of Gender in Victorian America.* 1985. New York: Oxford UP, 1986.

Spilka, Mark. *Dickens and Kafka.* Bloomington: Indiana UP, 1963.

Stallybrass, Peter, and Allon White. *The Politics and Poetics of Transgression.* Ithaca: Cornell UP, 1986.

Stepan, Nancy. *The Idea of Race in Science: Great Britain 1800–1960.* Hamden: Archon-Macmillan, 1982.

Stiebel, Lindy. "Imagining Empire's Margins: Land in Rider Haggard's African Romances." *Being/s in Transit: Travelling Migration Dislocation.* Ed. Liselotte Glage. Amsterdam: rodopi, 2000. 125–40.

Stocking, George W., Jr. *Victorian Anthropology.* New York: Free Press-Macmillan, 1987.

Stott, Rebecca. *The Fabrication of the Late-Victorian Femme Fatale.* Houndmills, Basingstoke, Hampshire: Macmillan, 1992.

———. "'Scaping the Body: Of Cannibal Mothers and Colonial Landscapes." *The New Woman in Fiction and in Fact: Fin-de-Siècle Feminisms.* Ed. Angelique Richardson and Chris Willis. New York: St. Martin's-Palgrave, 2001. 150–166.

Tanner, Tony. *Adultery in the Novel: Contract and Transgression.* Baltimore: Johns Hopkins UP, 1979.

Terry, Jennifer, and Jacqueline Urla. *Deviant Bodies: Critical Perspectives on Difference in Science and Popular Culture.* Bloomington: Indiana UP, 1995.

Thomas, Deborah A. *Hard Times: A Fable of Fragmentation and Wholeness.* New York: Twayne-Simon & Schuster Macmillan, 1997.

Thomas, Evan. "Explaining Lynndie England: How Did a Wispy Tomboy Behave Like a Monster at Abu Ghraib?" *Newsweek.* 15 May 2004. 2 Mar. 2005 <msnbc.msn.com>.

"Two Cents: On Martha Stewart." *San Francisco Chronicle.* 6 Mar. 2004. 3 Mar. 2005 <http://www.sfgate.com>.

Uzoigwe, G.N. *Britain and the Conquest of Africa: The Age of Salisbury.* Ann Arbor: U of Michigan P, 1974.

Walkowitz, Judith R. *Prostitution and Victorian Society: Women, Class, and the State.* Cambridge: Cambridge UP, 1980.

Walsh, Susan. "Bodies of Capital: *Great Expectations* and the Climacteric Economy." *Victorian Studies* 37.1 (1993): 73–98.

"Was Martha Stewart Targeted Because She Is a Major Democratic Contributor and a Woman? Where Is Ken Lay?" *Democracy Now!* 11 Mar. 2004. Hosted by Amy Goodman and Juan Gonzalez. 9 Mar. 2005 <http://www.democracynow.org>.

Waters, Catherine. "Ambiguous Intimacy: Brother and Sister Relationships in *Dombey and Son.*" *The Dickensian* 84 (Spring 1988): 8–26.

———. *Dickens and the Politics of the Family.* New York: Cambridge UP, 1997.

Watts, Cedric. *Thomas Hardy: Jude the Obscure.* London: Penguin, 1992.

Weeks, Jeffrey. *Sex, Politics and Society: The Regulation of Sexuality Since 1800.* 2nd ed. London: Longman, 1989.

———. *Sexuality and Its Discontents: Meanings, Myths & Modern Sexualities.* London: Routledge, 1985.

Welsh, Alexander. *The City of Dickens.* Oxford: Clarendon Press, 1971.

Williams, Raymond. *The Country and the City.* London: Hogarth Press, 1973.

———. "Dickens and Social Ideas." *Dickens 1970.* Ed. Michael Slater. London: Chapman & Hall, 1970. 77–98.

———. "The Reader in *Hard Times.*" *Writing in Society.* London: Verso. N.d. 166–174.

Wilson, Elizabeth. *The Sphinx in the City: Urban Life, the Control of Disorder, and Women.* Berkeley: U of California P, 1991.

Young, Robert J.C. *Colonial Desire: Hybridity in Theory, Culture and Race.* London: Routledge, 1995.

Index